CRUSHING THE JAPANESE SURFACE FLEET AT THE BATTLE OF THE SURIGAO STRAIT

CRUSHING THE JAPANESE SURFACE FLEET AT THE BATTLE OF THE SURIGAO STRAIT

THE LAST CROSSING OF THE T

WALTER S. ZAPOTOCZNY JR.

FONTHILL

For the sailors who never came home

Fonthill Media Language Policy

Fonthill Media publishes in the international English language market. One language edition is published worldwide. As there are minor differences in spelling and presentation, especially with regard to American English and British English, a policy is necessary to define which form of English to use. The Fonthill Policy is to use the form of English native to the author. Walter S. Zapotoczny, Jr. was born and educated in the U.S.; therefore, American English has been adopted in this publication.

Fonthill Media Limited
Fonthill Media LLC
www.fonthillmedia.com
office@fonthillmedia.com

First published in the United Kingdom and the United States of America 2022

British Library Cataloguing in Publication Data:
A catalogue record for this book is available from the British Library

ISBN 978-1-78155-873-7

Typeset in 10pt on 13pt Sabon
Printed and bound in England

Preface

"Crossing the T" is a classic naval warfare tactic used from the late nineteenth to mid-twentieth centuries, in which a line of warships crosses in front of a line of enemy ships, allowing the crossing line to bring all their guns to bear while receiving fire from only the forward guns of the enemy. It became possible to bring all of a ship's main guns to bear only in the late nineteenth and the early twentieth centuries with the advent of steam-powered battleships with rotating gun turrets, which were able to move faster and turn more quickly than sailing ships, which had fixed guns facing sideways. The tactic became largely obsolete with the introduction of missiles and aircraft as long-range strikes are less dependent on the direction the ships are facing.

When going into battle, ships would assume a battle-line formation called "line astern," in which one vessel follows another in one or more parallel lines. This allows each ship to fire over wide arcs without lofting salvos of projectiles over friendly vessels. Each ship in the line generally engages its opposite number in the enemy battle line, which moves in a parallel course.

However, moving ahead of the enemy line on a perpendicular course "crossing the T" enables a ship to launch salvos at the same target with both the forward and rear turrets, maximizing the chances for a hit. It also makes ranging errors less critical for the ship doing the crossing, while simultaneously more critical for the ship being crossed. In military terms, this is known as enfilade fire. The tactic, designed for heavily armed and armored battleships, was used with varying degrees of success with more lightly armed and armored cruisers and heavy cruisers.

Advances in gun manufacturing and fire-control systems allowed engagements at increasingly long range, from approximately 6,000 yards at the Battle of Tsushima in 1905 to 20,000 yards at the Battle of Jutland in 1916. The introduction of brown powder, which burned less rapidly than black powder, allowed longer barrels, which allow greater accuracy; because it expanded less sharply than black powder, it put less strain on the insides of the barrel, allowing guns to last longer and to be manufactured to tighter tolerances. The addition of radar allowed World War II-era ships to fire farther, more accurately, and at night. The last time the "T" was crossed was at the Battle of the Surigao Strait during the Battle of Leyte Gulf in World War II. This book examines the Battle of the Surigao Strait and the plans and actions that led up to it.

Contents

Abbreviations and Definitions

A-Day:	Landing day (Leyte landing)
AAA:	Anti-aircraft gun
AAC:	Anti-aircraft common
AAVT:	Anti-aircraft with proximity fuse
AGC:	General communications vessel
AK:	Cargo ship, auxiliary
AO:	Oiler, or fuel oil tanker
AP:	Armor-piercing
APA:	Attack transport
AP-T:	Armor-piercing projectiles that include a tracer (incendiary)
APH-TC:	Armor-piercing high-capacity tracer (incendiary)
ASW:	Flat-nosed anti-submarine shell
AT:	Ocean-going tug
AVP:	Small seaplane tender
BatDiv.:	Battleship division
BB:	Battleship
BB-XCV:	Hermaphrodite (dreadnaught) battleship, ICE class
CA:	Heavy cruiser
CANFSWPA:	Commander Allied naval forces, Southwest Pacific area
CarDiv.:	Carrier division
CA-XCVS:	Heavy cruiser, converted seaplane carrier
CCS:	Combined chiefs of staff
CIC:	Combat information center
C-in-C:	Commander-in-chief
C-in-CPac.:	Commander-in-chief, U.S. Pacific Fleet
CINCSWPA:	Supreme commander of the SWPA
CL:	Light cruiser

CNO: Chief of naval operations
COMINCH: Commander-in-chief, U.S. Fleet
Cdr.: Commander
ComTaskFor: Commander task force
Condition I: General quarters, all hands at battle stations
Condition II: Modified general quarters, ships to permit some relaxation among personnel
Condition III: Wartime cruising, generally one-third of the crew is on watch
Control Green: All guns hold fire on air targets
Control Yellow: All guns may fire on any air target identified as enemy
CP: Common pointed British designation for shell
CPBC: Common pointed ballistic cap—British designation for shells
CPC: Common pointed British designation for capped shells
Corpen: Change of course in which ships in company move their rudders sequentially
CortDiv.: Escort division
crh: Caliber radius head (the pointed head of a projectile)
CruDiv.: Cruiser division
CSA: Commander of support aircraft
CTF: Commander task force
CTG: Commander task group
CV: Aircraft carrier
CVE: Aircraft carrier escort
CVL: Aircraft carrier, small
DD: Destroyer
DE: Destroyer escort
DesDiv.: Destroyer division
DesRon.: Destroyer squadron
DP: Dual-purpose gun, surface and air
Explosive D: Ammonium picrate, a yellow crystalline material
Fall of Shot: The place where artillery rounds fired by a ship actually impact
FC: Fire control radar
FD: Anti-aircraft and dual-purpose battery director radar
FEAF: Far East air force
FH: Fire control radar
Flash Blue: Air attack probable, unidentified aircraft in vicinity
Flash Red: Air attack imminent, enemy aircraft in vicinity
Flash White: All clear, aircraft identified as friendly
fps: Feet per second
GHQ: General headquarters
HB: Heavy barrel
HBX: High blast explosive

HC:	High capacity
HE:	High explosive
HE-I:	HE projectiles that include an incendiary
HE-T:	HE shell with a tracer
HMAS:	His Majesty's Australian ship
IGHQ:	Imperial general headquarters
I:	India time zone
IJN:	Imperial Japanese Navy
IS:	Incendiary shrapnel round intended for anti-aircraft use
JCS:	Joint chiefs of staffs
LCI:	Landing craft, infantry
LSM:	Landing ship, medium
LST:	Landing ship, tank
OBB:	Old battleship
OTC:	Officer in Tactical Command
NC:	British term for nitrocellulose in tubular form
NEI:	Netherlands East Indies
PAC:	Pacific
PFHE:	Proximity-fused HE
POA:	Pacific Ocean area
PT:	Patrol vessel, motor torpedo boat
RAN:	Royal Australian Navy
RAP:	Rocket-assisted projectile
rpm:	Rounds per minute
Salvo:	The simultaneous firing of guns
SAP:	Semi-armor-piercing
SAPC:	Semi-armor-piercing capped
SBD:	Scout Bomber Douglas
SG:	Surface search radar
SK:	Air search radar
SOPUS:	Senior (U.S.) officer present
SP:	Smokeless powder
SPD:	Single-base smokeless powder stabilized with diphenylamine
SPDN:	Diphenylamine-stabilized smokeless powder with non-volatile materials
SPCG:	Multi-base smokeless powder stabilized with ethyl centralite
SS:	Submarine
SWPA:	Southwest Pacific area
T:	Beside compass degrees, indicating true heading
Taffy:	Code name for U.S. escort carrier group
TF:	Task force
TBD:	Torpedo Bomber Douglas

ULTRA:	Allied interception and decryption program against Japanese radio traffic
USS:	U.S. ship, naval vessel
XRAY:	Material condition that provides the least amount of protection
YMS:	Auxiliary motor minesweeper
YOKE:	Material condition that provides more protection than condition XRAY
ZEBRA:	Material condition that is set to isolate and control fires and flooding

Introduction

The battleship's bark was heard through the dark,
As they belched their heavy shell.
Let the enemy feel our hot white steel,
And hope they fry in hell...

From a poem by a sailor aboard USS *Louisville*

In late 1944, the war in the Pacific was going badly for Japan. The American military was determined to retake the Philippines. The U.S. Pacific Fleet had moved to the Mariana Islands in support of General MacArthur's army, which had landed on the east coast of Leyte in October. The U.S. Seventh Fleet, commanded by Admiral Thomas C. Kinkaid, was near the Surigao Strait off Leyte. The U.S. Third Fleet, under Vice Admiral Halsey had been divided into four task groups, each under Vice Admiral McCaine, Rear Admirals Sherman, Bogan, and Davison. These task groups were stationed to operate off Luzon. Sherman's group in the north, Davison's group in the south, and Bogan's in the middle. McCaine's group, which had five carriers, was ordered to Ulithi for resupply.

The Japanese strategy in the defense of Leyte was to entrap the U.S. Navy's Seventh Fleet by its naval forces from the north in the Sibuyan Sea, and with assault from the south from Surigao Strait. Admiral Halsey and the U.S. Navy's Third Fleet was to be lured northwards, away from the Leyte Strait by a decoy carrier force. The Japanese plan, named Shō-Go (short for *Shō-Itchi-Go*, Operation Victory One), called for the convergence of their two battleship forces from north and south on MacArthur's landing beach, catching the American troops and invasion ships in a pincer movement. To execute this strategy, the Imperial Japanese Navy formed four task forces under the overall command of Vice Admiral Jisaburo Ozawa, who himself was to lead the decoy carrier force with two battleships, three light cruisers, and nine destroyers. The southern and weaker of these battleship forces, commanded by Rear Admiral Nishimura, would penetrate through Surigao Strait just south of Leyte, tying up the American battleships, while the more powerful of the two battleship forces, the Central Force under the command of Vice Admiral Kurita, would penetrate through San Bernardino Strait, sail down the coast of Samar, and fall on the American invasion fleet from the northeast. Admiral Shima, with cruisers and destroyers acting as a second striking force, would follow Nishimura into the Surigao Strait. The Battle of the Surigao Strait was one of the four engagements that made up the Battle of Leyte Gulf, which was the biggest naval battle fought in the Pacific Theatre during World War II. It was also the last time the tactic of "crossing the T" was used in battle.

The commander of the American ships facing Rear Admiral Nishimura was Rear Admiral Jesse Oldendorf. In his book *Sea of Thunder*, Evan Thomas describes Oldendorf as "an unapologetic practitioner of the American war. He believed in massed firepower and overwhelming force." It was his boldness, the use of the basic philosophies of war, and the use of the classic naval tactic of "crossing the T" that defeated the Japanese at Surigao Strait. His tactics were considered to be sound. It was a naval officer's dream come true. The enemy had come to Oldendorf and could only come one way, north through the Surigao Strait. The enemy's "T" was crossed, and his ships destroyed. This played a significant role in winning the Battle of Leyte Gulf, and in so doing, it helped to secure the beachheads of the U.S. Sixth Army on Leyte against Japanese attack from the sea. The battle was decisive in that it destroyed much of the remaining Japanese surface fleet while virtually ending Japan's ability to move resources from Southeast Asia to the home islands.

In no battle of the entire war did the U.S. Navy make so nearly a complete sweep as in that of Surigao Strait, at so little cost. The Battle of Surigao Strait saw the end of the battleline in naval warfare. The development of the aircraft carrier meant that no line of battleships could withstand a sustained air attack.

1

Notable Battles in which Warships "Crossed the T"

Battle of Lissa (1866)

The Battle of Lissa took place on July 20, 1866 in the Adriatic Sea near the Dalmatian island of Lissa and was a decisive victory for an outnumbered Austrian Empire force over a numerically superior Italian force. It was the first major sea battle between ironclads and one of the last to involve deliberate ramming. The fleets were composed of a mix of unarmored sailing ships with steam engines, and armored ironclads also combining sails and steam engines. The Italian fleet of twelve ironclads and seventeen unarmored ships outnumbered the Austrian fleet of seven and eleven respectively. The Austrians were also severely outmatched in rifled guns and total weight of metal. A single turret ship took part in the action—the Italian IRN *Affondatore*. Piedmontese Count Carlo di Persano commanded the Italian fleet, while the Austrian fleet was commanded by *Konteradmiral* Wilhelm von Tegetthoff. Having ignored warnings from his pickets of suspicious ships in sight, Persano had effectively allowed the Austrians to ambush his force while it was still forming. Tegetthoff, seeing a gap opening between the 1st and 2nd Divisions, forced his fleet into it and concentrated on raking the Italians and ramming. This meant that he allowed his "T" to be crossed.

Battle of Tsushima (1905)

Japanese Admiral Tōgō Heihachirō, by use of wireless communications and the proper deployment of reconnaissance, had positioned his fleet in such a way as to bring the Russian fleet to battle. Tōgō had preserved for himself the interior lines of movement, while forcing the longer lines of movement upon his opponent, whichever course the Russian admiral should take; by his selected positioning, he had the effect of throwing the Russian broadsides more and more out of action. He had crossed his "T." The Russian admiral, other than retreat or surrender, had no other option except charging Tōgō's battle line or accepting a formal pitched battle. Admiral Zinovy Rozhestvensky chose the latter, resulting in his total defeat in the only decisive fleet action in naval history fought solely by modern battleships. Rozhestvensky was severely wounded during the battle and was taken prisoner. Seven battleships were sunk and one was captured by the Japanese.

Battle of Elli (1912)

The Battle of Elli took place near the mouth of the Dardanelles on December 16, 1912 as part of the First Balkan War between the fleets of Greece and the Ottoman Empire. It was the largest sea battle of the Balkan Wars. The Royal Hellenic Navy, led by Rear Admiral Pavlos Kountouriotis on board the flagship *Averof*, defeated the Ottoman Navy just outside the entrance to the Dardanelles. During the battle, Kountouriotis, frustrated by the slow speed of the three older Greek battleships *Hydra*, *Spetsai*, and *Psara*, hoisted the flag signal for the letter "Z," which stood for "Independent Action," and sailed forward alone at a speed of 20 knots, against the Ottoman fleet. Taking full advantage in her superior speed, guns, and armor, the *Averof* succeeded in crossing the Ottoman fleet's "T" and concentrated her fire against the Ottoman flagship *Barbaros Hayreddin*, thus forcing the Ottoman fleet to retreat in disorder.

Battle of Jutland (1916)

The Battle of Jutland was a naval battle fought by the Royal Navy's Grand Fleet against the Imperial German Navy's High Seas Fleet during World War I. The battle was fought on May 31 and June 1, 1916 in the North Sea near Jutland, Denmark. It was the largest naval battle and the only full-scale clash of battleships in the war. It was only the third ever fleet action between steel battleships, following the smaller but more decisive Battle of Tsushima during the Russo-Japanese War. The Grand Fleet was commanded by British Admiral Sir John Jellicoe and the High Seas Fleet by German Vice Admiral Reinhard Scheer. The High Seas Fleet's intention was to lure out, trap, and destroy a portion of the Grand Fleet as the German naval force was insufficient to successfully engage the entire British fleet. This formed part of a larger strategy to break the British blockade of Germany and to allow German mercantile shipping to operate. Meanwhile, the Royal Navy pursued a strategy to engage and destroy the High Seas Fleet, or keep the German force contained and away from Britain's own shipping lanes. By 6:30 p.m., the main battle fleet action was joined for the first time, with Jellicoe effectively crossing Scheer's "T." The officers on the lead German battleships, and Scheer himself, were taken completely by surprise when they emerged from drifting clouds of smoky mist to suddenly find themselves facing the massed firepower of the entire Grand Fleet main battle line, which they did not know was even at sea. Jellicoe's flagship *Iron Duke* quickly scored seven hits on the lead German dreadnought, SMS *König*.

Battle of Cape Esperance (1942)

The Battle of Cape Esperance—also known as the Second Battle of Savo Island and, in Japanese sources, as the Sea Battle of Savo Island—took place on October 11–12, 1942. It was a naval battle of the Pacific campaign of World War II between the IJN and U.S. Navy. The battle was the second of four major surface engagements during the Guadalcanal campaign and took place at the entrance to the strait between Savo Island and Guadalcanal in the Solomon Islands. On the night of October 11, Japanese naval forces in the Solomon Islands area—under the command of Vice Admiral Gunichi Mikawa—sent a major supply and reinforcement convoy to their forces on Guadalcanal. The convoy consisted of two seaplane tenders and six destroyers and was commanded by Rear Admiral Takatsugu Jojima. At the same time, but in a separate operation, three heavy cruisers and two destroyers, under the command of Rear Admiral Aritomo Gotō, were to bombard the Allied airfield on Guadalcanal the object of destroying Allied aircraft and the airfield's facilities. Shortly before midnight on October 11, a U.S. force of four cruisers and five destroyers, under the command of Rear Admiral Norman Scott, intercepted Gotō's force as it approached Savo Island near Guadalcanal. Taking the Japanese by surprise, Scott's warships sank one of Gotō's cruisers and one of his destroyers, heavily damaged another cruiser, mortally wounded Gotō, and forced the rest of Gotō's warships to abandon the bombardment mission and retreat. Admiral Norman Scott crossed the "T" of a cruiser-destroyer force under Aritomo Gotō.

2

The Strategic Setting in the Pacific in 1944

The Allied invasion of Leyte, which began on October 20, 1944, was the first major combined operation in the new Philippines campaign that would end with the liberation of the entire archipelago less than a year later. By then, the Allied forces had cut off Japan from its vital sources of raw materials in the south. From their bases on Luzon, the Allied airpower was able to neutralize the enemy airpower on Formosa. The Philippines were also used as a base for preparing the final Allied assault on the Home Islands.

The Philippines campaign was a result of the long, hard struggle the Allied forces had fought in the Pacific after the Japanese attack on Pearl Harbor. Within four months, the Japanese conquered Malaya, the Netherlands East Indies (NEI), the Philippines, and the southern part of Burma. The speed of these victories emboldened the Japanese High Command to expand Japan's power into the southern Pacific in early 1942.

By middle of the spring of 1942, the Japanese completed the conquest of the Philippines and extended their control into the eastern part of New Guinea, the Admiralties, the Bismarck Archipelago, and the Lower Solomons. However, they suffered their first major defeat in the Battle of the Coral Sea in May 1942, which ended their attempt to seize Port Moresby, New Guinea, by the sea. This operational success was followed by the U.S. Navy's major operational victory in the Battle of Midway in June. A month later, the Allies made a strategic decision to seize Guadalcanal in the Lower Solomons as the first move toward capturing Japanese positions in the entire Solomons Archipelago, ending with the capture of Rabaul.

On March 24, 1942, the CCS gave the U.S. the primary responsibility for waging war against Japan in the Pacific, including the Americas, China, Australia, New Zealand, and Japan but excluding operations in Sumatra and the Malayan Peninsula. In the spring of 1942, the U.S. JCS divided the Pacific into two *de facto* theaters of war—the Southwest Pacific area (SWPA) and the Pacific Ocean area (POA). On March 18, 1942, General Douglas MacArthur was appointed supreme commander of the SWPA. The POA was led by Admiral Chester W. Nimitz, formally appointed CINCPOA on April 3, 1942. He was also at the same time CINC of the U.S. Pacific Fleet (CINCPac.). MacArthur and Nimitz reported directly to the JCS through General George C. Marshall, the army's chief of staff, and Admiral Ernest J. King, chief of naval operations (CNO) and commander-in-chief, U.S. Fleet (COMINCH), respectively. With two commands in the Pacific, control of the entire theater was in fact vested in the hands of the JCS. The chiefs had to reconcile conflicting demands between these two theaters. On April 3, 1942, the JCS issued general strategic tasks to both MacArthur and Nimitz. The most important strategic tasks were to retain control of the key areas of Australia as bases for future offensive operations, stop the Japanese advance toward Australia, protect principal lines of communications, and exert economic pressure on the Japanese by destroying their shipping in the area. Other strategic tasks included maintaining the U.S. position in the Philippines, protecting Allied communications within the SWPA and its approaches, providing support of friendly forces in the POA and Indian theater, and preparing to take the offensive.

The Allies went on the strategic offensive in the Pacific with their landing on Guadalcanal on August 8, 1942. The struggle for control of that island and its approaches lasted until February 1, 1943 when the Japanese were forced to evacuate their remaining troops from Guadalcanal. The SWPA's forces started the New Guinea Campaign in late July 1942. By March 1943, MacArthur's forces captured Lae and Finschafen on the Huon Peninsula.

The JCS submitted a strategic plan aimed to ultimately force Japan to unconditional surrender. Approved by the CCS on May 19, 1943, it specifically called for the capture of successive island strongpoints, preferably those that would shorten Allied supply routes and also deny bases from which the Japanese might interfere with Allied sea lines of communication. MacArthur's forces were directed to advance along the coast of New Guinea to the island of Morotai in the Moluccas. By seizing Morotai, the Allies would obtain a major staging base from which to threaten Mindanao, about 300 miles away. Simultaneously, Nimitz's forces were directed to start a drive across the central Pacific, from the Gilberts to the Marshalls and the Marianas, and then to the western Carolines. The ultimate objective of that advance was to seize the Palaus, approximately 540 miles away from Mindanao.

The Allied advance in the Pacific forced the Japanese to shift their defense efforts from the outer perimeter to an inner zone. In September 1943, they established the so-called "absolute defense zone," encompassing the ocean and land areas west of the Marianas–Carolines–western New Guinea line. The Philippines would serve as a rear staging area for Japanese troops, supplies, and air reinforcements in support of operations conducted along the main defense perimeter. To protect the Home Islands, the Japanese planned to strengthen their defensive positions in the central Pacific and the Ryukyu Islands and on Formosa. They also planned to boost aircraft production and strengthen protection for Japanese maritime shipping.

On November 16, 1943, the JCS decided that the advance along the New Guinea–NEI–Philippines axis should continue concurrently with operations aimed at capturing the island chains in the central Pacific. Once the Marianas were captured, they would be used as bases for the Allied long-range heavy bombers to strike the enemy Home Islands. The JCS also planned to intensify the air bombardment of the enemy installations and facilities in the NEI. The U.S. Pacific Fleet would support successive operations along each strategic axis to prevent interference by the enemy heavy surface forces. The JCS believed that Nimitz's operations in the central Pacific promised a more rapid advance than MacArthur's operations toward Japan and its vital lines of communications, facilitating the capture of island positions relatively close to the Japanese Home Islands from which the Allies could conduct the strategic bombing of Japan. Also, advance along the central Pacific's axis, it was believed, would most likely precipitate a decisive battle with the Japanese fleet.

On March 2, 1944, the JCS decided that the primary strategic objectives in the Pacific theater would be the capture of Luzon, Formosa, and southern China's coast. The tentative target date for the capture of Formosa was February 15, 1945. However, the JCS left open the possibility that Luzon would be seized before Formosa if necessary—a deferred decision that would result in protracted and often contentious discussion in the coming months.

The JCS believed that it might be necessary to land on Luzon following the capture of Mindanao. This, in turn, would divert Allied forces that could be better employed in an attack on Formosa. The JCS's planners believed that lodgment on China's coast could be secured without seizing Formosa first. Yet that course of action would leave Allied lines of supplies open to attack. The enemy could deploy sufficiently strong forces to counter any Allied move against China's coast. Seizing Luzon, on the other hand, would give the Allies a base of operations for reinforcing a sea and air blockade of the Japanese Home Islands.

JCS Directive Number 713/4 of March 12, 1944 directed MacArthur to cancel his plan for invading Kavieng, New Ireland, and instead isolate the Rabaul–Kavieng area by using minimum forces. Manus, Admiralties, would be captured and developed as an air and fleet base. The JCS also directed capture of Hollandia, New Guinea, with the target date of April 15. Hollandia would be used afterward as the base for the Allied heavy bombers in attacking the Palaus and neutralization of the western New Guinea–Halmahera area. POA's forces were directed to neutralize Truk, central Carolines, and seize the southern Marianas with the target date June 15. The attack on the Palaus, western Carolines, target date September 15, was aimed to establish a fleet base and airfields in support of the Allied operations against Mindanao, Formosa, and China. The JCS's directive also envisioned the occupation of Mindanao, with a target date of November 15. This operation was designed to neutralize Japanese forces in the Philippines prior to an advance on Formosa, either directly or via Luzon, and strike enemy installations in the NEI. The capture of Formosa was still planned for February 15, 1945, though the JCS had not ruled out capturing Luzon first.

By the late spring of 1944, the Japanese "absolute defense zone" was penetrated at two vital points. In the south, the SWPA's forces advanced more than 1,000 miles along the north coast of New Guinea. After the capture of the Admiralties in March 1944, the Allies completely isolated enemy forces on New Britain and New Ireland. The SWPA's forces made a long hop along New Guinea's coast by landing at Hollandia on April 22 and then, four weeks later, landed at Sarmi and Wakde. In another landing, in late May, SWPA's forces seized Biak, the Schouten Islands, some 200 miles further west from Hollandia. The Allies also obtained bases for the land-based aircraft at Noemfoor (southwest of Biak), thereby obtaining a position from which to control the area of the Moluccas, the Palaus, and the sea approaches to the southern Philippines.

The parallel Allied thrusts into western New Guinea and central Pacific led to considerable changes in Japanese strategic plans. A study by Imperial General Headquarters (IGHQ) in March 1944 highlighted the importance of the Philippines in the defense of the empire. Japanese planners concluded that there was little likelihood of an enemy advance toward the Home Islands from the direction of the central Pacific because of a lack of land bases for enemy fighter aircraft. They correctly predicted that the most likely course of action for the enemy was to advance along the central Pacific and New Guinea axes toward the Philippines to cut off Japan's southern lines of supplies. Afterward, the enemy would use the Philippines as a major base to continue the advance northward toward Japan via the Ryukyus. Enemy land-based aircraft would support each successive stage of this advance.

In the late winter of 1943 and the following spring, Allied intelligence obtained evidence of the reduced effectiveness of enemy air power. There were also indications that the Japanese had strengthened their defenses of the southern Philippines and northern NEI. Reacting to such strategic realities, the JCS tried to find ways of accelerating the schedule of Allied operations in the Pacific. One option was to advance target dates for seizing major objectives in the SWPA before an attack on Formosa. Another option was to bypass these objectives and select new ones, including even an attack on the Japanese Home Islands. In the end, the planners concluded that the target dates for seizing major objectives could not be significantly sped-up.

One of the major strategic problems facing the JCS in the spring of 1944 was whether Allied strength in the Pacific would be employed against enemy forces on Luzon or Formosa and China's south coast, or against both objectives. Allied strategic planners did not seriously question the need to obtain a foothold in the Philippines before advancing further north toward Japan. However, serious differences of opinion existed about whether to seize Luzon or to bypass it and directly invade Formosa and part of China's mainland coast.

The need to control the Philippines and adjacent sea areas was well understood by both the Japanese and the United States before the start of the war in the Pacific. The Philippine Archipelago lies crossways to all sea routes from Japan to the "Southern Resources Area," rich in the rubber, tin, oil, and rice that were critical to the functioning of Japan's war economy. Allied control of the Philippines would not only cut off sea routes from Japan to the NEI but would also provide an excellent staging area for Allied attacks against Japanese positions in southern China, Formosa, and Japan proper. Luzon being the largest and most populous island in the Philippines, neutralization of enemy air bases there was a prerequisite for an assault on Formosa. Any delay in seizing Luzon would give the Japanese time to recover from the Allied attacks. General MacArthur insisted that Luzon, with its friendly Filipino population, would be a more suitable base for assembling Allied forces for the final assault on Japan than hostile Formosa, which the Japanese could readily reinforce from China.

Political factors also favored seizing Luzon before Formosa. The recapture of the Philippines would liberate Filipinos who, because of their long association with the United States, were sympathetic to the Allied cause. MacArthur believed that the United States was honor-bound to liberate the Philippines at the earliest possible date. U.S. prestige was on the line, not to mention MacArthur's personal prestige. The general was determined to return to the Philippines to avenge the humiliating defeat suffered by U.S. forces under his command in 1941–1942.

However, many top U.S. military planners favored bypassing the Philippines entirely and invading Formosa first. In their view, Formosa would provide an ideal springboard for an attack against the Chinese mainland and bases for an attack on the Home Islands. In addition, Allied control of the island would cut Japan off from its sources of war materials in the NEI. Opponents argued that this course of action would insert Allied forces between substantial Japanese strength deployed in the Philippines and the Ryukyus and on China's mainland coast.

Admiral King was a leading advocate of bypassing the Philippines and establishing a base either on China's mainland or in the Ryukyus for mounting the final assault on Japan. In contrast, Admiral Nimitz and other top naval commanders in the Pacific wanted to obtain control of the southern or central Philippines before moving on to Formosa. In their view, it would be impossible to secure Allied lines of communication to Formosa until Allied land-based aircraft from southern Philippine bases had neutralized enemy air power on Luzon.

In mid-1944, the JCS decided to accelerate the Pacific timetable and reopened the question of bypassing the Philippines. On June 15, in response to a JCS message inquiring about his plans for future operations, General MacArthur presented a two-phase plan. The first phase envisaged a landing at Sarangani Bay, southern Mindanao, on October 25, 1944 to establish a base for land-based aircraft. The second phase envisaged invasion of Leyte, Visayas, on November 15, aimed at seizing airfields and naval bases there.

On June 24, General Marshall informed MacArthur that all the information the Allies had received from the "Magic" (Magic was an Allied cryptanalysis project) radio intercepts indicated a steady buildup of enemy strength in Mindanao, Celebes, Halmahera, the Vogelkop Peninsula (New Guinea), and the Palaus. In Marshall's view, the enemy offensive that started in May 1944 had already threatened the Allied position in China. The successful conduct of war against Japan necessarily depended on the use of bases on China's coast. The Allies could not just stand by and see that region completely overrun and consolidated by the Japanese. This was the most important reason for drafting a plan aimed at the early capture of Formosa.

In his response to Marshall on July 4, Nimitz expressed great doubts as to whether forces under his command could meet scheduled target dates. The reason for his pessimism was strengthening of the enemy garrisons in the central Pacific. Nevertheless, both Nimitz and MacArthur agreed on the need to speed up Pacific operations. By mid-1944, the logistic resources of the SWPA were stretched to the limit to meet the fixed target date. The support of fast carrier forces would be required for the Morotai and Sarangani operations. This, in turn, would make it essential to base heavy bombers at Sarangani before the landing on Leyte. Otherwise, the neutralization of so many enemy airfields and land-based aircraft would be a difficult task by using carrier-based aircraft only. The Leyte operation, if successful, would secure Allied air superiority over the Philippines. In Nimitz's view, the basic concept of operations proposed by MacArthur, in which land-based aircraft, ground troops, and naval forces would advance together, was sound. However, unless the rate of attrition inflicted on enemy naval and air forces rose or the Allies obtained complete victory at sea, the success of a movement into the Formosa Strait area would depend on neutralizing Japanese air power in Luzon by land-based aircraft. Nimitz believed that the capture of Leyte and Mindanao would speed up subsequent operations.

The Japanese suffered a significant setback after the Allied landings on the Marianas in mid-June 1944. By capturing the Marianas, the Allies obtained a position about 1,500 miles south from Tokyo. Later that summer, from their newly established bases on the Marianas, the Allies started sending long-range heavy bombers against Kyushu, Manchuria, and Korea. The Allied attack on Japanese maritime transportation not only separated the Home Islands from the "Southern Resources Area" but also gradually isolated each district in the area, creating an acute shortage of material in Japan and long delays in troop and material reinforcements.

After the fall of Saipan on July 9, General Hideki Tōjō's cabinet was forced to resign. The new government, led by Kuniaki Koiso, also an army general, was sworn in. The Japanese anticipated that the enemy would continue its northwestern advance along New Guinea's coast and toward the Philippines. Another course of action open to the enemy was the invasion of Luzon. The Japanese believed that by using bases in northern Australia, the enemy would try to capture Halmahera and the Palaus around August and invade Mindanao by November 1944.

In the summer of 1944, Allied gains forced the Japanese to reexamine their strategic situation in the Pacific. IGHQ concluded that an Allied advance toward the Home Islands from the direction of the Marianas was possible but not likely because of the lack of bases and the difficulty of maintaining long supply lines. IGHQ believed that capturing the Philippines was the most probable enemy course of action and a prelude to any invasion of the Home Islands. Hence, the decision was made to strengthen maritime defenses along the Philippines–Taiwan–Nansei, Shoto–Home Islands–Kurils line. IGHQ directed preparations for a series of contingency plans, code-named Sho-Go, to defend strategic positions in Japan's inner zone of defense.

In July, MacArthur submitted to Marshall a summary of his latest version of the campaign plan for the liberation of the Philippines, code-named RENO-V. The plan aimed at capturing central and northern Luzon before the beginning of the 1945 rainy season and providing support to the planned operations to seize Formosa and southern China's coast. MacArthur planned to land at Vogelkop Peninsula and Morotai, northern Moluccas, followed by securing a foothold in the southern and central Philippines. The first major operation, the landing at Sarangani Bay, was planned for November 1, 1944. Its objective was to establish bases for land-based aircraft to augment carrier-based air support for the capture of Leyte. Next he envisaged capturing Luzon Pacific Fleet forces would be extensively employed to support this effort and consolidating control of the Philippines. This stage would be followed by an overland advance to the capital of Manila and the central plain.

A major conference dealing with the progress of the Pacific war was held in Honolulu on July 28, 1944, with President Franklin D. Roosevelt in attendance. However, none of the JCS's members attended the meeting. Nimitz presented Admiral King's plan of continuing an advance in central Pacific and bypassing Luzon and invading Formosa early in 1945. All U.S. forces in the SWPA except two divisions and a few air squadrons would be transferred to Nimitz. MacArthur opposed that plan both on military and political grounds. He insisted on seizing Luzon first, in his view an easier operation for the army. In the end, both theater commanders agreed that the final decision could be postponed until the fall of 1944. Though Roosevelt expressed a preference for MacArthur's course of action, he did not rule out an invasion of Formosa. He also did not make a final decision as to which operation should come first.

MacArthur was reassured by the president's comments. After returning to his headquarters, however, he found a message from the joint staff planners that implied that Luzon would be bypassed. He fired off a message to Marshall voicing strong objections that the lodgment in the Philippines would be used only to neutralize enemy air power in Luzon while the major part of his forces would be employed to augment POA's forces planned for invasion of Formosa. The major strategic objective should be the liberation of the Philippines, he contended, and Luzon was the most important element of that objective. Strategically, the continued Japanese occupation of the Philippines would deny the Allies access to Malaya, the NEI, Borneo, and the South China Sea. Moreover, any attempt to conduct a campaign in the vast expanses of the Pacific without establishing adequate bases would be fraught with danger.

Though planning for operations slowed down in August 1944 because of a lack of directive from the JCS, Nimitz directed his subordinate commanders to proceed with planning for future operations, using campaign plan Granite II, an outline plan for occupation of the Formosa area and part of southern China's coast, as their basis.

On August 18, Nimitz agreed to all of the SWPA operations then planned, including the capture of Leyte. However, he asked King to secure a JCS directive for the POA's plan to invade southern Formosa and seize Amoy on China's mainland coast (Operation Causeway). The plan required the employment of three marine divisions against Amoy. Two marine and four army divisions would secure the southwestern part of Formosa. Carrier strikes, combined with the Far East Air Force (FEAF)'s strikes from Leyte and Seventh Air Force's strikes from the Palaus, would tie up Japanese air strength in the Philippines.

On September 1, the JCS met again to discuss whether to seize Luzon or Formosa. As result, it directed the joint staff planners to prepare a directive for the Leyte operation as a matter of urgency. However, no agreement was reached concerning which operations would follow the capture of Leyte. The JCS decided that MacArthur's forces would occupy the Leyte–Surigao area, with a target date of December 20, 1944 and seize bases in the central Philippines for an advance to either Formosa or Luzon. Nimitz would provide support for the SWPA's operations and submit plans for the Formosa operation as well as for support of the Luzon operation. The decision as to whether Luzon would be seized before Formosa was delayed. On September 9, theater commanders were directed to submit their respective plans for the effective reduction of Japanese air strength on Luzon in support of a POA attack on Formosa.

At the Second Quebec Conference in mid-September, the CCS twice changed the timetable for Pacific operations. MacArthur's forces would capture Morotai and Nimitz's forces would seize Peleliu in September. Nimitz's forces would invade Yap and Ulithi in October and then move into Talaud. In November, MacArthur would seize Sarangani Bay. In December, MacArthur and Nimitz would jointly capture Leyte, followed by the landing on Luzon or Formosa. The second change was prompted by events in the Pacific. Aircraft of the Third Fleet struck Yap and the Pala us on September 7 and 8 and for the next two days Mindanao as well. In the wake of these attacks, Admiral William F. Halsey, commander of the Third Fleet, informed Nimitz and MacArthur that few serviceable Japanese aircraft were left in the Philippines. The bulk of the enemy oil supplies were destroyed. There was no shipping left to sink and, in his view, the entire area was wide open for an Allied attack. He recommended that the Pacific Fleet and the Seventh Fleet jointly invade Leyte on October 20—two months ahead of schedule. Nimitz on his part recommended that the intermediate operations against Yap, Talaud, and Sarangani Bay be canceled, as Leyte could be captured easily and without any intermediate operation.

Marshall asked MacArthur for his opinion on the proposed change to the target date. MacArthur's chief of staff, Lieutenant General Richard K. Sutherland, then with GHQ SWPA at Hollandia, New Guinea, radioed to Marshall in MacArthur's name (who was *en route* to Morotai and was observing radio silence) that although information that there were no Japanese troops on Leyte was false, the intermediate operations could be canceled. When the message was received, Marshall was at a dinner with Canadian Prime Minister Mackenzie King. Marshall, together with Admiral King and Admiral William D. Leahy, chief of staff to President Roosevelt and senior member of the JCS, decided to cancel the intermediate operations for seizing Yap, Talaud, and Sarangani. They directed MacArthur and Nimitz to coordinate their plans and invade Leyte on October 20.

Afterward, in order not to overshadow the D-Day for the Normandy invasion, MacArthur designated the day of the Leyte invasion as A-Day. He reportedly said that Leyte would be the anvil against which he hoped to hammer the Japanese into submission in the central Philippines—the springboard from which he could proceed to the conquest of Luzon or the final assault against Japan itself.

By the time the decision to invade Leyte was made, the Allied forces had considerably reduced the area in the Pacific under effective Japanese control. Since April 1944, the POA's forces seized control of the central Pacific by moving 1,625 nautical miles from the Marshalls to the Palaus or to a distance of some 3,250 nautical miles from Hawaii. The Allies employed in the effort nine army divisions, an equivalent of an army division, one Marine division, plus the Seventh and the Third Fleets. The SWPA's forces advanced some 1,300 nautical miles from the Huon Peninsula to Morotai. All these successes were achieved at relatively small costs for the Allied forces: 20,000 combat casualties including 3,600 killed in action or missing. The Japanese losses were much higher: 43,000 men including about 40,000 killed. Some seven Japanese divisions and the equivalent of another division were destroyed. In addition, the Japanese lost an entire air army.

In retrospect, the strategic decision to invade Leyte first instead of Mindanao was a bold, although risky move. MacArthur's forces would be inserted into the central part of the Philippine Archipelago and thereby obtain a commanding position to neutralize the enemy's air power on Luzon. The enemy forces on Mindanao would be isolated. By canceling the Sarangani operation, the potentially long and costly struggle for control of Mindanao would be avoided. Another advantage of advancing the target date was to deny the enemy enough time to prepare his defenses, and especially to reconstitute combat potential of his carrier forces. Because Leyte was located beyond the effective range of the SWPA's land-based aircraft, it was critical that the U.S. Third Fleet provide reliable and timely cover and support. Advancing the original date for the Leyte operation by about two months was bound to create rather serious problems for the Allied operational planners and complicate logistical support and sustainment.

3

U.S. Naval Doctrine in Confronting the Japanese Fleet

The basic strategic problems confronting the U.S. Navy during the interwar years of the 1920s and 1930s were how to move a large fleet across the Pacific, absorb or avoid Japanese attacks, seize forward bases for further operations, and retain sufficient fighting strength to defeat Japan's Combined Fleet. Japanese and American policies in Asia were in conflict, and war was an inevitable result. The U.S. Navy planned to win by destroying Japan's navy, imposing a blockade, and forcing Japan's surrender. Details of the strategic dilemma were the focus of interwar plans, large fleet maneuvers, and complex war games at the Naval War College, in Newport, Rhode Island. By the time war arrived in 1941, the concept of an advance across the Pacific had become the subject of extensive and detailed strategic planning. However, the fleet that advanced through the Pacific in World War II was not the fleet of prewar plans.

The prewar navy had centered on a battle fleet, a battleship-centric formation that, concentrated together with a large fleet, would move as a unit, seizing objectives along its path. By early 1943, a new and more effective fleet organization had become available. Fast carrier task forces had demonstrated their ability to form powerful striking forces, maneuver independently of slower assault shipping, and force a decision on their own. The fleet that took the war to Japanese shores was built around carrier task forces. It is generally assumed that the change from a battleship-centric formation to carrier task forces invalidated the strategic and tactical planning carried out before the war, but this is not necessarily the case. The continuity in the navy's strategic planning can be found in tactical plans and doctrine.

Although the relatively high speed and flexibility of carrier task forces gave them operational maneuverability significantly greater than that of the battleship formations that preceded them, the basic tactical principles that the navy employed in its battle doctrines remained unchanged. The changes were confined to the method of applying and distributing these principles. Two important factors combined to temper the prewar concepts and produce a new approach. The first was the flexibility afforded by carrier task forces and the way they could concentrate against multiple targets simultaneously or against a single target without becoming a single target themselves. The second factor was wartime experience. By late 1942, the navy's prewar approach to the development and dissemination of tactical doctrine had shown serious flaws. Ships and men were going into battle without the proper indoctrination, limiting their effectiveness. A new approach was needed. The navy's Pacific Fleet was the first to synthesize all three elements: the necessity of a new approach to tactical doctrine; the challenge introduced by fast carrier task forces; and existing prewar doctrinal concepts.

These were married together by new tactical manuals, new fleet organizations, and refined battle plans. Together, these elements enabled success in the rapid string of offensives that moved through the Central Pacific, returned American forces to the Philippines, and crushed Japan as a naval power.

In early 1943, the Pacific War was entering a new phase. The Pacific Fleet, under Admiral Chester W. Nimitz, had defeated the Japanese in the attritional struggle for Guadalcanal and forced them onto the strategic defensive. It was essential that Nimitz's forces seize the opportunity afforded by their success and begin a strategic offensive, if they were to maintain the initiative. The Central Pacific would be the objective of the new offensive. Before the war, both sides had recognized the strategic importance of the Marshall, Caroline, and Mariana island groups, collectively known as the Mandates. The islands occupied a central position and provided numerous bases. The navy could use these to support further offensives in the direction of the Philippines, Formosa, or Japan itself. It was estimated that the seizure of the Mandates would make available approximately twenty airfields, fifteen seaplane bases, eight submarine bases, and ten fleet anchorages. Accordingly, in June 1943, Nimitz was directed by the JCS to develop a plan to penetrate the Japanese perimeter. The initial target would be the Marshall Islands.

The campaign plan Nimitz and his staff developed stressed two specific operational goals: a rapid pace of operations that would pressure the Japanese and keep the initiative firmly within the Pacific Fleet's grasp, and a decisive showdown with the Japanese fleet. Granite, as the plan was code-named, stressed both of these objectives, emphasizing the need to maintain unremitting pressure against Japan and seeking the destruction of the Japanese fleet at an early date. The fast pace of operations presented several challenges. It would be necessary to keep the striking arm of the fleet in forward areas almost continuously. This required a new approach to logistics.

Increased tempo also required a new approach to the development and dissemination of tactical doctrine. The prewar concept of a fleet that would move through the Pacific as a cohesive unit had to be discarded. To sustain the rapid pace of operations, individual ships and small task units would have to be interchangeable. They would have to move out of forward areas without disrupting the pace of the offensive. They would have to move into the combat zone and be effective immediately. They could not be expected to spend adequate time training with their cohorts. Further exacerbating these issues was the need for ships of the Pacific Fleet to support two major offensives in two theaters simultaneously.

A new tactical manual, *Current Tactical Orders and Doctrine, U.S. Pacific Fleet*, known as PAC 10, would help resolve these issues. Victory in a major fleet action is commonly assumed to have been a tactical objective of the Pacific Fleet, but the Granite plan illustrates that it was a strategic goal. All operations will be conducted as to maintain maximum readiness to take advantage of opportunities to bring important enemy naval forces to action. The Japanese fleet was a credible fighting force, and so long as it could sortie and threaten the success of an amphibious operation, it would limit the Pacific Fleet's freedom of maneuver. Operational and tactical plans had to account for this contingency. Thus, Granite assumed that a major fleet action, although it may delay amphibious operations for a brief period, will greatly accelerate them thereafter.

The movement into the Mandates was expected to draw out the Japanese fleet and enable its destruction. Every subsidiary operation plan to Granite—including Galvanic for the invasion of the Gilberts, Flintlock and Catchpole for the Marshalls, Hailstone for Truk, Longhop for Manus, and Forager for the Marianas—therefore had to account for the possible opportunity of decisive action. Tactical and operational plans were developed to meet this contingency.

The navy's existing tactical doctrine provided a backdrop for offensive preparations. Sophisticated and nuanced after refinement in the interwar period, this doctrine emphasized major fleet action and relied on several fundamental principles, including tactical concentration and coordinated action against the enemy. The doctrine's set of major tactics, those for a large fleet in battle, were thorough and flexible. They covered a variety of contingencies apart from the main fleet action. Cruisers and destroyers were drilled in night search and attack procedures, designed to locate and damage an enemy battle fleet the night before a battle.

Battle-line aircraft carriers operated with the battle fleet, providing air cover for the battleships and fleet train. Independent carrier task forces performed reconnaissance and targeted their opposite numbers to establish aerial superiority. Submarines scouted ahead and attacked enemy surface vessels. But the main emphasis of major tactics was the complex ballet of a battle-line action. Battle plans emphasized the cooperation of all fleet units to destroy the main objective—the enemy battle line. The publication of *Tentative Fleet Dispositions and Battle Plans, 1930* introduced a new level of complexity and coordination. For the first time, the navy had standard plans to govern the entire fleet in action. The new plans were further refined by *General Tactical Instructions, United States Navy in 1934* and by *General Tactical Instructions, United States Navy in 1940*. Battle plans were designated by a system of coded numbers and letters. The first number would determine the overall type of action to be fought. A normal action on similar courses—that is, with the navy's battle line steaming in the same direction as that of the enemy—was indicated by "1." The numeral "2" indicated a reverse action, with the navy's battle line moving in the opposite direction and chasing the enemy's tail. Reverse actions were believed to offer significant advantages, because the Japanese were expected to put fast and powerful forces at the head of their line. If the battle moved away from them, their effectiveness would be reduced.

Other numbers were used for more complex situations. After the number followed a letter that prescribed a specific range band: "E" indicated a fight at extreme range, 27,000 yards and above; "L" signified long range, 21,000–27,000 yards; "M" was for medium range, 17,000–21,000 yards; and "C" meant close range, 17,000 yards and below. Other letters provided details on the use of supporting forces. Common plans, such as 1L, a normal action at long range, and 2M, a reverse action at medium range, were described in detail. All these scripted plans assumed the same basic battle formation, a focused concentration of offensive power. Battleships were positioned in the center, with their broadsides facing the enemy. Light forces—groups of cruisers and destroyers—were positioned on either flank.

A group of destroyers was generally retained with the battle line to provide close protection against enemy destroyers and submarines. Carriers and ships of the fleet train would position themselves on the far side of the battle line from the enemy. The intent was to allow all elements of the fleet to cooperate, to fight as a unit toward the common goal of destroying the enemy battle line. Concentration of the battle fleet was particularly vital to success in a gunnery action, and the battle formation reflected this. Although the range and accuracy of battleship guns increased during the interwar period, battleships had to group together to maximize their fighting power. Experiments during tactical exercises were conducted with distributed formations, but results had repeatedly shown that dispersion invited defeat in detail. Accordingly, concentration had become a doctrinal tenet. A concentrated formation maximized the offensive power of not only the battle line but also the other fighting units that made up the battle fleet. The lessons of the interwar period had also led to an emphasis on combined arms, coordinated attacks on the enemy formation by all elements of the fleet, including battleships, destroyers, and airplanes.

For a time, submarines and minelayers were even considered important elements of a major fleet action. All available weapons were to be used in concert. Admiral Harris Laning, writing in his 1933 pamphlet on fleet action, emphasized this point: "With so many weapons carried on such different types of ships it is apparent that if we are to get the maximum effect of all weapons and make our blow the sum total of the blows of all, there must be perfect coordination between the types carrying them."

The effectiveness of each individual attack, then, was expected to be increased by coordination with other types. This was particularly true of attacks by airplanes and destroyers. Under normal circumstances enemy battleships were believed capable of thwarting them through a combination of defensive fire and maneuver, but when combined with battleship gunfire, aircraft and destroyers were considered to be far more effective.

Coordinated attacks using planes, destroyers, and the guns of battleships were a recurring feature of the navy's Fleet Problems and tactical exercises. The idea of using aircraft and surface ships in concert to destroy an enemy fleet became an essential feature of the navy's plans for decisive battle. Submarines were another important element of the navy's plans in the interwar period. They had long been considered for use in major actions, but the specifics of how they were to be employed had not been resolved. Early plans had envisioned using them as a tactical scouting force for the fleet, sailing ahead to report on and attack approaching enemy ships. This proved difficult to implement as submarines were too slow. In general, their usefulness in fleet operations proved limited. Wartime commanders would adopt a new solution.

Opportunities for the employment of major tactics were lacking in the two years following Pearl Harbor. The combat that did occur—furious battles of light forces and long-range carrier duels—revealed flaws in the navy's prewar approach to the development and dissemination of tactical doctrine. In contrast to preparations for decisive battle, minor tactics—those that would govern the employment of smaller forces—were neglected before the war. Very limited doctrinal guidance was provided for minor actions at the fleet level. Instead, individual squadron and task force commanders were expected to develop combat doctrines and battle plans themselves for the employment of their forces. This mechanism worked well under prewar conditions, when formations were cohesive and had time to drill under individual commanders. Where these circumstances held in wartime, the navy's light forces were effective in battle.

In the latter half of 1942, however, combat losses, the pace of operations in the Pacific, and the demands of a two-ocean war made this increasingly difficult. The climactic battles for Guadalcanal in November 1942 saw ships thrown together in haste. Commanders had no time to develop common doctrine or plans, and the resulting losses were severe. It became obvious that the development of minor tactics could not be left to commanders at sea. The Pacific Fleet's initial approach to addressing this problem was inadequate. Tactical bulletins and confidential letters on specific topics were produced and distributed to fleet units. These documents modified, enhanced, or introduced procedures that reflected lessons of combat and experience with new tactics and techniques. They covered a variety of topics—major action plans, night battle tactics, the use of radar, and the introduction of the combat information center. Their proliferation, however, led to redundancy and inconsistency.

By 1943, war experience had shown that a comprehensive revision of tactical manuals was necessary. The navy's carrier battle doctrine was effective enough to allow operational, if not tactical, success in all the major carrier battles of 1942. However, lessons from combat illustrated that improvement was necessary, particularly in the coordination of multiple carriers within a single formation. The navy had limited experience with task forces containing multiple carriers. For much of the interwar period, the navy had had only two large carriers for experiments and exercises—USS *Lexington* and USS *Saratoga*. During Fleet Problems, they were regularly placed on opposite sides. When teamed together, they operated in independent task groups or were tied to the battle line.

Technological factors also contributed to the navy's lack of experience in this respect. Before the advent of radar and effective fighter-direction techniques, carriers were best protected by keeping them hidden. A carrier that had been located could be struck and rendered inoperable by an enemy attack. Dispersing carriers into separate strike forces, away from the main body and each other, was a logical defensive measure. The war and the advance of technology changed the situation. Improved radars to detect incoming strikes and more effective techniques for vectoring fighters to intercept them allowed groups of carriers to pool resources and offer mutual support.

The navy's carrier task force doctrine was revised on the basis of these developments and of lessons from the 1942 battles. Single-carrier formations were abandoned. Task forces were formed around multiple carriers operating together. Even more fundamental changes would occur. Fast carrier task forces became the basis of the offensive power of the Pacific Fleet. The shift to carrier task forces and away from a battle fleet offered opportunities. For instance, because each of the carrier task forces could operate independently, it was possible to disperse them and strike multiple targets simultaneously. This would help achieve one of the major operational goals of the offensive, a rapid tempo. However, this was not without risk. Carriers were still considered vulnerable to surface action, and they needed support during their thrusts into the enemy's defensive perimeter. The new, fast battleships were ideally suited to provide this support, and they would be made part of the carrier task forces. The dispersal of battleship strength, however, ran counter to the principle of concentration the navy had emphasized for decades. It introduced the risk that a lone carrier task force might be isolated and destroyed. It also made it essential that the carrier task forces concentrate prior to major fleet action in order to bring the battleships together. Thus, although dispersal enabled the rapid pace of operations, it hindered the second goal, the need to bring the Japanese fleet to decisive action. An approach that balanced the two factors was necessary.

A combination of approaches was used to satisfy the operational goals of the Central Pacific offensive. New fleet-wide tactical manuals were developed that covered minor tactics and the operations of small task forces. The common doctrines they established allowed for the interchangeability of ships and task units demanded by the rapid operational tempo. Operation plans called for the seizure of multiple objectives but also acknowledged the need to concentrate for decisive action. Tactical plans emphasizing concerted action against the enemy prepared the navy for the expected battles. Together, these methods ensured the success of the offensive in the Central Pacific.

In April 1943, Admiral Nimitz created a board to revise the Pacific Fleet Cruising Instructions. The officers of the board were ordered to review current doctrinal publications, examine combat reports, interview officers returning from combat zones, and produce a new set of cruising instructions. They would in fact exceed this authority. By drawing on operational goals of the coming campaign, existing principles of the navy's doctrine, and doctrinal flaws exposed by wartime experience, the board produced a new doctrinal manual for the Pacific Fleet, and the most important one issued by the wartime navy.

Although carrier airpower would dominate the coming offensive, Nimitz chose three surface officers for the board and only one aviator. The senior member, Rear Admiral Robert M. Griffin, was an experienced surface warfare officer. He left the board before it completed its work, going on to command Battleship Division 3. Captain E. M. Crouch replaced Griffin. As commander of Destroyer Division 57, Crouch had survived the initial Japanese offensives in the South Pacific. Captain Roscoe F. Good also became a senior member of the board with Griffin's departure. Later in the war, he would command the battleship USS *Washington*. The aviator was Captain Apollo Soucek, who had served with distinction on the carrier USS *Hornet*, and at the time of its loss had been its executive officer. It was their labors that produced the current *Tactical Orders and Doctrine, U.S. Pacific Fleet* (PAC 10), issued in June 1943, which provided the navy with what it had been missing—a common set of tactical principles for the cooperation of small forces and detached units in battle. It corrected the under emphasis on minor tactics, granting them the same detailed treatment that major actions had received for over a decade.

The coded system of letters and numbers used for major actions was recycled and applied to small task forces. Compact battle formations developed specifically for combat by such forces were presented. Existing battle formations for light forces in night combat were retained. Instead of having to create and distribute their own tactical doctrines, small task group commanders could now develop battle plans rapidly, having a common doctrine to which they could refer. This streamlined the process, relieved small-unit commanders of an unnecessary burden, and ensured a common approach. Now, new ships could familiarize themselves with PAC 10 as they prepared to join the fleet and, because the manual applied to all task forces in all Pacific combat zones, it became possible to move ships from group to group or theater to theater without reequipping them with lengthy instructions by their new commanders. This was an extremely important development, and it was stressed in the manual's introduction. PAC 10 was intended to obviate necessity for special instructions under ordinary circumstances and to minimize them in extraordinary circumstances.

The ultimate aim was to obtain essential uniformity without unacceptable sacrifice of flexibility. It must be possible for forces composed of diverse types, and indoctrinated under different task force commanders, to join at sea on short notice for concerted action against the enemy without exchanging a mass of special instructions. Successors to PAC 10 built upon the foundation that the original provided. In February 1944, the U.S. Fleet followed the lead of its Pacific arm and issued *Current Tactical Orders and Doctrine, U.S. Fleet*, known as USF 10A. USF 10A built directly upon PAC 10. Its format, structure, and the majority of its contents were unchanged from the Pacific Fleet's publication. Although its title implied that it was an amendment of the prewar USF 10, *Current Tactical Orders and Doctrine, United States Fleet*, the new manual shared very little with its predecessor and provided far more tactical detail.

With PAC 10, the fleet solved two significant problems. First, the creation of a single, common doctrine allowed ships to be interchanged between task groups, and this in turn enabled the rapid operational tempo Nimitz desired. Second, shifting the development of small-unit tactical doctrine to the fleet level and out of the hands of individual commanders increased the effectiveness of all units, particularly the fast-moving carrier task forces. Tactical and operational plans for the coming offensive were built on this foundation.

Although the JCS directive ordered the seizure of positions in the Marshalls, Nimitz considered a thrust directly into the island group too dangerous. Too little was known about Japanese positions. Experience had demonstrated the importance of reconnaissance before amphibious landings, and the Marshalls were too far away for land-based planes to photograph the targets.

An intermediate objective was needed. Admiral Nimitz and his planners chose the Gilbert island group, formerly a British possession, recently seized by the Japanese. The code name for the operation was Galvanic. Nimitz's Central Pacific Force, augmented by ever-growing numbers of new ships and aircraft, was by November 1943 ready to begin major offensive operations. Vice Admiral Raymond A. Spruance had assumed command on August 5. The relative inexperience of the growing fleet had made a comprehensive doctrine for tactical operations imperative. Most of the ships of the force were new, the majority of their officers were reservists, and many of the men had never been to sea before. These ships could not operate as a cohesive unit without a doctrine to guide them, particularly if the Japanese sought a fleet action. The possibility of fleet action heavily influenced plans for Galvanic.

The Central Pacific Force would seize three atolls: Tarawa, Makin, and Abemama. Possession of these would guarantee American dominance of the Gilbert Islands and provide airfields from which to reconnoiter and attack the Marshalls. Although long-range bombers and reconnaissance aircraft could reach the Gilberts, the extreme range forced Spruance to provide direct air support for the invasion forces with his fast carrier task forces. This severely limited the carriers' freedom of maneuver. In prewar exercises, combat forces caught while supporting amphibious assaults had been damaged by attritional raids and then defeated by major attacks. At Savo Island, the Japanese had reinforced these lessons by decimating an Allied covering force. Japanese responses in the Central Pacific were expected to be even more powerful.

Minor raids could be handled by the invasion forces, using PAC 10 as a guide, but a major Japanese response would be a serious threat. Spruance's Galvanic plan accounted for this possibility. The main objectives would be seized simultaneously, Tarawa by the Southern Attack Force and Makin by the Northern. The atolls were expected to be occupied before the Japanese could mount a major response. Simultaneous attacks divided his forces, but the best defense against the threat of attack in the middle of an amphibious operation was to overwhelm the objectives quickly, granting the fleet freedom to maneuver; this also satisfied the desire for a rapid operational tempo. The potential for a major action was very real. Powerful Japanese forces based at Truk in the Caroline Islands could quickly move into the Marshalls and challenge the invasion. Estimates suggested that the Japanese could oppose the attack with ten battleships, seven aircraft carriers, and supporting forces.

Intelligence indicated the presence of the major portion of the Japanese Fleet in the Truk area. Whether the fleet can or will be used to interfere with Galvanic was unclear. Over 100 miles separated Tarawa and Makin. The forces covering the assaults were too far apart to provide mutual support, unless Spruance had timely warning of a Japanese approach. He was extremely apprehensive that a powerful attack would fall on a portion of his force and defeat it in detail. Of the two island objectives, Makin was closer to the Marshalls and much more vulnerable to a Japanese response. Spruance expected air searches to give him adequate warning and allow concentration of the Central Pacific Force. If weather patterns were unfavorable, however, storm systems could prevent aerial searches in the direction of the Mandates. Admiral Spruance considered delaying the attack on Makin if such circumstances developed.

Even if they did not, however, the forces around Makin had to be ready to defend themselves. Spruance placed significantly more firepower in his northern groups. The old battleships in the Northern Attack Force, USS *Idaho*, USS *Mississippi*, and USS *New Mexico*, had been extensively modified before the war and were the most powerful of the old battleships available. In addition, all six fast battleships supporting the operation were near Makin, evenly divided between the carrier task group providing direct support to the attack and the interceptor carrier group. The latter, under the direct command of Rear Admiral Charles A. Pownall, Spruance's carrier force commander, was positioned to intercept Japanese aerial attacks and provide early warning of enemy forces approaching from the Marshalls. Spruance urged these carrier groups to remain concentrated: "Carrier Task Groups which are screened by fast battleships and are supporting the attack on Makin and covering our northern flank will ... be operated in as close tactical support as possible of each other and the combatant units of the Northern Attack Force."

If the Japanese sought battle, the nine battleships in the north could separate from their task groups and unite to form a powerful battle line under Rear Admiral Willis A. Lee. But this was not Spruance's desired approach. He wanted a margin of superiority over his foe, and his battle plan called for the entire Central Pacific Force to come together to counter any major Japanese move. Three old battleships and additional ships supporting the landing at Tarawa would join the forces around Makin, giving Spruance a battle fleet of twelve battleships, nine heavy cruisers, three light cruisers, and twenty-eight destroyers. This battle fleet drew not only from the fast carrier groups but also from the invasion forces. As it would form on the spot, common doctrine would be essential. Spruance's Galvanic plan emphasized the importance of destroying the Japanese fleet, and it echoed the goal of the Granite campaign. If a major portion of the Japanese Fleet were to attempt to interfere with Galvanic, it is obvious that the defeat of the enemy fleet would at once become paramount. Without having inflicted such a defeat on the enemy, they would be unable to proceed with the capture and development of Makin, Tarawa, and Apamama. The destruction of a considerable portion of Japanese naval strength would go far toward winning the war.

In fact, the Japanese too anticipated a major fleet action. Prior to Galvanic, when Central Pacific carrier task forces had raided Tarawa, Makin, and Wake Island, Admiral Mineichi Koga, commander-in-chief of the Combined Fleet, correctly anticipated that these actions signaled the start of an offensive. Twice, in September and again in October, he moved the bulk of his forces from his main base at Truk to Eniwetok in the Marshalls, ready to counter Spruance. Each time, when the expected offensive did not occur, Koga returned to Truk. By the time of the landings on November 20, Koga was no longer prepared. In late October, faced with a threat to his southern flank by Allied advances toward Bougainville, Koga reinforced the bastion of Rabaul. He sent his carrier squadrons there, along with most of his cruiser forces. Nimitz's rapid operational tempo was delivering results. Frequent raids had kept the Japanese guessing about where the first blow would fall, and, pressured on two fronts, they chose to reinforce their southern flank. When Spruance moved into the Gilberts, stripped of its air squadrons and cruiser scouts, there was little the Combined Fleet could do. The desired decisive action did not materialize.

With the success of Galvanic, attention quickly shifted to the Marshalls. The important question was how best to continue the rapid pace of the offensive and quickly neutralize Japanese positions in the island group. The essential initial objective was an airfield that could support bombers. There were bomber airfields on Wotje and Maloelap in the eastern portion of the Marshalls. A phased approach, breaking the capture of the Marshalls into eastern and western operations, was considered and endorsed by the JCS. Nimitz and his planners rejected this idea though. They did not want the offensive to degenerate into an attritional struggle like the fighting in the Solomons. As plans for the Marshalls were refined, concurrent raids struck Japanese positions. PAC 10 facilitated these minor operations.

Lee's fast battleships were detached from the carrier task forces and moved to the South Pacific; along the way, they bombarded the Japanese base on Nauru, west of the Gilberts. Pownall led two of his carrier groups into the heart of the Marshalls, attacking the Kwajalein and Wotje Atolls. Raids like these sustained the operational tempo. Pownall's strikes destroyed planes, sank ships, and damaged installations, but their most valuable achievement was a photograph of a large airstrip the Japanese were constructing on Kwajalein Island. This proved what none had expected—that a bomber airfield could be built on Kwajalein. Plans to capture the Marshalls in one operation were quickly finalized. Kwajalein, the centerpiece of the Japanese defensive position, would be seized. The eastern Marshalls would be isolated and left to wither on the vine.

Flintlock, as the operation was code-named, required three attack forces. The first two would strike Kwajalein. The northern element would assault the twin islands of Roi-Namur, while the southern would capture Kwajalein Island, on the southern end of the atoll. The third force would occupy undefended Majuro Atoll, which would become a local anchorage for assault forces, and be an operational reserve. The reserves would be held ready to assist in the capture of Kwajalein. If not needed there, they would take part in Operation Catchpole, the assault on Eniwetok. The fast carrier task forces, now designated Task Force 58, had a new commander for Flintlock, Rear Admiral Marc A. Mitscher. As in Galvanic, they had to operate in direct support of the assault forces, but the previous approach of teaming a carrier task force to an assault objective was discarded. Pinning carriers to physical objectives restricted their mobility, and the decision had been criticized. Mitscher would operate his carriers offensively in the Marshalls, rotating between supporting landings and neutralizing Japanese air bases. Two of these carrier groups were kept near the main objectives at Kwajalein Atoll, close enough to concentrate quickly for mutual support.

On January 29, 1944, Task Groups 58.2 and 58.3 attacked Kwajalein. The next day, Task Group 58.1 replaced Task Group 58.3, and the latter moved to Eniwetok, farther to the west and closer to Truk. These relative positions were held until TG 58.3 retired to fuel on February 3. The use of Task Group 58.3 as the advanced guard was deliberate. That group contained the two newest battleships, USS *Iowa* and USS *New Jersey*. The fastest and most powerful in the fleet, these two battleships constituted Battleship Division 7. Their high speed, over 32.5 knots, allowed them to keep pace with the fast carriers. With Battleship Division 7, Task Group 58.3 could outfight any enemy surface force it could not outrun. If a major Japanese counterattack ensued, the task group would fall back on Kwajalein. The remaining six fast battleships were divided evenly between Task Groups 58.1 and 58.2. Major action was once again anticipated. This was the first advance into the Mandates, which were known to be an important element of Japanese defensive strategy. In prewar plans, Admiral Husband E. Kimmel had expected to entice the Japanese to battle in the Central Pacific by threatening their position in the Marshalls.

Now Nimitz expected to do the same with the much larger and more powerful Central Pacific Force. Spruance's battle plan for Flintlock again called for the concentration of all fifteen available battleships, new and old, into a single battle line. Supporting units would be drawn from both the invasion fleet and the carrier groups. To guide the fleet in battle, Spruance planned to employ major action plans. These provided a mutually understood frame of reference and required the minimum of signaling—though if necessary, Spruance would develop his own battle plans and distribute them by signal. Admiral Lee would command the battle line, as before. Catchpole and Hailstone, the anticipated Japanese response to Flintlock, did not occur. Majuro, Roi-Namur, and Kwajalein were all seized without interference from Japanese surface units. The reserve force moved to Eniwetok, initiating Operation Catchpole. Admiral Spruance set his sights on the Combined Fleet. Aerial reconnaissance of Truk showed that major elements of the Japanese fleet were in the Carolines. A powerful attack, Hailstone, was planned to cover the landings at Eniwetok by neutralizing Truk and destroying any forces encountered.

If the Japanese fleet did not come out to fight, Spruance would take the fight to it. Unlike previous major operations involving the fast carriers, Hailstone did not have an amphibious component; Catchpole was a separate operation. Hailstone, however, was not just a raid but a deliberate attempt to destroy a large portion of the Combined Fleet. All the fast battleships were concentrated into a single carrier group, Task Group 58.3, ready to deploy quickly and engage the enemy in the anticipated fleet action. The old battleships were left behind. By the time of the initial air strikes on February 17, 1944, the Japanese had withdrawn their heavy units from Truk, but a large amount of shipping was discovered and attacked in the lagoon. When a group of Japanese light forces attempted to escape through the northern passage, Spruance detached a high-speed surface striking force, Task Group 50.9, to intercept. Battleship Division 7 formed its core; two heavy cruisers and four destroyers were attached in support. This was the first employment of the new battleship division in a role that would often be assigned to it—pursuit and destruction of enemy ships. The high speed of the battleships made them especially well-suited for it, and on this occasion, they were able to destroy four Japanese ships; a lone destroyer escaped. The creation and detachment of *ad hoc* units like this, with no opportunity to train together, had produced unfortunate results fifteen months before off Guadalcanal.

PAC 10 and the recently issued USF 10A had made an important difference, enabling tactical commanders to seize opportunities presented by the rapid operational tempo. The ships of Task Group 50.9 were not the only ones waiting to strike Japanese cripples. Ten submarines had been sent to prowl the waters around Truk in concert with the operation. On February 16, USS *Skate* sighted and torpedoed the cruiser IJN *Agano*, sinking it. The submarine's place in the decisive battle had been found. In future operations, commanders ashore would strategically position submarines to provide distant reconnaissance and to attack targets of opportunity. Additional carrier raids followed. After the successful strike on Truk and the enemy withdrawal from the Carolines, Spruance was free to range deeper into the Japanese defensive system. On February 23, 1944, Task Force 58 struck Japanese air bases in the Marianas, attacking the islands of Guam, Saipan, Tinian, and Rota.

On March 31 and April 1, the fast carriers hit Palau and Yap. The rapid pace of operations emphasized in the Granite plan was being sustained, and it was keeping the pressure on the Japanese. The invasion of Hollandia on the northern coast of New Guinea was a southwest Pacific operation, not a Central Pacific one, but the JCS had decreed that the fast carriers would support it. Seizure of the Japanese base complex between Tanahmerah and Humboldt bays would provide General Douglas MacArthur's Southwest Pacific Force with an ideal position from which to further its advance along the northern coast of the island. Admiral Nimitz remained, however, focused on the destruction of the Japanese Combined Fleet, the primary aim of Granite.

On March 23, during a visit to Brisbane, he emphasized the navy's priorities to the general and made it clear that if the Japanese came out to fight, their fleet would become the primary objective of the fast carrier force. The participation of TF 58 in the operation was code-named Desecrate II. Admiral Mitscher was in command. (Spruance and the Central Pacific Force's amphibious elements remained behind, preparing for the invasion of the Marianas.) As in Flintlock, the fast carriers were to provide direct support to the assault forces and suppress nearby Japanese airfields. Mitscher used three carrier task groups: TG 58.1, which had no battleships, would range to the west and attack Japanese airfields at Wakde, Sawar, and Sarmi; Task Group 58.2, with the two fast battleships of Battleship Division 7, was to support the landings in Humboldt Bay; and TG 58.3, with four other fast battleships, would cover the landings in Tanahmerah Bay.

This arrangement positioned the bulk of Mitscher's surface striking power in the center, facilitating concentration if the Japanese appeared in force. Should a powerful battle fleet be required for a major action, six battleships, ten heavy cruisers, three light cruisers, and twenty-two destroyers were to concentrate under Admiral Lee; a carrier group, Task Group 58.1, would operate in direct support, under Lee's command. In battle, Lee expected to leverage plans and dispositions from FTP 188 and USF 10A. The remaining two carrier groups, stripped of the bulk of their escorts, would remain under Mitscher's command and operate in distant support. Two additional plans were developed, for minor action, should the Japanese challenge with small forces. One teamed Lee's six battleships with two destroyer squadrons. The other was a pursuit force built around Battleship Division 7, very similar to Task Group 50.9, which Spruance had sent around Truk; this time, the two fast battleships would be matched with two heavy cruisers and seven destroyers. Their preferred battle plan was 1E2, from USF 10A—an engagement on parallel courses at extreme range, with light forces on both flanks operating defensively.

By June 1944, Japanese bases in the Marshalls and Carolines had been seized or neutralized, the major base at Rabaul had been rendered untenable, and the Allies were rapidly advancing along the northern coast of New Guinea. It seemed as if the Japanese were content to let their defensive perimeter crumble without risking major fleet units, but this was about to change. The third major offensive of Spruance's force, officially designated the Fifth Fleet on April 29, 1944, was the seizure of the Marianas. Operation Forager comprised the capture of Saipan, Tinian, and Guam. Saipan would be attacked first, on June 15. Landings on Guam were initially scheduled for three days later.

The assault on Tinian would follow, but the specific date remained flexible. Because the capture of the Marshalls and Carolines had not produced a fleet action, the prevailing opinion was that the Japanese navy would not fight for the Marianas. But Spruance had to be prepared for that contingency, and his battle plan for the Marianas changed little from those developed for earlier operations.

As before, he expected to concentrate all his battleships into one formation. Seven old ones supporting the amphibious assaults were to combine with seven fast battleships from the carrier groups to give a total of fourteen. Supporting ships would be drawn from the carrier task groups and assault forces. Concentration and employment of his entire force remained fundamental elements of Spruance's plan. Concentration was also still a guiding principle of the employment of the fast battleships specifically in acting as a covering force have carrier task groups which are screened by fast battleships operate in as close tactical support of each other as the nature of their tasks and enemy action will permit.

The increasing number of escort carriers in the invasion forces allowed the primary focus of the fast carriers to become the suppression of enemy air bases, rather than direct air support for the invasion. The plan called for the carriers to start their attacks three days before the landings, but this date was advanced a day because of the "large, estimated strength of enemy aircraft in the Marianas." On June 11, planes from Mitscher's Task Force 58 struck Japanese positions on Saipan, Tinian, Guam, Rota, and Pagan. These attacks continued for the next two days. The carriers operated in four task groups: Task Group 58.1 attacked Guam, and the other three hit Saipan and Tinian. The fast battleships were kept concentrated: TG 58.2 contained the two high-speed battleships of Battleship Division 7, Task Group 58.3 the other five fast battleships. Finally, Task Groups 58.1 and 58.4 were supported by cruisers. The night before the landings, these two groups were sent north to attack the islands of Chichi Jima and Iwo Jima. The two other groups, with their battleships, remained to cover the landing beaches and assault forces. In the meantime, the Japanese had resolved to contest the landings.

On June 12, having received word of the strikes in the Marianas, the new commander-in-chief of the Combined Fleet, Admiral Soemu Toyoda, issued orders to execute Operation A-Go, his plan for a major fleet action. Three days later, he made his intention explicit: "The Combined Fleet will attack the enemy in the Marianas area and annihilate the invasion force. Activate A-Go Operation for decisive battle." A powerful fleet was assembled under the command of Vice Admiral Jisaburo Ozawa, including nine carriers, five battleships, and eleven heavy cruisers. This force approached the Marianas in two main groups. The carriers and three battleships, with Ozawa embarked, left their base at Tawi-Tawi in the southern Philippines and sailed through the archipelago, transiting the San Bernardino Strait. A second force, with the large battleships IJN *Yamato* and IJN *Musashi*, came north from Batjan in the Moluccas and rendezvoused with Ozawa in the Philippine Sea. Spruance received word of these movements from submarines and realized that a major action was possible if the Japanese continued their approach.

During the night of June 14–15, he ordered Task Groups 58.1 and 58.4 to cut short their attacks on Chichi Jima and Iwo Jima and return for a rendezvous near Saipan on June 18. On June 16, he postponed the invasion of Guam and held a conference with Vice Admiral Richmond K. Turner, commander of the invasion force. The two developed a plan of action to deal with the approaching threat. Two aspects of the developing situation presented particular challenges for Spruance. The battle for Saipan was still going on and limited his mobility, but he had expected that the Japanese would strike before one or more of the islands were secure all along. The fact that the Japanese were approaching in two distinct groups was a more significant problem. Spruance's original plan had anticipated that the Japanese might have two formations, a carrier group and an advanced guard, but he had expected them to be within supporting distance.

The sightings so far suggested instead two independent formations. Therefore, rather than concentrating the entire Fifth Fleet as per the plan, Spruance and Turner elected to strengthen Task Force 58 with five heavy cruisers, three light cruisers, and twenty-one destroyers detached from the invasion forces. The old battleships, three cruisers, and five destroyers were formed into a blocking force and sent west of Saipan. This plan had two advantages: the blocking force provided close cover for the Saipan beachhead, and Task Force 58 retained its mobility by separating itself from the slower old battleships.

On June 17, in preparation for a surface action, Admiral Mitscher recommended detaching the battleships entirely from the carrier task groups and placing them into a separate formation. This would prevent the confusion that would inevitably result if the battleships and their escorts had to form in the middle of an air battle. Spruance concurred; the resulting Task Group 58.7 was placed under command of Admiral Lee. It contained seven battleships, four heavy cruisers, and thirteen destroyers. Spruance then issued his battle plan. It called for air strikes to disable the enemy carriers and surface action by the battle line: "Our air will knock out enemy carriers … then will attack enemy battleships and cruisers to slow or disable them. Task Group 58.7 will destroy enemy fleet either by fleet action if enemy elects to fight or by sinking slowed or crippled ships if enemy retreats."

Early on June 18, when Task Groups 58.1 and 58.4 were to rejoin, a new submarine contact suggested the Japanese were close enough for a surface action that night. Mitscher asked Lee if he desired a night action. Lee declined emphatically: "Do not, repeat, do not believe we should seek night engagement." Lee's response reflected both his own experience and the limited training of his command. He had fought and won a night battle and knew how quickly such an action could degenerate into a melee, particularly if the forces involved lacked cohesion. Lee's formation, formed on the spot from four different task groups, could operate together in daylight, by virtue of the common doctrines of USF 10A, but it was not prepared for night action. Lee's comments after his earlier battle provide clues as to his state of mind at this point: "Our battleships are neither designed nor armed for close range night actions with enemy light forces. A few minutes intense fire … from secondary battery guns can, and did, render one of our new battleships deaf, dumb, blind and impotent through destruction of radar, radio and fire control circuits."

Soon after Lee responded, Spruance decided against night action. He did not want to get too far from the forces at Saipan and risk defeat in detail. It is likely that he also wanted to ensure the concentration of all elements of Task Force 58. Task Groups 58.1 and 58.4 had not yet rejoined. In his response, Spruance mentioned concern at the prospect of a diversionary attack on the flank. Most interpretations take this to mean that Spruance worried that a Japanese southern force would slip beyond him to raid the invasion beaches, but there is another possibility. Captured Japanese planning material, which Spruance had reviewed, discussed flanking, but in another context—attacking an opposing carrier force after its attack planes had been committed to another, less important, target.

The Japanese believed they had been flanked in this sense at Midway, in that their carriers had been struck by surprise from an unanticipated direction while preoccupied with attacking Midway Island. They hoped to do the same to the Americans in future battles, and since Spruance had come into possession of a Japanese document discussing this approach, it is likely that he expected to face such tactics. This explains his preference for remaining concentrated and not striking in force until the Japanese had shown their hand. Spruance's emphasis on concentration continued to influence the developing action. He did not accept Mitscher's recommendation to detach Task Group 58.1 and operate it to the northwest in order to cut off Ozawa's escape route to the home islands.

When a direction-finding fix from Pearl Harbor on June 18 placed the Japanese formation approximately 355 miles to the west, Mitscher recommended closing at night to launch a morning strike and get the battleships into position. Spruance again refused, citing the possibility of an end run. With that decision, the chance for a decisive action was lost. The details of the ensuing battle are well known. The Japanese sent a series of air strikes against Task Force 58, but none succeeded in causing major damage. Their losses in planes and pilots were tremendous. Unable to sustain the attacks, Ozawa turned toward Japan and began to withdraw. Spruance pursued, and on the evening of the next day a long-range strike succeeded in sinking the carrier IJN *Hiyo*, but Spruance again refused to detach task forces.

Before the action, Vice Admiral Charles A. Lockwood, commander of the Pacific Fleet's submarines, stationed four of his boats in a square surrounding the area in which he believed Ozawa's forces would operate. On June 19, two of them found their targets. Albacore sighted and torpedoed Ozawa's flagship, IJN *Taiho*, just after it had completed launching its first strike. Eight hours later, IJN *Taiho* sank, destroyed by the fires that ensued. In the interim, three torpedoes from USS *Cavella* sank carrier IJN *Shokaku*. The outcome in the battle of the Philippine Sea, however, was not decisive, even when the successes of submarines are considered. The Japanese were soundly defeated, but the majority of their fleet units, including most of their carriers and all their battleships, withdrew to fight again. Nonetheless, the first phase of the decisive naval battle of the Pacific War, the carrier duel, was over. The battleship war was yet to come.

4

The U.S. Invasion of the Philippines

To take Leyte, American and Allied forces mounted the largest amphibious operation to date in the Pacific. The JCS designated General MacArthur supreme commander of sea, air, and land forces drawn from both the Southwest Pacific and Central Pacific theaters of operation. Allied naval forces consisted primarily of the U.S. Seventh Fleet, commanded by Vice Admiral Thomas C. Kinkaid. With 701 ships, including 157 warships, Kinkaid's fleet would transport and put ashore the landing force.

The U.S. Sixth Army, commanded by Lieutenant General Walter Krueger, and consisting of two corps of two divisions each, would conduct operations ashore. Major General Franklin C. Sibert's X Corps included the 1st Cavalry Division and the 24th Infantry Division, the latter less the 21st Infantry, which had been temporarily organized as an independent regimental combat team. Major General John R. Hodge's XXIV Corps included the 7th and 96th Infantry Divisions, the latter less the 381st Infantry, also organized as a regimental combat team in army reserve. The Sixth Army reserve would include the 32nd and 77th Infantry Divisions and the 381st Regimental Combat Team. Of the six divisions, only the 96th Infantry Division had not yet seen combat.

On March 12, 1944, the JCS directed General MacArthur to plan an invasion of Mindanao, the southernmost island of the archipelago, starting on November 15. The general responded in June with a two-phase operational plan, which included the seizure of southern Mindanao on October 25 to serve as a staging area for a larger amphibious assault against Leyte three weeks later. Luzon, the largest island in the archipelago and the location of the headquarters for Japanese forces in the islands, would eventually have to be taken to secure the Philippines. However, Mindanao and Leyte had features that made them desirable, if not necessary, preliminary operations to the liberation of Luzon. For one, both islands were accessible. Generally exposed coastlines—Mindanao to the south and Leyte to the east—would allow American forces approaching from either direction to preserve uninterrupted lines of communication from recently secured bases. In contrast, an amphibious strike directly against Luzon in the northern Philippines would be more difficult to support. Second and critical to forces operating together for the first time, both islands were known to be defended by garrisons much smaller than that on Luzon. MacArthur's staff estimated Japanese combat strength on Mindanao to be 50,000 with another 50,000 in the Visayas, the central Philippine Islands which included Leyte. They estimated that Luzon had 180,000 defenders.

Preparation for the invasion of the Philippines was greatly assisted by Operation Ultra, the Allied top secret interception, decryption, and dissemination program against Japanese radio traffic. Acting on tip-offs from Ultra, American submarines and aircraft had been ambushing Japanese shipping in the Western Pacific and interfering with enemy exploitation of resources in the East Indies for many months. In June 1944, Ultra revealed that Tokyo had decided to greatly strengthen its Philippine defenses to block the expected American route of advance northward toward the home islands. That knowledge and subsequent intercepts had allowed the Allied high command to focus submarine and air attacks against Japanese shipping routes and flight paths to the Philippines. But despite increasing losses, the Japanese buildup in the islands continued through the summer and fall of 1944.

For the Allies, the sooner the invasion began, the better. But the availability of amphibious shipping, fleet fire support, and air support became major obstacles to accelerating the invasion date. Logistical studies by different headquarters gave conflicting answers to the question of whether or not there was enough shipping in the Pacific to support major landings on both Mindanao and Leyte. By the end of summer, the JCS could no longer wait to fix the timetable for the assault. On September 8, the chiefs directed MacArthur and Nimitz to take the Leyte and Surigao Strait area beginning December 20.

The issues of objectives and operational scheduling were finally settled by fleet-covering operations in support of the invasion of the Palaus and Morotai. Beginning on September 7, 1944, carrier task forces from Admiral William F. Halsey's Third Fleet struck Yap and the Palaus, as well as Mindanao and islands in the central Philippines. Air strikes continued in October against Japanese airfields on Okinawa, Formosa, and Luzon, as well as enemy shipping in adjacent waters. American planners estimated that these attacks destroyed more than 500 enemy aircraft in the Philippines and a similar number elsewhere, in addition to about 180 seagoing merchant ships. The aerial successes convinced them that a major landing on Mindanao was no longer necessary and that available shipping and logistical strength could now be concentrated on Leyte. Accordingly, the JCS directed MacArthur and Nimitz to cancel intermediate operations and accelerate planning to carry out an invasion of Leyte on October 20.

Meanwhile, Japanese imperial headquarters received a completely different impression of what had been occurring. With their naval pilots forwarding wildly exaggerated reports of downing 1,200 American aircraft and sinking eleven aircraft carriers, Tokyo became increasingly optimistic. Although senior naval officers grew suspicious of these claims, other military authorities in Tokyo accepted them. In their eyes, the supposed American losses made it possible to decisively defeat the Americans wherever they landed in the Philippines, if Japan could concentrate its resources there. American planners, however, continued to regard Leyte as a mere steppingstone to the more decisive campaign for Luzon. This conceptual difference would greatly increase the stakes at Leyte or wherever the Americans landed first.

One of the larger islands of the Philippine archipelago, Leyte extends 110 miles from north to south and ranges between 15 and 50 miles in width. The land surface presented features both inviting and forbidding to U.S. military planners. Deep-water approaches on the east side of the island and sandy beaches offered opportunities for amphibious assaults and close-in resupply operations. The interior of the island was dominated by a heavily forested north–south mountain range, separating two sizable valleys, or coastal plains. The larger of the two, Leyte Valley, extends from the northern coast to the long eastern shore and at the time, contained most of the towns and roadways on the island. Highway 1 ran along the east coast for some 40 miles between the town of Abuyog to the northern end of San Juanico Strait between Leyte and Samar Islands. The roads and lowlands extending inland from Highway 1 provided avenues for tank-infantry operations, as well as a basis for airfield construction.

The only other lowland expanse, Ormoc Valley, is on the west side of the island connected to Leyte Valley by a roundabout and winding road. From the town of Palo on the east coast, Highway 2 ran west and northwest through Leyte Valley to the north coast, then turned south and wound through a mountainous neck to enter the north end of Ormoc Valley. The road continued south to the port of Ormoc City, then along Leyte's western shore to the town of Baybay. There it turned east to cross the mountainous waist of the island and connected with Highway 1 on the east coast at Abuyog. Below Abuyog and Baybay, the mountainous southern third of Leyte was only sparsely inhabited and contained no areas suitable for development.

Mountain peaks reaching to over 4,400 feet as well as the jagged outcroppings, ravines, and caves typical of volcanic islands offered formidable defensive opportunities. In addition, the late-year schedule of the assault would force combat troops and supporting pilots, as well as logistical units, to contend with monsoon rains. On a favorable note, the population of over 900,000 people, most of whom engaged in agriculture and fishing, could be expected to assist an American invasion, since many residents already supported the guerrilla struggle against the Japanese in the face of harsh repression.

Supplementing these forces were a battalion of Rangers and a support command specially tailored for large amphibious operations. The task of the 6th Ranger Infantry Battalion was to secure outlying islands and guide naval forces to the landing beaches. The new Sixth Army Service Command, commanded by Major General Hugh J. Casey, was responsible for organizing the beachhead supplying units ashore, and constructing or improving roads and airfields. General Krueger had under his command a total of 202,500 ground troops. The tasks of the commander of Allied naval forces, SWPA:

1. Transport and establish landing forces ashore in the Leyte Gulf–Surigao Strait area, as arranged with the commanding general, Sixth U.S. Army.
2. Support the operation by:
    a. Provide air protection for convoys and naval task forces and direct air support for the landing and subsequent operations, supplemented as arranged with the commander of the Third Fleet and the commander of Allied air forces.
    b. Arrange direct air support and cover with carrier aircraft for minesweeping and preliminary landings in the Leyte Gulf Area during the period A-2 to the time escort carriers assume the mission of direct support of A-Day (landing day).
    c. Transporting supporting troops and their supplies as required to the Leyte Gulf–Surigao area, in naval assault shipping.
    d. Denying Japanese reinforcement of the Leyte Area from Samar, western Visayas and northwestern Mindanao.
    e. Clearing the Surigao Strait area of hostile naval forces, and shipping, and sweeping the Surigao Strait to open it for naval operations and shipping in the Camotes Sea and adjacent waters, in conjunction with operations of the Sixth U.S. Army.
3. Provide submarine offensive reconnaissance a long probably routes of hostile naval forces and or water borne reinforcements and supplies.
4. Provide lifeguard service as required.
5. Transfer to the commander of Allied air forces the mission of direct air support when land-based fighters and the light bombers are established in the Leyte area, at a time as arranged with the commander of Allied air forces.
6. Escort and protect shipping on the lines or communication into the Leyte and Samar areas.
7. Establish in Visayan waters naval forces required to support current and future operations by:

a. During the period A-1 to A-7, effect carrier strikes on Okinawa and Formosa and northern Leyte objectives. Selection of targets to be dependent upon intelligence data and the strategic situations obtaining at that time.

b. During the period A-4 and including A-Day, to effect carrier strikes on the Luzon–Bicols area, the Leyte–Cebu–Negros area, and in support of the landing in the Leyte area.
c. Beginning on A plus 1 and thereafter to operate in strategic support of the operation, effecting strikes as the situation at the time required.
d. It was anticipated that the shore-based air forces, Central Pacific, would operate in the general Bicols area as soon as effective from Palau.

To accomplish the assigned task, forces already serving in the Seventh Fleet were greatly augmented by units from Central Pacific and the Third Amphibious Force, under Vice Admiral Wilkinson, was made available in its entirety. The new organization, under the overall command of the commander of Seventh Fleet, consisted of three task forces, numbers 77, 78, and 79. Task Force 77 was divided into fire support group, escort carrier group, minesweeping and hydrographic group, and service group; Task Forces 78 and 79 were the amphibious attack forces. The landings and other missions were carried out as planned, with the result that Allied forces became securely entrenched in the Central Philippines.

Air support for the Leyte operation would be provided by the Seventh Fleet during the transport and amphibious phases, then transferred to Allied air forces, commanded by Lieutenant General George C. Kenney, when conditions ashore allowed. More distant-covering air support would be provided by the four fast carrier task forces of Admiral Halsey's Third Fleet, whose operations would remain under overall command of Admiral Nimitz.

The Sixth Army mission of securing Leyte was to be accomplished in three phases. The first would begin on October 17, three days before and some fifty miles east of the landing beaches, with the seizure of three islands commanding the eastern approaches to Leyte Gulf. On October 20, termed 'A-day,' the X and XXIV Corps would land at separate beaches on the east coast of Leyte, the former on the right (north), the latter 15 miles to the south. As quickly as possible, the X Corps would take the city of Tacloban and its airfield both just one mile north of the corps beachhead secure the strait between Leyte and Samar Islands, then push through Leyte Valley to the north coast. The XXIV Corps' mission was to secure the southern end of Leyte Valley for airfield and logistical development. Meanwhile, the 21st Regimental Combat Team would come ashore some 70 miles south of the main landing beaches to secure the strait between Leyte and Panaon Islands. In the third phase, the two corps would take separate routes through the mountains to clear the enemy from Ormoc Valley and the west coast of the island at the same time placing an outpost on the island of Samar some 35 miles north of Tacloban.

Preliminary operations for the Leyte invasion began at dawn on October 17 with minesweeping operations and the movement of the 6th Rangers toward three small islands in Leyte Gulf. Although delayed by a storm, the Rangers were on Suluan and Dinagat by 12:30 p.m. On Suluan, they dispersed a small number of Japanese defenders and destroyed a radio station, while they found no enemy on Dinagat. On both, the Rangers proceeded to erect navigation lights for the amphibious transports to follow three days later. The Rangers occupied the third island Homonhon, without opposition the next day. Meanwhile, reconnaissance by underwater demolition teams revealed clear landing beaches for assault troops on Leyte itself.

Accordingly to plan, on October 11, the slow minesweepers sortied from Manus and on October 12, the Dinagat force left Hollandia. They rendezvoused near Palau and were joined on October 15 by Task Groups 77.2, 77.4 (with twelve CVEs), and 77.6, which together had sortied from Manus on October 12. These groups proceeded to their stations off Leyte Gulf, arriving during a storm on the evening of October 16. A few minesweepers were delayed by high seas but were able to arrive on A-3 day in time to effect sweeps. At 1 p.m. on A-3 day, Task Unit 77.2.3 and Task Group 78.4 advanced from the main body towards their targets. The other ships, including the escort carriers, cruised east and southeast of Leyte Gulf, waiting on appointed hours to commence their respective missions. Bad weather prevented any air activity from the carriers until 5:30 a.m. on October 18, by which time the weather was excellent, the sea was moderate to smooth and the ceiling was 8,000 feet.

The main landings on Leyte Island were preceded by minesweeping, seizure of Suluan, Dinagat, and Homonhon Islands, underwater reconnaissance of beach areas and aerial and ship bombardment. The objective was to destroy any enemy personnel, installations, and facilities that might interfere with the landings.

Several enemy planes attacked the fire support group in the early morning of October 20 and anti-aircraft fire was instituted immediately. One bomber dropped two bombs toward USS *Louisville,* but they exploded in the water and did no damage. Minor attacks continued sporadically during the day.

Following four hours of heavy naval gunfire on A-Day, October 20, Sixth Army forces landed on assigned beaches at 10 a.m. Troops from X Corps pushed across a 4-mile stretch of beach between Tacloban airfield and the Palo River. Some 15 miles to the south, XXIV Corps units came ashore across a 3-mile strand between San José and the Daguitan River. Troops in both corps sectors found as much or more resistance from swampy terrain as from Japanese fire. Within an hour of landing, units in most sectors had secured beachheads deep enough to receive heavy vehicles and large amounts of supplies. Only in the 24th Division sector did enemy fire force a diversion of follow-on landing craft. But even that sector was secure enough by 1:30 p.m. to allow General MacArthur to make a dramatic entrance through the surf and announce to the populace the beginning of their liberation, "People of the Philippines, I have returned! By the grace of Almighty God, our forces stand again on Philippine soil."

By the end of A-Day, the Sixth Army had moved inland as deep as two miles and controlled Panaon Strait at the southern end of Leyte. In the X Corps sector, the 1st Cavalry Division held Tacloban airfield and the 24th Infantry Division had taken the high ground commanding its beachheads on Hill 522. In the XXIV Corps sector, the 96th Infantry Division held the approaches to Catmon Hill, the highest point in both corps beachheads; the 7th Infantry Division had taken the town of Dulag, forcing General Makino to move his 16th Division command post 10 miles inland to the town of Dagami. These gains had been won at a cost of forty-nine killed, 192 wounded, and six missing.

In the days that followed, the Sixth Army made steady progress inland against an enemy that resisted tenaciously at several points but was unable to coordinate an overall island defense. In the process, the 1st Cavalry Division, commanded by Major General Verne D. Mudge, secured the provincial capital of Tacloban on October 21. Two days later, General MacArthur presided over a ceremony to restore civil government to Leyte.

5

Japanese Naval Doctrine

The main factors that drove the formulation of the Japanese naval doctrine during World War II are first, who is the anticipated enemy, and second, what is their relative economic and military strength. Clearly, Japan viewed the U.S. as the only real impediment to its domination in the western Pacific. America would undoubtedly be the main foe. It was also accepted that Japan's economic and resource base would never match that of the U.S. Even if Japan established secure sources of raw materials, these sources would always be vulnerable. Moreover, whatever military advantage Japan could establish over the U.S. would eventually disappear once America was fully committed to war.

From these two main factors, two divergent doctrines emerged. The first doctrine assumed that the primary way to secure victory was through a decisive battle waged against the enemy fleet. The second view focused on a defensive posture, which relied on a relatively small number of ships to extend a controlling influence without ever leaving port. Both views had supporters in the Imperial Navy. The defensive posture was mostly favored by the naval general staff. Prominent senior officers such as Takijiro Onishi, Shigeyoshi Inouye, and Nagano Osami firmly believed that a defensive, attrition-based doctrine would afford the best opportunity for victory.

The opposing view, which favored a decisive victory doctrine, was championed by the Combined Fleet Staff and, perhaps more importantly, counted Admiral Isoroku Yamamoto as its most influential support. This doctrine inherently embodied a more aggressive, offensive strategy. But even Admiral Yamamoto had mixed views towards this doctrine. On one hand, he realized that the Japanese Navy could not win with a purely defensive posture because it would give the initiative to the Americans who could determine when and how to meet the Imperial Fleet. Conversely, he noted that in previous war games, a decisive victory was never achieved, and the games were suspended when it became clear that Japanese for would be gradually whittled away.

Both of these doctrines were born out of a sense of material inferiority that the Japan felt throughout the 1920s and 1930s. This sense of material inferiority and the underdog mentality that resulted, influenced many naval officers and affected all phases of naval planning from strategy to weapons design and procurement. The inability to firmly commit to either doctrine is evidenced by the types of weapons the Japanese designed and procured. While the keels for the super battleships IJN *Yamato* and IJN *Musashi* were being laid, plans were put in motion to increase the submarine force. As a result, by the end of the war, over 126 submarines were built. While the battleship reflected a weapon capable of winning the decisive battle as it was envisioned by the Japanese in late 1930s, the submarine, as the Japanese would come to employ it, was thought to be primarily a weapon of interception and attrition.

By December 1941, through the influence of Admiral Yamamoto, the decisive battle doctrine prevailed. The opening salvo in the Pacific war, the impressive attack on Pearl Harbor, was affirmation that this doctrine was in force. When interviewed after the war, Captain Toshikzu Ohmae remarked that, "he believed too much emphasis was put on the offensive in our Japanese naval thinking and in our War College Training." Moreover, this doctrine will drive the strategy that directed all of the Japanese operational plans. But as we shall see from the case studies, the inability of the Japanese naval leadership to firmly commit to either doctrine will complicate their war plans and sow the seeds of failure. The decisive battle doctrine, in large part, defined the tactics which would be used to execute the operational plans. Tactics, in a broad sense, exists at the strategic, operational, and tactical levels of war.

The operational level tactics used by the Imperial Navy can be distilled into two overall categories: surprise and outranging. Surprise was an essential operational tactic used throughout the war in the Pacific and can be sub-divided into two key components—secrecy and deception. Integral to virtually every operational plan was the use of the element of surprise. The caricature of the "sneaky oriental" common in wartime propaganda is a gross misrepresentation. Nonetheless, the Japanese sought to fold into their operational plans the best elements of the Sun Tzu style of war fighting. In each of the case studies of Japanese actions, surprise, secrecy, and deception are significant elements.

Outranging is the second primary operational tactic which most of the Japanese plans were built around. Outranging permeated practically every aspect of naval planning in the air, on the surface, and undersea. On the surface, the idea was to deploy large, heavily armored, unsinkable battleships and battle cruisers to engage the enemy outside his effective weapons range. Japan could only afford to build a small number of big ships with big guns, thus quality, not quantity, was the rule. This fit in nicely with the decisive battle doctrine wherein a large ship could mass superior firepower upon the enemy. However, the big ship idea did not fit in well with attrition-style warfare where it is assumed a few units will be sacrificed in the course of the overall campaign. In addition, the emphasis on night fighting, with large ships slugging it out in the dark, was incorporated into operational tactics as early as 1927. Japanese training also stressed this concept.

By 1937, Japan no longer adhered to the Washington or London Treaties, which put severe restrictions on the number, size, and strength of naval combatants Japan could build. The pinnacle of the outranging concept by surface ships was reflected in the *Yamato*-class battleship, which carried 18.1-inch guns with a range of 40,000 meters. These behemoths, though running counter to the new emphasis on aviation, were monuments to the strength of the outranging idea. They were certainly capable of outranging and out gunning any ship afloat in a conventional surface-to-surface fleet engagement.

Outranging as an operational tactic in undersea warfare could also be used to support either the decisive battle or attrition doctrines. As a weapon of attrition-interception, the submarine relied on the torpedo as its main weapon. At a range of 40,000 meters running at 32 knots, the type 91 oxygen torpedo had more than five times the range of U.S. and British torpedoes. With this range and speed, it was a potent weapon against a surface combatant in either attrition warfare or as an element in the decisive battle. In addition, in 1933, the navy began work on a midget submarine which tacticians believed, if properly developed, would give the inferior Japanese fleet an edge in the decisive battle. Thus, the Imperial Navy was well positioned to utilize the submarine in a wide range of missions encompassing either the decisive battle or attrition interception doctrines.

Similar to undersea warfare, operational tactics using aircraft could support the outranging concept in either a decisive battle or attrition-based doctrine. The Japanese stressed the outranging concept in all of their aircraft at the start of the war included the Mitsubishi Zero, which range was 1,930 nautical miles; the Aichi Val dive bomber, with a range of 970 nautical miles; and the Yokosuka Judy, with a range of 1,320 nautical miles. Compared to the Grumman F4F Wildcat, with a range of 721 nautical miles; Douglas TBD Devastator, range 435 nautical miles; and Douglas SBD Dauntless, with a range of 464 nautical miles, Japanese aircraft could outrange any U.S. aircraft. Only later in the war, using large land-based bombers, could the U.S. exceed the ranges achieved by Japanese aircraft.

While it is clear that Japanese aircraft could clearly outrange American aircraft, the more relevant debate revolved around the primacy of the aircraft carrier as the central capital ship. Many influential officers in the Imperial Navy argued that aircraft had overtaken the battleship. By 1939, the attack range of a Japanese combined air wing was about 200 nautical miles, far beyond the range of any big gun. The debate continued throughout the war and the subsequent division in thinking would become a critical element in operational planning. The Japanese incorporated other operational tactics into their plans. However other elements of operational level tactics such as maneuver, massing of force, phasing, and sequencing can all be seen to support the outranging concept.

Overall training for the Japanese was quite good. Throughout the war, they continued to demonstrate excellent seamanship and airmanship even in the face of tremendous adversity. Their surface training continued to stress the decisive night engagement. This skill was amply demonstrated throughout the war, most notably during the Battle of Savo Island in August 1942. Japanese aviation training was excellent at the start of the war. They had commenced formal flight training in 1920 and by December 1941, over 3,500 naval aviators and 2,500 army aviators were ready for combat. At the start of the war, navy and army pilots entered combat with over 700 and 500 flight hours respectively. However, both the quantity and quality of pilot production decreased as the war progressed so that by the end of the war most navy and army pilots entered combat with less than 100 flight hours. And as most aviators will agree, that is barely enough time to feel comfortable in the cockpit.

Besides the declining quality of aviators reaching the fleet, Japanese naval aviation suffered in two additional key areas, which were directly related to training. First, reconnaissance and, more importantly its sister skill, recognition was very poor throughout the war. It is difficult to accurately identify ships at sea from any air platform, especially in a combat situation. But couple this inherent difficulty with a lack of proper recognition and reporting training, and the likelihood of generating inaccurate reconnaissance reports is substantially increased. Second, while the early cadre of aviators received night carrier landing training, they were far from proficient and contributed to the failure of their operational plans. As a result of the limited quantity and quality of aviation training, the *kamikaze* units emerged. The Japanese will come to draw upon the *bushido* warrior spirit in an act of selfless sacrifice to compensate for shortfalls in training and dwindling aircraft assets. A similar shortfall occurred in the submarine force as a result of training and submarine design. The main focus of submarine design was on making a formidable war machine, not on habitability. The confined quarters might have been adequate if there had been enough men to rotate the crews for proper rest and rehabilitation after each mission. But there were never enough trained men. As time passed, the efficiency of submarines deteriorated even faster than their numbers decreased, and the results were disastrous. Lastly, training stressed unquestioning obedience at all levels and all ranks. This training included standing prohibitions against rebut, surrender and being taken alive. While this intense devotion to duty and unwavering discipline is a tremendous asset to the commander in the field, at the higher levels of planning and policymaking, it hinders effective debate, stifles legitimate criticism, and prevents probing evaluation of plans and policies. This intense obedience existed, to varying degrees, among the Japanese officers charged with formulating operational plans. The result is that operational plans with essential flaws were often initiated without anyone clearly and forcefully challenging their validity and applicability.

Leadership styles vary considerably among individual commanders and only fragmentary information exists on Japanese wartime naval leaders. Except for Yamamoto and other select naval leaders, little is known. However, from their actions in battle, three general qualities emerge. First, in part, due to their early training, they displayed intense obedience and devotion to duty. Their sense of commitment and unswerving dedication was unsurpassed. Time after time, they engaged U.S. forces even when the odds were decidedly against them, which occasionally paid-off. However, this had a negative side too. Often when it appeared that there was not a logical or operational reason to press ahead, many Japanese naval leaders may have needlessly endangered their units, there by jeopardizing vital assets which could have been used more effectively elsewhere. Second, it is clear from a review operational studies, and other key naval engagements, that Japanese commanders were skilled and accomplished seamen. They were very capable of executing complex naval maneuvers and following operational plans. Third, many Japanese leaders possessed an underlying sense of apprehension born of the material inferiority most had lived through during the 1920s and 1930s. Perhaps this thought never left them and emerged at critical junctions in several key battles. It is this tension, created by their intense sense of duty and commitment on one side, and this underlying apprehension on the other that makes Japanese leaders so complex and challenging to fully understand. Nonetheless, it is an important element, one which will directly impact the Japanese in their operational planning.

It is worth noting that the navy sent its most promising officers to tours of duty in Washington as naval *attachés*. Admiral Yamamoto and Vice Admiral Nagumo both had tours in the U.S. Many other officers had the same opportunity. This gave the Japanese naval leadership direct understanding and a unique insight into America that few U.S. wartime leaders had of Japan. It is important to recognize the spiritual and moral leadership Admiral Yamamoto provided to the Imperial Navy. It was through his strength of character and influence that many critical debates on policy and strategy were resolved in the first years of the war. His initial reluctance to go to war with the U.S. is acknowledged by many and was based on his personal and accurate assessment of projected American war fighting potential. But once Japan was committed to war, he was determined to win the decisive naval battle. When the transport plane he was embarked on was shot down in April 1943 by U.S. P-38s, the Imperial Navy suffered a major defeat. No other naval leader could completely take his place and the unifying effect he provided was lost.

6

The Japanese Philippines Defensive Plan

So ominous for Japan's future war prospects were the defeats inflicted by Allied arms in the Marianas and Western New Guinea in the early summer of 1944 that, in mid-July, they culminated in the second shake-up of the army and navy high commands in five months, and the first major political crisis since the Tōjō government had taken the nation into war.

On July 17, Admiral Shigetaro Shimada resigned as navy minister in the Tōjō cabinet, and a day later, simultaneously with the public announcement of the fall of Saipan, General Tōjō tendered the resignation of the entire cabinet, yielding not only his political offices as premier and war minister, but also stepping down as chief of army general staff. General Kuniaki Koiso (retired), then governor-general of Korea, formed a new cabinet on July 22 with Field Marshal Sugiyama as war minister and Admiral Mitsumasa Yonai as navy minister. General Yoshijiro Umezu was named chief of army general staff. The shake-up was not finally completed until August 2 when Admiral Shimada also yielded his post as chief of navy general staff to be replaced by Admiral Koshiro Oikawa.

While these changes in Japan's top-level war command were still taking place, the planning staffs of the army and navy sections of imperial general headquarters were already giving urgent attention to the revision of future war strategy in the light of the new situation created by the parallel Allied thrusts into Western New Guinea and the Marianas. Strategically, as well as in virtually every other respect, the situation was darker than at any time since the outbreak of the Pacific War.

The absolute defense zone defined by imperial GHQ in September 1943 had in fact been penetrated at two vital points. In the south, General MacArthur's forces, within six months of their breakthrough via the Vitiaz and Dampier Straits, had pushed one arm of the Allied offensive more than 1,000 miles along the north coast of New Guinea, bypassing and isolating huge numbers of Japanese troops along the axis of advance. The capture of Hollandia gave the Allies a major staging area for further offensive moves, and his land-based air forces, with forward bases on Biak and Noemfoor, were in a position to extend their domination over the Moluccas, Palau, and the sea approaches to the southern Philippines.

In the Central Pacific, the northern prong of the Allied offensive had bypassed the Japanese naval stronghold at Truk to penetrate the planned defense perimeter at a second vital point in the Marianas, only 1,500 miles from the home islands themselves. The seizure of Saipan not only placed the Volcano and Bonin Islands within easy range of Allied tactical bomber aircraft, but threatened Japan itself with intensified raids by the new B-29, already operating from western China. More serious still, the crippling losses suffered by the navy in the Philippine Sea Battle, especially in air strength, gave the Allies unquestioned fleet and air supremacy in the Western Pacific.

Because of the vast expansion of the areas menaced by Allied sea and air activity, it was necessary to abandon all projects for the dispatch of major reinforcements to segments of the outer defense line which still remained intact, notably Palau and Halmahera. Japanese lines of communication with the southern area were pushed back into the inner waters of the South and East China Seas, and even these relatively protected, interior routes were now subject to increased danger since the acquisition of new bases in the Marianas enabled Allied submarines to step up and prolong their operations against convoys moving along the inner shipping lanes.

Transport losses due to Allied undersea attacks, particularly in the waters adjacent to the Philippines, had already assumed grave proportions before the loss of the Marianas. Vital military and raw materials traffic between Japan and the southern area was seriously affected, and by the summer of 1944, fuel reserves in the homeland had dwindled to a critically low point, while southbound troops and materiel began to pile up at Manila, the central distribution point for the entire southern area, for lack of transport. Personnel replacement depots in the Manila area were so overcrowded that local food supplies ran short and the troops had to be placed on reduced rations.

The shortage of fuel reserves in Japan had a hampering effect on the operational mobility of Japan's remaining fleet strength. Soon after returning to home bases from the Philippine Sea Battle, the First Mobile Fleet was obliged to split its forces, dispatching most of its surface strength to Lingga anchorage, in the Dutch East Indies, where sufficient fuel was available, while the carrier forces remained in home waters to await aircraft and pilot replacements.

With the main Pacific defense line breached at two points and its remaining segments incapable of being reinforced adequately to ensure successful resistance to Allied assault, it was obvious that Japan must now fall back upon its inner defenses extending from the Kuriles and Japanese Islands through the Ryukyu Islands,

Formosa, and the Philippines to the Dutch East Indies. Plans and preparations had to be swiftly be completed with a view to the eventual commitment of the maximum ground, sea, and air strength that Japan could muster in a decisive battle to halt the enemy advance when it reached this inner line. Because of their key strategic position linking Japan with the southern area of natural resources, the Philippines naturally assumed a position of primary importance in the formulation of these plans. Just as their initial conquest had been necessary to guard the Japanese line of advance to the south in 1941–1942, so was their retention of paramount importance to the defense of the empire in 1944.

Were the Philippines lost, the already contracted supply lines over which flowed the fuel and other resources essential to continued prosecution of the war would be completely severed, and all of Japan's southern armies from Burma to the islands north of Australia would be cut off from the homeland. At the same time, the Allies would gain possession of a vital steppingstone toward the heart of the empire and a staging area adequate to accommodate the vast build-up of forces and materiel required for mounting the final assault upon the Japanese home islands. Imperial GHQ estimates of Allied offensive plans also underlined the importance of the Philippines. As early as March 1944, a careful study of the Allies' probable future strategy arrived at the conclusion that there was only slight possibility of a direct advance upon Japan from the Central Pacific, primarily because the absence of land bases within fighter range of the main islands would make effective air support of an invasion via that route extremely difficult. Instead, it was considered most probable that the enemy offensives from New Guinea and the Central Pacific would first converge upon the Philippines in order to sever Japan's southern line of communications, and that, with these islands as a major base, the advance would then be pushed northward toward Japan via the Ryukyu Island chain. Land-based air power would be able to support each successive stage of this advance.

The Allied thrust into the Marianas in June caused imperial GHQ to reexamine the possibilities of a direct advance upon the homeland from that direction, but while a capability was accepted, the high command did not diverge from its previous estimate that the enemy's most probable course would be to undertake reconquest of the Philippines as a prior requisite to the invasion of the Japanese homeland.

On the basis of these estimates, imperial GHQ decided that top priority in preparations for decisive battle along the inner defense line must be assigned to the Philippines. It was anticipated that the Allies would launch preliminary moves against Palau and Halmahera about the middle of September in order to secure advance supporting air bases, and that the major assault on the Philippines would come sometime after the middle of November. With the short space of only four months remaining before the anticipated invasion deadline, all Japan's energies had to be concentrated on the task of transforming the

Philippines into a powerful defense stronghold capable of turning back and destroying the Allied forces.

For almost a year and a half following the completion of the Japanese occupation of the Philippines in June 1942, little attention had been given either by imperial GHQ or by the occupying forces to preparations against an ultimate Allied reinvasion. Japan's full war energies were thrown into the outer perimeter of advance to meet steadily intensifying Allied counter-pressure, and the development of a strategic inner defense system went neglected until the establishment in September 1943 of the absolute defense zone embracing areas west of Marianas–Carolines–Western New Guinea line. Under the plans worked out for this zone, the Philippines were to play the role of a rear base of operations as an assembly and staging area for troops and supplies and a concentration area for air reserves, to support operations at any threatened point on the main defense perimeter from the Marianas south to Western New Guinea and the Banda Sea area. To implement these plans, imperial GHQ in October directed the Fourteenth Army to complete the establishment of the necessary base facilities by the spring of 1944. Major emphasis in this program was laid upon the construction of air bases. The army alone planned to build or improve thirty airfields in addition to thirteen already in operational use or partially completed. The navy projected twenty-one airfields and seaplane bases to be ready for operational use by the end of 1944, expanding its total number of Philippine bases to thirty-three. Line of communications and other rear area base installations were also to be expanded and improved.

To speed up the execution of the program, imperial GHQ dispatched additional personnel to the Philippines in November, and ordered the reorganization and expansion of the 10th, 11th, and 17th Independent Garrison Units, currently stationed on Mindanao, the Visayas, and northern Luzon respectively, into the 30th, 31st, and 32nd Independent Mixed Brigades, with a strength of six infantry battalions each, plus normal supporting elements. In addition, the 33rd Independent Mixed Brigade was newly activated at Fort Stotsenberg, Luzon, by combining various garrison units.

Between October 1943 and March 1944, military preparations in the Philippines remained confined to the development of the islands as a rear operational base for support of decisive battle operations along the Marianas–Carolines–Western New Guinea line. No plans were yet considered for fortifying the Philippines themselves against enemy invasion, partially because Japan's resources were already heavily taxed in order to complete preparations along the main forward line, and partially because of belief that the Allied advance could be stopped at this forward barrier.

In March, however, the first indications of a change in strategic thinking with regard to the Philippines appeared. On March 27, imperial GHQ army section ordered a revision of the command set-up for the southern area, expanding

Southern Army's operational control to take in the Fourteenth Army in the Philippines, the Second Area Army in Western New Guinea and the eastern Dutch East Indies, and Fourth Air Army. The same order directed Fourteenth Army to institute defense preparations, particularly on Mindanao, and on April 4, imperial GHQ transferred the 32nd Division to Fourteenth Army for the purpose of reinforcing the southern Philippines.

Although the Philippines were expected to be the first of these inner areas to be attacked, imperial GHQ also had to consider the possible contingency that the enemy might strike alternatively at Formosa or the Ryukyu Islands, or possibly even at the Japanese home islands themselves. Comprehensive operational plans therefore had to be worked out to cover all these possibilities.

The basic strategic principle adopted as the foundation of these plans was that whichever of the inner areas first became the object of invasion operations by the main strength of the Allies would be designated as the decisive battle theater, and that as soon as this theater was determined, all available sea, air, and ground forces would be swiftly concentrated there to crush the invading force. Because of the necessity of central control and coordination, the decision as to when and where to activate decisive battle operations was reserved to the highest command level, the imperial GHQ.

Following the issuance of the army's basic Shō-Go operations order on July 24, the navy section of imperial GHQ on July 26 issued a new directive fitting its previous outline of naval policy for urgent operations into the framework of the Shō-Go operations plan. To implement both these directives, the Combined Fleet on August 1 issued Combined Fleet Top Secret Operations Order Number 83, which specified the following general missions of the naval forces in the Shō-Go operations:

1. Operational Policy: The Combined Fleet will cooperate with the army according to the operational procedures specified by imperial GHQ for the Shō-Go operations in order to intercept and destroy the invading enemy in decisive battle at sea and to maintain an impregnable strategical position.
2. Outline of Operations:

a. Preparations: (1) air bases will be prepared as rapidly as possible in the Philippines to permit deployment of the entire air strength of the First and Second Air Fleets. Air bases in the Clark Field and Bacolod areas will be organized rapidly in accordance with the Army-Navy Central Agreement.

b. Operations: (1) enemy aircraft carriers will be destroyed first by concentrated attacks of the base air forces. (2) Transport convoys will be destroyed jointly by the surface and air forces. If the enemy succeeds in landing, transports carrying reinforcements and the troops already on land will be the principal targets so as to annihilate them at the beachhead.

(3) Surface forces will sortie against the enemy landing point within two days after the enemy begins landing. All-out air attacks will be launched two days prior to the attack by the surface forces.

Combined Fleet Top Secret Operations Order Number 84, also issued on August 1, fixed the new tactical grouping of naval forces for the Shō-Go operations. Almost the entire surface combat strength of the fleet was included in a task force placed under the overall command of the First Mobile Fleet commander, Vice Admiral Jisaburo Ozawa. This force was broken down into three tactical groups:

1. The task force main body, directly commanded by Vice Admiral Ozawa and consisting of most of the Third Fleet (carrier forces).
2. The First Striking Force, commanded by Vice Admiral Takeo Kurita and made up of the Second Fleet with part of the 10th Destroyer Squadron attached.
3. The Second Striking Force commanded by Vice Admiral Kiyohide Shima and composed of the Fifth Fleet plus two destroyer divisions and the battleships *Fusō* and *Yamashiro*.

The manner in which these tactical forces were to be employed in the planned decisive battle operations was set forth in more detail in an outline of operations annexed to Combined Fleet Top Secret Operations Order Number 85, issued on August 4. The gist of this outline applying to surface force operations was as follows:

1. Disposition of forces: The First Striking Force will be stationed at Lingga Anchorage, while the task force main body and the Second Striking Force will be stationed in the western part of the Inland Sea. However, if an enemy, attack becomes expected, the First Striking Force will advance from Lingga Anchorage to Brunei, Coron, or Guimaras; the task force main body and the Second Striking Force will remain in the Inland Sea and prepare to attack the north flank of the enemy task force.
2. Combat operations: If the enemy attack reaches the stage of landing operations, the First Striking Force, in conjunction with the base air forces, will attack the enemy in the landing area.
   a. If the enemy attack occurs before the end of August, the Second Striking Force, plus the 4th Carrier Division and part of the 3rd Carrier Division, will facilitate the operations of the First Striking Force by launching effective attacks against the enemy and diverting his task forces to the northeast.
   b. If the enemy attack occurs after the end of August, the Second Striking Force will be incorporated under the command of the task force main body as a vanguard force. The main body will then assume the mission

> of diverting the enemy task forces to the northeast in order to facilitate the attack of the First Striking Force and will also carry out an attack against the flank of the enemy task forces.

During August, the navy section of imperial GHQ also took action to give the Combined Fleet more unified operational control of naval forces in order to facilitate the execution of the Shō-Go plans. On August 9, the General Escort Command and units assigned to naval stations were placed under operational command of the Combined Fleet, and on August 21, the China Area Fleet was similarly placed under Combined Fleet command.

While army and navy air forces prepared themselves for battle, the widely dispersed naval surface forces also continued preparations for the vital role they were to play in the Shō-Go operations. At Lingga Anchorage, south of Singapore, the First Striking Force concentrated on training in night attacks and the use of radar fire control, the latter of which had not been extensively employed previously. The task force main body and the Second Striking Force remained in the Inland Sea, the former still occupied primarily with the replenishment and training of its carrier air groups.

On August 10, the 1st Carrier Division, reorganized around two newly commissioned regular carriers, was added to the task force main body. Vice Admiral Ozawa, task force commander, meanwhile set October 15 as the target date for completion of the reorganization and training of the 3rd and 4th Carrier Division air groups. Concurrently with these preparations, steps were taken to strengthen the anti-aircraft armament of combat units.

The Allied options were equally apparent to the Imperial Japanese Navy. Combined Fleet Chief Toyoda Soemu prepared four victory plans. Shō-Go 1 was a major naval operation in the Philippines, while Shō-Go 2, Shō-Go 3, and Shō-Go 4 were responses to attacks on Formosa, the Ryukyu, and Kurile Islands respectively. The plans were complex, aggressive operations committing all available forces to a decisive battle, ignoring Japan's strategic immobility because of a lack of oil.

Thus, when on October 12, 1944, Nimitz launched a carrier raid against Formosa to make sure planes based there could not intervene in the Leyte landings, the Japanese put Shō-Go 2 into action, launching waves of attacks against the carriers, losing 600 planes in three days, almost their entire air force in the region. Following the American invasion of the Philippines, the Japanese Navy transitioned to Shō-Go 1.

Shō-Go 1 called for Vice Admiral Jisaburo Ozawa's fleet, known as Northern Force, to lure the U.S. Third Fleet away from the landings using an obviously vulnerable force of carriers, which were in fact mostly empty of aircraft. The Allied landing forces, lacking air cover, would then be attacked from the west by three Japanese forces. Vice Admiral Takeo Kurita's command, Center

Force, based in Brunei, would enter Leyte Gulf and destroy the Allied landing forces. Rear Admiral Shōji Nishimura's and Vice Admiral Kiyohide Shima's fleets, collectively called Southern Force, would act as mobile strike forces. All three forces would consist of surface ships. The plan was likely to result in the destruction of one or more of the forces, but Toyoda later justified it to his American interrogators as follows:

> Should we lose in the Philippines operations, even though the fleet should be left, the shipping lane to the south would be completely cut off so that the fleet, if it should come back to Japanese waters, could not obtain its fuel supply. If it should remain in southern waters, it could not receive supplies of ammunition and arms. There would be no sense in saving the fleet at the expense of the loss of the Philippines.

7

The Battle of Leyte Gulf

Army General Douglas MacArthur's 1942 pledge to return to the Philippines prompted high-level discussion regarding the advisability of seizing the Philippines or Formosa. For a variety of reasons, including a national debt to the long-suffering Filipino people, a huge amphibious force set its sights on Leyte Gulf that fall. The stage was being set for the Battle of Leyte Gulf.

The engagement, fought in waters near the Philippine islands of Leyte, Luzon, and Samar, took place from October 23 to October 26. The Allies were American and Australian forces against the Imperial Japanese Navy. Historians consider the battle to be the largest naval battle of World War II and perhaps the largest naval battle in history. Four separate engagements took place: the Battle of the Sibuyan Sea, the Battle of Surigao Strait, the Battle of Cape Engaño, and the Battle of Samar. Because Japan had fewer aircraft than the Allies had sea vessels, it was the first battle in which Japanese pilots carried out organized *kamikaze* attacks.

The U.S. Third Fleet sought to weaken Japan at the periphery before striking the Philippines. Therefore, carriers hit Okinawa on October 10 and Formosa on October 12. Carrier aircrews estimated they destroyed 650 planes at Formosa, while Japan admitted half as many, still a heavy blow. Yet Tokyo, still believing its own propaganda, announced sinking three dozen American ships, including battleships and carriers. Even the normally level-headed *kamikaze* chief, Vice Admiral Matome Ugaki, thought his airmen had destroyed three carriers and three other ships. In truth, two U.S. cruisers were badly damaged but survived.

Admiral Halsey's Third Fleet arrived off the Philippines with Task Force Thirty-Eight's four groups deploying sixteen fast carriers. From bases in Japan and the East Indies the Imperial Navy launched a three-pronged response with carriers, battleships, and scores of escorts. The sprawling, four-day extended exchange of heavy blows began on October 24. Halsey had released two groups to head eastward for replenishment when the crisis broke. He recalled Rear Admiral Gerald Bogan's task group, while allowing Vice Admiral John McCain to proceed to Ulithi, taking five aircraft carriers out of action until late in the battle. Thankfully, Marc Mitscher's fast carriers were not the only aircraft carriers involved. Vice Admiral Thomas C. Kinkaid, who had commanded at Santa Cruz, led Seventh Fleet including eighteen CVEs for close air support and antisubmarine patrol.

In the Sibuyan Sea, another front of the Battle of Leyte Gulf located on the western side of the Philippines, carrier airpower destroyed one of the largest battleships afloat. Three fast carrier groups launched multiple strikes against Vice Admiral Takeo Kurita's five battleships, twelve cruisers, and fifteen destroyers. Aircraft swarmed the 64,000-ton IJN *Musashi* for more than five hours, hammering her with seventeen bombs and nineteen torpedoes, from USS *Enterprise* and USS *Franklin*'s air groups. Ten aircraft fell to Japanese anti-aircraft fire, but it was the first-time carrier planes sank a battleship underway, unassisted by surface combatants. It would not be the last.

Kurita had already lost two cruisers to submarines and another turned back with bomb damage, but after regrouping, he continued his mission to enter Leyte Gulf, unknown to Halsey. Meanwhile, Japanese land-based aircraft posed a serious threat to the fast carriers. Winging seaward in three large formations, they were intercepted by relays of F6F Hellcats well managed by fighter-direction officers. But fighters were spread thin. In Task Group 38.3, USS *Essex*'s last two available Hellcats were launched with hostiles inbound, putting Commander David McCampbell and Lieutenant Junior Grade Roy Rushing onto a mix with the Japanese aircraft. In the next ninety minutes, McCampbell claimed nine kills, the all-time U.S. one-day record, and Rushing claimed six kills. In all, USS *Essex*'s Fighter Squadron 15 was credited with forty-three kills that day.

In the same group, USS *Princeton*'s shark-mouthed VF-27 Hellcats fought hard for its ship, splashing thirty-six raiders. But a single Yokosuka Judy put a 550-pound bomb through the flight deck, igniting ordnance on the hangar deck. The light cruiser USS *Birmingham* came alongside to take off survivors when a huge secondary explosion swept the would-be rescuer, inflicting nearly 700 casualties. USS *Princeton* was scuttled after an eight-hour ordeal, losing 108 men. She was the first American fast carrier sunk since USS *Hornet* was sunk during the brutal battle of the Santa Cruz Islands and remained the last. Carrier aviators claimed 270 kills on October 24, the second highest count of the war.

"October 24, 1944 was the longest day of my life," wrote retired Captain James A. Shirley in a letter to a shipmate thirty-six years later. It was a day on which he experienced the highest of highs for any fighter pilot, shooting down five Japanese aircraft to become an ace in a day. Yet it also marked the lowest of lows for anyone who has ever put to sea as a Japanese bombing attack sank Shirley's ship, the light carrier USS *Princeton* while she operated in support of the invasion of Leyte in the Philippines. The day had begun in the predawn darkness as Shirley led his division of F6F Hellcats off the flight deck to fly combat air patrol. His squadron, Fighter Squadron VF-27, had been flying off Princeton since June 1944, but as the official squadron history noted, its big day came on October 24.

As Shirley and his fellow aviators climbed to altitude, they received word of radar contact being made with a large group of bogeys approaching from Luzon, which prompted the launch of more squadron aircraft, eventually bringing the total number of VF-27 Hellcats in the air to twenty. In a wide-ranging action that included intercepts of enemy bombers and fighters, the VF-27 planes were credited with shooting down thirty-six enemy aircraft against the loss of one of their squadron mates. Shirley was credited with five of the enemy planes and described the air-to-air combat: "Just after daylight, I began to make out an unusually large formation of planes of every Japanese make stacked in altitudes from 6 to 25 thousand feet and headed for our fleet." Shirley recalled: "We started in head-on at our altitude of about 23,000 feet and worked our way down as we had to. We first reversed course with an overhead run and each of us took out one or more planes on their first pass. Our speed advantage was about 50 knots, so we repeatedly made runs in through their formation."

With fuel dwindling and ammunition gone, Shirley's division retired and set course back to the carrier. For his actions, he would be awarded the Navy Cross. After recovery and debriefing, Shirley headed to the flight deck to monitor the installation of new gun barrels on the F6F Hellcat he had flown in the air-to-air action when he spied a lone plane entering a dive overhead. The time was 9:39 a.m. when he and the men around dived to the starboard side to the space between the forward gun mount and the island. He was about fourth from the bottom and there were others on top of him.

The attacker dropped a bomb that penetrated the flight deck and hangar bay before exploding beneath a number of fully armed and fueled TBM Avengers. With fuel pouring out of them, a violent fire erupted, filling the ship with thick clouds of smoke. As the day passed, violent explosions rumbled throughout the flattop, including one in the late afternoon that blew off the carrier's stern and heavily damaged the light cruiser USS *Birmingham*, which was alongside rendering assistance.

After the bomb hit, Shirley had made his way below decks to the ready room to await instructions and hopefully retrieve his pistol and flight logbook. When the order came down to abandon ship, he went over the side wearing his Mae West life vest, which was fortunate given the choppy seas into to which he jumped. Spent from swimming away from the carrier, Shirley could not pull himself up a rescue ladder when he finally reached the destroyer USS *Irwin*, two sailors literally pulling him onto the deck. He was one of 646 men from USS *Princeton* rescued by the destroyer. From the destroyer, the aviator watched the futile efforts to save the ship and her final slipping beneath the waves in the late afternoon after USS *Irwin* fired a spread of torpedoes to hasten the inevitable.

But the Imperial Navy was not ready to give up the Battle of Leyte Gulf. Under cover of darkness on October 24-25, Kurita transited San Bernardino Strait between Luzon and Samar, eastbound, intending to fall upon MacArthur's vulnerable transports in the gulf. The navy's first full-time night flying unit, Air Group 41 in light carrier USS *Independence*, had Grumman TBF-1 Avengers airborne that night, tracking the large enemy force. Mitscher assumed that Third Fleet had the information, but for reasons still unclear, Halsey ignored it.

Additionally, that afternoon, Task Force Thirty-Eight search teams had found Ozawa's four carriers off Luzon's northeast coast. That information, later combined with USS *Independence*'s report of Kurita's eastward course, bothered some senior officers, who correctly deduced Ozawa's purpose—to draw the fast carriers north, clearing the way for Kurita's center force. Mitscher, informed of the developing situation, declined to intervene with Halsey.

Well to the south, the third prong of Tokyo's offensive met Seventh Fleet units in Surigao Strait separating Leyte and Mindanao with everything from PT boats to battleships. In the world's last major surface engagement, the annihilation was nearly complete, leaving the dogged Kurita pressing eastward while Jisabuo Ozawa, survivor of the Marianas, lurked well to the north with four partly equipped carriers.

Shortly past dawn on October 25, Vice Admiral Kinkaid's three escort carrier groups had patrols airborne. An Avenger sighted large ships with pagoda masts emerging from San Bernardino strait and radioed the alarming news. All that stood in Kurita's path was Rear Admiral Clifton Sprague's Task Group, with six CVEs and seven escorts, off Samar's east coast. "Taffy Three" turned away, making smoke, launching aircraft, and hollering for help. Sprague faced four battleships, eight cruisers, and eleven destroyers. But support from "Taffy Two" added more Avengers and Wildcats to Sprague's numbers. As the destroyers attacked with torpedoes and 5-inch gunfire, aviators made repeated runs with bombs, torpedoes, and strafing passes. One Wildcat pilot made twenty-six runs, most of them without ammunition.

Unable to outrun the enemy, the 19-knot CVEs were chased down. USS *Gambier Bay* succumbed to cruiser guns, as did three of the escorts. After HMS *Glorious* in 1940, she was only the second aircraft carrier sunk by surface ships. But Kurita, impressed with the ferocity of the escort carriers' response, and mindful of the pummeling he had taken the day before, called off the chase. Just as an historic victory lay on the horizon, he disengaged. Kinkaid's transports and MacArthur's source of supply were safe.

Still, Taffy Three remained in peril. That afternoon, USS *Saint Lo*, originally named USS *Midway*, was attacked by a single Zero that made no effort to pull out of its dive. Wracked by fire, the little flattop went down, first victim of the Special Attack Corps (*kamikazes*). Six more CVEs were tagged that day. While the drama played out near Samar, the Japanese waved an irresistible target under Halsey's nose. Ozawa's four carriers steamed off the northeast Philippines, seemingly representing the third major threat after the surface forces in San Bernardino and Surigao straits. Once the commander of Third Fleet got the news, Halsey reacted predictably. He rushed to destroy Tokyo's remaining flattops. In his haste, he committed a severe blunder, leaving San Bernardino unguarded. He assumed that battleships of Vice Admiral Willis Lee's powerful Task Force Thirty-Four would prevent an enemy force from entering the gulf. He did not realize as he steamed north that all seven battleships and their screens in Lee's contingency force remained integrated into the fast carrier task groups.

Bull Halsey was more a fighter than a thinker. An instinctive warrior, he rode to where he imagined the guns were sounding. Only when the stunning news arrived of Japanese battleships pounding Taffy Three did he realize that he had been fooled. Worse, he wasted an hour or more ranting and sulking before deciding on a course of action. Ozawa lay more than 400 miles from the Taffies, and Halsey was in between. Halsey finally ordered Lee's battlewagons, racing ahead of the carriers, to reverse helm and move southward, although everyone knew it was far too late.

The four carriers in Ozawa's Mobile Fleet had deployed with just 116 aircraft, but by the morning of October 25, they retained only twenty-nine. The ensuing clash could only go one way. Starting at 8 a.m., USS *Mitscher* launched 180 aircraft, the first of six strikes totaling more than 500 sorties. The on-scene coordinators were air group commanders from TG 38.3, first from USS *Essex*, then from USS *Lexington*. The F6Fs brushed aside the dozen or so Zeros trying to defend their flight decks. USS *Lexington* and USS *Langley*'s aircrews wrote the final log entry for IJN *Zuikaku*, survivor of Coral Sea, Eastern Solomons, and Santa Cruz. Other air groups sank CVLs IJN *Chitose* and IJN *Zuiho* as well as a destroyer. Ozawa shifted his flag to cruiser IJN *Oyodo*. That morning, USS *Essex*'s air group commander, David McCampbell, directed strikes that sank the light carrier IJN *Chitose*. Relieving him as target coordinator was the *Lexington*'s commander, Hugh Winters, controlling some 200 aircraft. He recalled: "There was no chance for surprise, as the Japs were already bleeding some, so we didn't have to shoot on sight, so to speak. We wanted all the carriers, with maybe a BB or CA for the cherry on top." Winters directed his squadrons against IJN *Zuikaku*, IJN *Zuiho*, and the larger escorts. He noted:

> The heavy haze of AA smoke trailing off the quarter gave good windage for our dive bombers as we pushed over.... The ships were using new anti-aircraft stuff with wires and burning phosphorous shells which put up all different-colored fire and smoke around our planes. But we had faced so much deadly AA for so

> many lousy targets that it didn't bother us too much, hunting this big game. The boys were as cool as any professionals working in a hospital or law office.

Winters assigned subsequent air groups according to his target priority, and watched IJN *Zuiho* sink, then IJN *Zuikaku* capsize. "No big explosions, no steam from flooded firerooms, no fire and smoke—just a few huge bubbles. Quietly, and it seemed to me, with dignity."

Thus perished the last survivor of the Pearl Harbor attackers. The light carrier IJN *Chiyoda* lingered a bit longer. Hugh Winters and wingman Ensign Barney Garbow had witnessed something unprecedented. They saw three aircraft carriers sink during one mission. Halsey dispatched four cruisers and nine destroyers as a pickup team to complete the execution. They sank IJN *Chiyoda* late that afternoon and pummeled a remaining destroyer. Carrier planes continued scouring Philippine waters during October 26–27, picking off a light cruiser and four more destroyers. It brought Japanese losses in the four-day battle to twenty-six combatants, totaling 300,000 tons.

The Battle of Leyte Gulf officially entered the books as the Second Battle of the Philippine Sea, though most of the action occurred nearly 1,000 miles from the June turkey shoot. Whatever the battle's official name, after October 1944, the Imperial Navy was finished.

Fleets and Commanders

Allies

Admiral William Halsey
Vice Admiral Thomas Kinkaid
8 fleet carriers
8 light carriers
18 escort carriers
12 battleships
24 cruisers
141 destroyers and destroyer escorts

Japanese

Admiral Soemu Toyoda
Vice Admiral Takeo Kurita
Vice Admiral Shōji Nishimura
Vice Admiral Kiyohide Shima
Admiral Jisaburo Ozawa
1 fleet carrier
3 light carriers

9 battleships
14 heavy cruisers
6 light cruisers
35-plus destroyers

Losses

Allies: 1 light carrier, 2 escort carriers, 2 destroyers, 1 destroyer escort, approximately 200 aircraft.

Japanese: 1 fleet carrier, 3 light carriers, 3 battleships, 10 cruisers, 11 destroyers, approximately 300 aircraft.

Sibuyan Sea

Beginning on October 23, the Battle of Leyte Gulf consisted of four primary meetings between Allied and Japanese forces. In the first engagement on October 23–24, the Battle of the Sibuyan Sea, Kurita's Center Force was attacked by the American submarines USS *Darter* and USS *Dace* as well as Halsey's aircraft. Engaging the Japanese around dawn on October 23, Darter scored four hits on Kurita's flagship, the heavy cruiser IJN *Atago*, and two on the heavy cruiser IJN *Takao*. A short time later, USS *Dace* hit the heavy cruiser IJN *Maya* with four torpedoes. While IJN *Atago* and IJN *Maya* both sank quickly, IJN *Takao*, badly damaged, withdrew to Brunei with two destroyers as escorts.

Rescued from the water, Kurita transferred his flag to IJN *Yamato*. The next morning, Center Force was located by American aircraft as it moved through the Sibuyan Sea. Brought under attack by aircraft from 3rd Fleet's carriers, the Japanese quickly took hits to the battleships IJN *Nagato*, IJN *Yamato*, and IJN *Musashi* and saw the heavy cruiser IJN *Myōkō* badly damaged. Subsequent strikes saw IJN *Musashi* crippled and drop from Kurita's formation. It later sank around 7:30 p.m. after being hit with at least seventeen bombs and nineteen torpedoes.

Under increasingly intense air attacks, Kurita reversed his course and retreated. As the Americans withdrew, Kurita again changed course around 5:15 p.m. and resumed his advance towards the San Bernardino Strait. Elsewhere that day, the escort carrier USS *Princeton* was sunk by land-based bombers as its aircraft attacked Japanese air bases on Luzon.

Cape Engaño

At 4:40 p.m. on the 24th, Halsey's scouts located Ozawa's Northern Force. Believing that Kurita was retreating, Halsey signaled Admiral Kinkaid that he was moving north to pursue the Japanese carriers. By doing so, Halsey was leaving the landings unprotected. Kinkaid was not aware of this as he believed Halsey had left one carrier group to cover the San Bernardino Straight.

At dawn on October 25, Ozawa launched a seventy-five-plane strike against Halsey and Mitscher's carriers. Easily defeated by the American combat air patrols, no damage was inflicted. Countering, Mitscher's first wave of aircraft began attacking the Japanese around 8 a.m. Overwhelming the enemy fighter defense, the attacks continued through the day and ultimately sank all four of Ozawa's carriers in what became known as the Battle of Cape Engaño.

Samar

As the battle was concluding, Halsey was informed that the situation off Leyte was critical. Toyoda's plan had worked. By Ozawa drawing away Halsey's carriers, the path through the San Bernardino Straight was left open for Kurita's Center Force to pass through to attack the landings. Breaking off his attacks, Halsey began steaming south at full speed. Off Samar (just north of Leyte), Kurita's force encountered the Seventh Fleet's escort carriers and destroyers.

Launching their planes, the escort carriers began to flee, while the destroyers valiantly attacked Kurita's much superior force. As the melee was turning in favor of the Japanese, Kurita broke off after realizing that he was not attacking Halsey's carriers and that the longer he lingered the more likely he was to be attacked by American aircraft. Kurita's retreat effectively ended the battle.

The fourth primary meetings between Allied and Japanese naval forces took place in the Surigao Strait. It is during this meeting that the last crossing of the "T" occurred.

8

The Last Crossing of the "T" at Surigao Strait

Shō-Go 1 was like most Imperial Japanese Navy plans of World War II—a decoy force would lure the Americans in one direction, while the real punch would come from other directions in a complex series of coordinated movements. This time, the decoy force was Japan's surviving aircraft carriers, under Vice Admiral Jisaburo Ozawa, steaming down from the home islands. With barely 100 planes between them, these carriers lacked offensive punch, but the Japanese believed the aggressive U.S. Admiral Halsey would race after them with his entire Third Fleet. While Halsey was drawn off, the powerful battleships and heavy cruisers of the Imperial Navy, mostly based at Lingga Roads near Singapore and the Borneo fuel stocks, would strike east and ravage the Seventh Fleet's amphibious forces while they lay in Leyte Gulf. The surface ships would pound the Seventh Fleet to death with torpedoes and shells, isolating the American invaders on shore. The combination of a trapped army in the Philippines and a smashed navy in the Pacific might at least buy Japan time, or even persuade America to make peace.

The battlewagons at Lingga were commanded by Vice Admiral Takeo Kurita and consisted of a powerful force. They were headed by two immense dreadnoughts, the IJN *Yamato* and IJN *Musashi*, sister ships that packed the heaviest armament ever loaded on a battleship, 18.1-inch guns. They were supported by five more dreadnoughts and a screen of cruisers and destroyers, all of which wielded the legendary Type 95 Long Lance torpedo, one of the best in the world. The Imperial Japanese Navy may have been worn down by war, but it was still a powerful force with highly skilled sailors and officers well trained in night fighting.

Toyoda and Kurita planned a pincer attack on Leyte Gulf with their battleships. Kurita would take one force, with five battleships, including IJN *Yamato* and IJN *Musashi*, through the San Bernardino Strait to hit Leyte Gulf from the north. A second force, under Vice Admiral Shōji Nishimura, a veteran sailor accustomed to the sea, would steam through the Surigao Strait and smash into Leyte Gulf from the south, the anvil to Kurita's hammer, just before dawn. A Naval War College graduate of 1911, Nishimura had commanded destroyers in the invasion of the Philippines and the Dutch East Indies in 1941. His son, Teiji Nishimura, a naval aviator, had been killed in the former invasion. In 1942, Nishimura commanded cruisers in the grueling struggle for Guadalcanal, suffering some bad luck but displaying skillful planning and lion-like fury in battle.

On September 10, 1944, Admiral Nishimura was given command of Battleship Division 2, which consisted of the dreadnoughts IJN *Fusō* and IJN *Yamashiro* and their destroyer escorts. The two battleships dated back to 1911 and were known throughout the fleet for their tall pagoda masts (44 meters above the waterline) and for having sat out most of the war in home waters, mostly as training vessels. The emperor's brother had served on IJN *Fusō* twice.

These battleships had never fired their guns in battle. They were the first battleships built with Japanese engines and guns, the most powerful dreadnoughts in the world at the time. But IJN *Fusō* and IJN *Yamashiro* were slow and outdated by 1944's standards, armed with six 14-inch guns each. They were sister ships, but not twins, and regarded as the ugliest ships in the Imperial Navy. Both had crews of about 1,600 officers and men. IJN *Yamashiro* flew Admiral Nishimura's flag.

Supporting Admiral Nishimura's force were four destroyers, IJN *Michishio*, IJN *Yamagumo*, IJN *Asagumo*, and IJN *Shigure*, and a veteran heavy cruiser, the IJN *Mogami*. Studying his war maps, Toyoda did not think that Nishimura had quite enough punch, so he added a second task force to the southern wing, under Vice Admiral Kiyohide Shima, swinging down from the Pescadore Islands off Formosa. The second striking force would consist of the heavy cruisers IJN *Nachi* and IJN *Ashigara*, both veteran ships; the light cruiser IJN *Abukuma*, which had escorted Japan's carriers to Pearl Harbor; and four destroyers, IJN *Shiranuhi*, IJN *Kasumi*, IJN *Ushio*, and IJN *Akebono*. Unlike Admiral Nishimura, Admiral Shima was a desk sailor. Like Nishimura, Shima had graduated from the Naval War College in the class of 1911. He had served in a variety of shore posts, mostly in communications.

Neither force commander coordinated his movements with the other. Nor were any orders given to do so. Neither commander was fully briefed about the other's operations. As far as historians could tell, Nishimura was to clear a path with his battleships so that the cruisers and destroyers behind could finish off the transports with torpedoes. Admiral Nishimura's group was called the Third Section, while Admiral Shima's group was the Second Striking Force. With the Americans moving on Leyte, the Japanese launched their intricate countermoves. Ozawa sortied from Japan, Shima from the Pescadores, and Kurita and Nishimura from Lingga Roads, headed for a refueling stop at Brunei.

On October 20, the Americans invaded Leyte with massive power. By A-Day 2, there had been no apparent enemy air or naval reaction to the U.S. landings, other than relatively light air attacks. The U.S. Third Fleet under Admiral Halsey was in supporting position, and his carrier task groups had bombed and strafed enemy air bases in central and southern Luzon and the Visayas. The aircraft of Carrier Task Group 77.4 had attacked enemy land installations and airfields, maintained a continuous combat air patrol and anti-submarine patrol, and supported landing and subsequent advance of troops.

In order to give prompt and early warning of movements of enemy forces, particularly major units approaching from the Brunei–Singapore area, submarines of the Seventh Fleet had been ordered to maintain strong patrols in Makassar Strait and western entrances to Celebes and Sulu Seas and off Hainan–Luzon area in coordination with the commander of Submarines Pacific. Carrier task forces of the Third Fleet and air searches of Central Pacific Forces from Palau and Saipan were relied upon to give early information of the approach of hostile forces east of the Philippines. The U.S. Central Philippines Attack Force responsible for the Surigao Strait was organized as follows:

77.2 Bombardment and Fire Support Group: Rear Admiral Oldendorf
77.2.1 Fire Support Unit North: Rear Admiral Weyler
- 1 OBB *Mississippi* (BatDiv.3): Rear Admiral Ruddock
- 2 OBB *Maryland, West Virginia* (BatDiv.4): Rear Admiral Oldendorf
- 3 DD *Aulick, Cony, Sigourney*

77.2.2 Fire Support Unit South: Rear Admiral Oldendorf
- 3 OBB *Tennessee, California, Pennsylvania* (BatDiv.2): Rear Admiral Chandler
- 3 CA *Louisville, Portland, Minneapolis* (CruDiv.4): Rear Admiral Oldendorf
- 1 CL *Honolulu* (CruDiv.9): Rear Admiral Ainsworth
- 2 CL *Denver, Columbia* (CruDiv.12): Rear Admiral Hayler
- 10 DD *Leutze, Newcomb, Bennion, H.L. Edwards, Halford, R.P. Leary, Robinson, Ross, A.W. Grant, Bryant, Halford* (DesRon.56): Captain Smoot
- 3 DD *Claxton, Thorn, Welles* (DesDiv. XRAY): Commander Hubbard
- 1 AVP *San Carlos*

77.3 Close Covering Group: Rear Admiral Berkey
- 2 CL *Phoenix, Boise* (CruDiv.15): Rear Admiral Berkey
- 2 CA *Australia, Shropshire*
- 5 DD *Bache, Beale, Hutchins, Daly, Killen* (DesDiv.47): Captain McManes
- 2 DD *Arunta, Warramunga* (RAN ships)

After the U.S. troop landings, Admiral Kurita summoned his senior officers to a conference on his flagship, the heavy cruiser IJN *Atago*. Kurita explained his plans to the assembled admirals, including the decision to split off Nishimura's force to head for the Surigao Strait. If the complex ship movements worked, the two forces would slam into the American Seventh Fleet just before dawn on October 25. The next morning, the Imperial Japanese Navy's battle line headed out for sea for the very last time, with Kurita and his five dreadnoughts steaming north to the Sibuyan Sea and the San Bernardino Strait. At 3:30 p.m. on October 22, Nishimura's ships left Brunei after Kurita. Shima's ships were already *en route*. All through the afternoon and night, the two forces steamed along unimpeded into the Sulu Sea. Not so Kurita's force, which was spotted by two American submarines, which slapped torpedoes into three of Kurita's cruisers, sinking two—including his flagship IJN *Atago*—and damaging the third. Kurita shifted his flag to the battleship IJN *Yamato* and sailed on.

The first report of the movement of Japanese naval forces approaching the southern entrance to Surigao Strait was received at 2 a.m. on October 22 from the submarine USS *Darter*, which had been assigned to cover the southern entrance to Palawan Passage. This submarine reported three unidentified large ships, estimated to be cruisers, but contact was lost. Despite extensive and prolonged air searches no sightings were reported by aircraft. At 2 a.m. on October 23, USS *Darter* reported three probable battleships moving on course 040°(T) and at 3 a.m. reported a force of eleven combat ships, on course 039°(T), speed 15 knots. At 4:30 a.m., USS *Bream* reported two *Aoba*-class cruisers and a destroyer on course toward Verde Island Passage, speed 19 knots. They obtained two hits on one of the cruisers. At 6:30 a.m., USS *Darter* reported the sinking of an *Atago*-class cruiser and four hits on another, from a force including at least three battleships, four *Atago*-class cruisers and three other vessels.

As Admiral Nishimura steamed toward the Surigao Strait, he knew that his chances for victory were slim. From his flag ship the *Yamashiro*, he evaluated the force facing him and knew that the success of the Japanese depended on his commitment to the Shō-Go plan. He had to tie up the American fleet committed to his destruction and spare Admiral Kurita's Center Force. Nishimura counted on the battleships IJN *Fusō* and IJN *Yamashiro*. At 9:05 a.m. on October 24, Nishimura's force was sighted by aircraft from the Third Fleet carriers USS *Enterprise* and USS *Franklin* of Rear Admiral Davison's task group. Shima's Second Striking Force was located by a U.S. Army Air Force bomber at 11:55 a.m. The search/strike element from Davison's group which first located Nishimura attacked at 9:18 a.m. and inflicted bomb hits on the flagship IJN *Yamashiro* and on the destroyer *Shigure*, but these hits caused little damage and Nishimura continued his advance undeterred.

Neither Admiral Nishimura nor Admiral Shima's received any further air attacks during daylight on October 24 since Admiral Halsey had transferred

Admiral Davison's fast carrier group to the attack on Admiral Kurita's Centre Force. Also, the Seventh Fleet's escort carriers were too busy with their duties around Leyte Gulf to be able to launch attacks on the Japanese forces. Admiral Kinkaid and his staff correctly surmised that the Japanese Southern Force would attempt to reach Leyte Gulf through Surigao Strait. Shortly after noon Kinkaid alerted every ship of the Seventh Fleet to prepare for a night action.

The submarine USS *Dace*, which had been assigned to cover the western approaches of Balabac Strait, reported at 7 a.m. that it had probably sunk a *Kongo*-class battleship in a force of eleven ships, including battleships, cruisers, destroyers, and a carrier. It was later determined that USS *Darter* and USS *Dace* had sunk the heavy cruisers IJN *Atago* and IJN *Maya* and damaged the heavy cruiser IJN *Takao*. At 10:15 p.m., USS *Angler* reported a large force, including three battleships, on an easterly course. A large force, presumably the same, was reported on October 24 heading south through Mindoro Strait at 3:30 a.m.

As a result of these reports, the commander of Third Fleet, Admiral Halsey, directed three reinforced air search to be made by his fast carrier groups early the morning of October 24, to cover the Manila, Verde Island Passage, and Sibuyan Sea areas, and the southern Visayas and central Sulu Sea area. These searches located the Japanese Central Force at 8:40 a.m. moving northeastward into Tablas Strait, and at 12 p.m., it was reported moving on a general easterly course, north of Tablas Island. Aircraft from Task Force 38 attacked, at about 2:30 p.m., positions in the Sibuyan Sea about 30 miles north of Sibuyan Island. Aircraft reports indicated the force was seriously damaged and badly organized.

At 9:05 a.m. on October 24, aircraft reported the Japanese Southern Force, including two battleships, a cruiser, and destroyers, southwest of Leyte and claimed four bomb hits on each battleship and rocket hits on destroyers. This force was again attacked at 10 a.m. in approximately the same position and later the same morning by other aircraft of Tack Force 38. However, a plane search at dusk in the Mindanao Sea failed to locate the Japanese Southern Force. In addition to the damage inflicted, it is considered that these submarines and air attacks succeeded in slowing and confusing the enemy Central Force to such an extent that they were unable to coordinate their attacks on U.S. surface units in the Battle off Samar Island.

At 3:12 p.m. on October 24, Admiral Halsey issued a dispatch to all Third Fleet subordinate commands, stating that a force of battleships, cruisers, and destroyers, was being formed as Task Force 34, presumably to engage the Japanese Central Force. The commander of Task Force 38 reported at 6:52 p.m. that planes had sighted, at 4:40 p.m., another Japanese Force, called Northern Force, on course 270°(T), speed 15 knots. At 8:24 p.m., Halsey advised the commander of Task Force 77 that the enemy Central Force was moving on a course of 120°(T) in the Sibuyan Sea toward the northwest tip of Masbate Island. He stated further that he was proceeding with three groups to attack the enemy carrier force (Northern Force) at dawn.

Throughout day on October 24, enemy aircraft attacked the U.S. naval forces with steadily increasing intensity. By nightfall, it was certain that the U.S. was being confronted by three large hostile forces. The disposition of the Japanese Southern Force as observed on October 24 indicated a probable attack on Leyte Gulf through Surigao Strait. At 2:43 p.m. on October 24, the commander of Task Force 77 ordered the commander of Task Group 77.2, Rear Admiral Oldendorf, to prepare for a probable night engagement. Task Group 77.3, Close Covering Group, was assigned to Oldendorf to augment his battle forces. Destroyer Squadron 54, which was operating as picket or guard force in Surigao Strain South, was also placed under Oldendorf's command. Motor torpedo boats were ordered to scout the enemy in eastern Mindanao Sea and Surigao Strait below latitude 10°10′N and to report all contacts and to attack if possible.

On the afternoon of October 24, thirty-nine Seventh Fleet torpedo boats moved at high speed through Leyte Gulf and Surigao Strait into the Mindanao Sea south of Leyte, and by dusk, they were in position on their patrol lines. As Seventh Fleet had no night patrol aircraft, and the Third Fleet's night carrier *Independence* had been taken northwards with the rest of the Third Fleet to attack the Japanese Northern Force, Oldendorf was dependent on the motor-torpedo boats for advance warning of the Japanese approach. Nishimura, advancing towards Surigao Strait, at about 6:30 p.m. received Kurita's signal that the latter's powerful Centre Force had been delayed by heavy air attacks in the Sibuyan Sea, which meant the Admiral Nishimura could not hope to be supported by Kurita in his attack on Leyte Gulf.

As he approached Leyte, Nishimura sent Mogami and three destroyers ahead to reconnoiter. The PT boats' first contact was with the battleships rather than with the IJN *Mogami* group though. At 10:36 p.m., *PT-131* of Section One, off the island of Bohol, made visual contact at a range of 3 miles, and shortly after were sighted by Shigure. At 10:54 p.m., Admiral Nishimura ordered an emergency turn towards the boats, and at 10:56 p.m., the Japanese ships turned on their searchlights and opened fire. The boats attempted to close in for a torpedo attack but were driven off by the Japanese gunfire, two of them having been hit and damaged. *PT-130* of Section One closed with the nearby Section Two and got *PT-127* of the latter section to relay a contact report. This report reached Admiral Oldendorf at 12:26 a.m. on October 25 and was the first concrete information of the enemy's position received by the admiral since 10 a.m. the previous morning.

The heavy cruiser IJN *Mogami* and her three accompanying destroyers got past PT Sections One and Two undetected. At 10:30 p.m., Admiral Nishimura radioed Admirals Kurita and Shima that he was advancing as scheduled while destroying enemy torpedo boats. In the lead were two destroyers. Some 4 km behind them were the two battleships and the cruiser IJN *Mogami* in line ahead, with a destroyer on each flank. The last action between the motor-torpedo boats and the Japanese force ended at 2:13 a.m. on October 25. As the battle between

Nishimura and the PT boats was ending the battle between his force and the American destroyers was beginning.

Rear Admiral Oldendorf, commanding Kinkaid's Bombardment and Fire Support Group, was ordered to the northern entrance of Surigao Strait with his very powerful force, and to prepare to meet the enemy ships. After Rear Admiral Oldendorf had formed his battle plan, he called Rear Admirals Weyler, commanding the battle line, and Rear Admiral Berkey, commander of the right flank cruisers and, destroyers aboard his flagship USS *Louisville* for a conference to discuss the plan and to ensure all commanders understood his intent.

Oldendorf had anticipated the order to prepare for battle. Since the first notice of enemy reaction to the invasion was received, he had made precautionary battle dispositions after sunset in Leyte Gulf. In these dispositions, light forces were located on an east–west line, 4 miles east of Taytay Point, and heavy forces with destroyer screen were deployed several miles to the northwest. The dispositions provided coverage against enemy attack through either Surigao Strait South or Surigao Strait East. Preparations for the night engagement entailed changes in the dispositions but no fundamental change in the concept of the battle plan.

The U.S. plan of attack was predicated on the use of torpedoes and heavy gunfire, the former to slow down the enemy, the latter to destroy him completely. The general shortage of ammunition, particularly armor-piercing, necessitated the employment of what they had at only the most effective ranges. Therefore, fire was to be held until the destroyers had launched torpedoes and the enemy had closed to within 17,000–20,000 yards of the battle line.

At 6 a.m. on October 24, the nearest carriers to Nishimura, the veteran USS *Enterprise* and the new USS *Franklin*, launched reconnaissance planes to fan out over the Sulu Sea, hunting for Japanese warships.

At 8:30 a.m., a USS *Enterprise* search team under Lieutenant Raymond E. Moore spotted Nishimura's battleships and identified them correctly. A strike group of twelve bombers and sixteen fighters headed for the dreadnoughts. For USS *Enterprise* Ensign Robert J. Barnes, seeing the massive battleships beneath him was "something you dream about as a dive-bomber pilot. The anti-aircraft fire was terrific."

On the Japanese ships, signal halyards and bugle calls summoned everyone to battle stations; the 14-inch guns loaded Type 3 antiaircraft ammunition and opened fire. The barrage of shells shook IJN *Asagumo*'s Chief Engineer Tokichi Ishii in his engine room. On IJN *Fusō*, Yeoman 2nd Class Hideo Ogawa, in the powder magazine, considered that if the battleship were hit his end would be quick, as he was surrounded by main battery powder canisters.

The American planes swooped down on the Japanese warships, subjecting them to bombing, strafing, and rockets. On IJN *Yamashiro*, twenty men died from strafing. A bomb scored a direct hit on IJN *Fusō*, bouncing No. 1 turret on its barbette. It crashed through the deck and killed everyone in the secondary battery. Another bomb hit IJN *Fusō*'s quarterdeck, setting two floatplanes ablaze and gutting the wardroom. Another bomb grazed the IJN *Shigure*'s No. 1 turret.

Lieutenant Commander Fred Bakutis, skipper of USS *Enterprise*'s fighter squadron, was shot out of the sky during the battle and had to ditch. Luckily, the Japanese did not spot him, and he spent seven days in a life raft before he was spotted and picked up by the submarine USS *Hardhead*, dehydrated, hungry, blistered, but otherwise in good shape. He recovered to resume flying. The American planes flew off, and damage control parties on the Japanese ships went to work. Both battleships suffered from burst seams and minor damage. Nishimura ordered his ships to proceed with their mission. He fired off IJN *Mogami*'s scout planes to check on the enemy. One of them reported four battleships, two cruisers, four destroyers, fifteen aircraft carriers, fourteen PT boats, and eighty transports in Leyte Gulf, a close approximation of the defense. At 4 p.m., Nishimura blinkered his battle plan. IJN *Mogami* and the four destroyers would steam ahead and mop up the enemy PT boats, then reassemble, and all ships would charge up Surigao Strait.

Advancing across the Pacific toward Leyte, battleship main and secondary battery fire control parties continued drilling for surface action, as they carried the armor-piercing shells for the big guns and what were called "common shells" for the secondary guns. The common shells were especially designed for use against thin-skinned vessels as destroyers and submarines. They would penetrate, but not too much. The armor-piercing shells had been known to pass completely through an unprotected target ship, creating fine stories, but relatively small damage.

The turret crews had fired so much in bombardment, it was almost routine. For surface action, the crews merely had to substitute the armor-piercing for the high-capacity shells and use full-servicing propelling charges rather than the reduced bombardment loads. Secured below each turret and standing chest high, the armor-piercing projectiles were an impressive sight. For example, on USS *Maryland*, the 16-inch armor-piercing shells weighed 2,240 pounds but contained only 35 pounds of explosive. That was sufficient when it detonated after penetration in a confined space. The service propelling charge consisted of five 125-pound powder bags, each with the black powder ignition charge attached to the base.

The propelling charge was not just a bag of random small granules as might be imagined. Instead, each particle was a carefully designed small cylinder with several holes running longitudinally. The purpose was to produce a controlled burn in the gunpowder chamber. This resulted in a powerful but steady push up the bore, rather than a violent, uncontrolled explosion.

USS *Maryland*'s 16-inch main battery guns had the same basic design as the 51-caliber secondary battery guns. The interior of the breeches had interrupted screw threads. The breech plugs had matching threads with mated with the breech threads when the plugs were inserted and rotated. In both guns, the plugs carried a mushroom16-inch shaped steel piece. When the guns fired, gas pressure forced the mushroom aft against the seal. This seal compressed and expanded in diameter to prevent the gasses from escaping.

In both guns, hot gasses and burning embers remained in the powder chambers from a previous round were expelled by high-pressure gas ejection compressed air. The air was automatically injected when the breech plugs were opened. Both guns were fired by a combination percussion and electric primer, which was inserted into the firing lock prior to each round. This lock was mounted at the center of the after side of the plug.

Aboard the battleships, sailors polished the breech of the guns. For most men who made up the compliment of a ship, duty consisted largely of unglamorous, yet necessary jobs as this. Every inch of the ship must be kept in top working order—scrubbed, oiled, painted, or polished—and that took a lot of elbow grease. With the possibility of a fight at any time as the fleet was in combat waters, there could be no hitch in the functioning of anything aboard the ships. However menial their jobs might have seemed, the navy could not get along without the sailors who swabbed the deck and polished the gun breeches. Sailors stripped to the waist for comfort loaded powder bags into the battleship's big guns. While the aircraft carrier had without doubt stolen the show in the Pacific from the bristling yet lumbering battle wagons in this war as the importance of air supremacy had become more and more apparent, the performance of the giants of the fleet could not be underestimated. Without their protective power, the vulnerable aircraft carriers would hardly have dared to strike so deeply within the enemy controlled waters. The worth of the battleships was about to be proved yet again.

Minesweepers swept ahead as the fleet prepared to enter Leyte Gulf. As the column of ships advanced, all hands topside kept a careful watch for mines. During the afternoon of October 24, the battleship crews were in their foretop general quarters stations when about twenty motor torpedo boats raced by. The battleships and cruisers launched all their observation planes. There was no official word, but the crews began to understand that the torpedo boats were speeding toward Surigao Strait.

At 2:43 p.m. on October 24, 1944, Rear Admiral Jesse B. Oldendorf received a dispatch from Vice Admiral Thomas C. Kinkaid, commander of the Central Philippines Attack Force. The message was straightforward and direct, "Prepare for night engagement," and was duly logged aboard Oldendorf's flagship, the heavy cruiser USS *Louisville*. Admiral Oldendorf, commander of the Leyte invasion fire support warships, was not surprised by the order. Naval intelligence had already been apprised of the fact that a Japanese force was on its way toward Leyte Gulf.

At the height of the Battle of Leyte Gulf, Admiral Oldendorf, a stocky man with a cheerful disposition, was to intercept Japanese naval Force C, under the command of Vice Admiral Shōji Nishimura. That morning, Nishimura's task group had been spotted by aircraft from the carriers USS *Enterprise* and USS

Franklin. Another task group was sighted less than three hours later. This was Second Striking Force, under Vice Admiral Kiyohide Shima. The main force, the First Striking Force under Vice Admiral Takeo Kurita, had been intercepted by the submarines USS *Darter* and USS *Dace* the day before.

The three Japanese task groups were to rendezvous at Leyte Gulf, with Kurita entering from the north and Nishimura and Shima from the south and attack the American transports and their escorts off the Philippine island of Leyte where American forces under General Douglas MacArthur had landed on October 20. If everything went according to the Japanese plan, the three task groups would arrive at Leyte Gulf at dawn on October 25, sink the American support ships off Leyte, and isolate the American troops on the island.

When he received the order to prepare for a night battle, Admiral Oldendorf decided that his best course of action would be to block Surigao Strait. The northern end of the strait leads into Leyte Gulf, and Oldendorf intended to place a battle line "squarely across the Leyte exit of the strait," blocking Japanese access to the gulf. And he had enough warships at his disposal to accomplish what he had in mind.

The heart of Oldendorf's battle line were the old U.S. battleships USS *Mississippi*, USS *Maryland*, USS *West Virginia*, USS *Tennessee*, USS *California*, and USS *Pennsylvania*. All but USS *Mississippi* were veterans of Pearl Harbor and had been either sunk or badly damaged by the Japanese attack. Now they were going to be given the chance to return the compliment. The rest of the American force consisted of four heavy cruisers, including the Australian HMAS *Shropshire*, four light cruisers, and at least twenty-eight destroyers including HMAS *Arunta*. The Japanese Navy was well known for its lethal night torpedo attacks, and Oldendorf planned to overwhelm the enemy with superior numbers. The Battle of Savo Island, fought by American and Japanese warships off Guadalcanal in August 1942, was one of the most humiliating defeats in the history of the U.S. Navy, and four Allied cruisers had been sunk. This time, nothing was being left to chance. Oldendorf's force comprised six elderly battleships, four heavy cruisers, four light cruisers, and twenty-eight destroyers. These ships were disposed in three groups, as follows:

Battle line (T.U. 77.2.1)

Battleship Division 4
USS *Mississippi*
USS *Maryland*
USS *West Virginia*

Battleship Division 2
USS *Tennessee*
USS *California*
USS *Pennsylvania*

Destroyer Squadron XRAY
USS *Claxton*
USS *Cony*
USS *Thorn*
USS *Aulick*
USS *Sigourney*
USS *Welles*

Left Flank (T.U. 77.2.2)

Cruiser Division 4
USS *Louisville*
USS *Portland*
USS *Minneapolis*

Cruiser Division 12
USS *Denver*
USS *Columbia*

Destroyer Squadron 56
Section I
USS *Newcomb*
USS *Richard P. Leary*
USS *Albert W. Grant*
Section 2
USS *Robinson*
USS *Halford*
USS *Bryant*
Section 3
USS *Heywood L. Edwards*
USS *Leutze*
USS *Bennion*

Right Flank (T.U. 77.2.3)

USS *Phoenix*
USS *Beale*
HMAS *Shropshire*

Destroyer Division 47 (Destroyer Squadron 24)

Section I
USS *Hutchins*
USS *Daly*
USS *Bache*
USS *Boise*

Section II
HMAS Arunta
USS *Killen*

Picket Patrol

Destroyer Squadron 54
USS *Remey*
USS *McGowen*
USS *Melvin*
Mertz

Destroyer Squadron 108
USS *McDermut*
USS *Monssen*
USS *McNair*

Task Group 70.1

Motor Torpedo Boats

PT-127 PT-191 PT-330
PT-128 PT-192 PT-331
PT-129 PT-194 PT-489
PT-130 PT-195 PT-490
PT-131 PT-196 PT-491
PT-132 PT-320 PT-492
PT-134 PT-321 PT-493
PT-137 PT-323 PT-494
PT-146 PT-324 PT-495
PT-150 PT-326 PT-497
PT-151 PT-327 PT-523
PT-152 PT-328 PT-524
PT-190 PT-329 PT-526

PT boats were organized in thirteen sections of three boats each. The sections were disposed to the following locations:

Southeast Amagusan Point, off Kanihaan Island
Midchannel off Kanhatid Point
Dinagat Island, off Sumilon Island
Southeast tip Panaon Island
Bilaa Point, Mindanao
Southwest tip Panaon Island
Patrol between Agio Point to Bahol Island to past Camiguin Island to Sepaca Point, Mindanao.

Note: 1. See Appendix I for details of the Allied Fleet at the Surigao Strait
2. See Appendix II for details of the Allied Naval Weapons at the Surigao Strait

Admiral Oldendorf's plan was fairly simple. First, every available PT boat would be stationed at the southern entrance to Surigao Strait. There would be thirty-nine PT boats on patrol in the strait after dark. Their instructions were to report the approach of the enemy and to attack with torpedoes. Next, the destroyers would attack with their torpedoes. The cruisers and battleships would then open fire with their large-caliber guns when the enemy came within range.

Throughout the battle line, preparations continued. The busiest sailors on the battleships were the men on the shell decks below the turret gunrooms. They were setting aside the high-capacity bombardment shells and loading the shell hoists with tough, steel-nosed armor-piercing projectiles. In the powder magazines other men made ready the full-service powder charges. Chief warrant gunners traversed the magazine areas, taking room temperatures, checking the ammunition and the ammunition handlers and adjusting ammunition supply plans to the anticipated needs of the forthcoming engagement.

The navigators and their assistants studied the charts of the probable battle area, spotting reefs and other dangers to navigation, checking tide levels and currents and looking at visibility, wind, and sea conditions. In the plotting rooms below the armored decks the main battery control officers and their assistants calculated their initial ballistics. Combat information center personnel checked their equipment and prepared to pick up, track, evaluate, and report all incoming surface and air contacts and process submarine reports from destroyers and search aircraft.

The damage control men laid out firefighting and damage-repair equipment while damage control officers reviewed the status of fuel and water tanks for possible counter-flooding to quickly remove any list resulting from underwater damage. They knew that extreme lists to the firing side would reduce the maximum ranges of the main and secondary batteries. The doctors and hospital corpsmen prepared the operating rooms for causalities. The engineering departments had all boilers on line, prepared for maximum speed, emergency maneuvers, and possible damage to any units of firerooms, turboelectric alternators, propulsion motors, shafts, bearings, screws, condensers, switchboards, pumps, etc. The radiomen received all encrypted traffic and decoded it. All the communications were standing by for possible emergency messages in the clear and uncoded. There were no signal flags at night, but the crew on the signal bridges were on alert for possible sightings of signal flares, identification lights, or emergency riding lights.

The machinery quietly hummed, the radar men concentrated on their scopes, the lookouts endlessly scanned the horizon. The helmsmen steered their courses and stood waiting at their tillers for sudden orders. The chaplains, often the best-liked officers aboard, were everywhere. Their mere presence reassured the crews.

Admiral Nishimura's force, which would be moving north toward Leyte Gulf, consisted of the old battleships IJN *Fusō* and IJN *Yamashiro*, the heavy cruiser IJN *Mogami*, and four destroyers: IJN *Michishio*, IJN *Yamagumo*, IJN *Asagumo*, and IJN *Shigure*. Added armor protection, new boilers, and other improvements modernized both IJN *Fusō* and IJN *Yamashiro* in the 1930s, but both were still considered too old and slow for an active role in the fleet. After Pearl Harbor, however, warships were needed for the confrontation with the U.S. Navy, and IJN *Fusō* and IJN *Yamashiro* were recalled from their training duties in the Inland Sea. IJN *Fusō* was part of the Aleutian force during the Battle of Midway and took part in the reinforcing of Truk in 1943. Nishimura's ships were disposed in two groups as follows:

Third Section: Vice Admiral Nishimura

Battleship Division 2:
Vice Admiral Nishimura
IJN *Yamashiro*
IJN *Fusō*
IJN *Mogami*

Destroyer Division 4:
Captain Takahashi
IJN *Michishio*
IJN *Asagumo*
IJN *Yamagumo*
IJN *Shigure*

Second Striking Force: Vice Admiral Shima

Cruiser Division 21:
Vice Admiral Shima
IJN *Nachi*
Ashigara

Destroyer Squadron 1:
Rear Admiral Kimura
IJN *Abukuma*

Destroyer Division 7: Captain Iwagami
IJN *Akebono*
IJN *Ushio*

Destroyer Division 18: Captain Inoue
IJN *Kasumi*
IJN *Shiranuhi*

Notes: 1. Destroyer Squadron 21 did not participate, as it was assigned transport duty.
2. See Appendix III for details of the Japanese Fleet at the Surigao Strait.
3. See Appendix IV for details of the Japanese naval weapons at the Surigao Strait

Admiral Nishimura's force was much smaller than the American fleet it would be facing, but Admiral Oldendorf was not about to show any leniency. "If my opponent is foolish enough to come at me with an inferior force," he later said, "I'm certainly not going to give him an even break." Also, one of his destroyer squadron commanders, Captain Jesse Coward, had faced the Japanese at night off Guadalcanal. He knew what the Japanese were capable of doing with their long lance torpedoes and night tactics and was not about to let them do the same thing at Surigao Strait. At 10:36 p.m. on October 24, the crew of *PT-131* picked up Nishimura's group on radar. Visual contact was established fourteen minutes later. About two minutes after this, the destroyer USS *Shigure* sighted the PT boats and began shooting. One shell hit *PT-130* but failed to explode. The boat's captain broke off contact at maximum speed and sent his contact report.

Aboard his flagship USS *Louisville*, Admiral Oldendorf received the report just after midnight on October 25. Each PT squadron in the Strait went through the same sequence of events: making contact with the enemy; usually sending a contact report; firing torpedoes that missed; coming under fire from Japanese destroyers; and retiring behind a smoke screen.

Admiral Oldendorf followed the progress of the PT reports closely. They confirmed the Japanese anticipated movement and he did not need to make any changes to his battle plan. Of the boats that came under fire, ten were hit and one was sunk. Total casualties were three killed and twenty wounded.

Admiral Nishimura paid no attention to the PT attacks and kept advancing northward toward Leyte Gulf. Admiral Nishimura's column had its four destroyers in the lead, followed by IJN *Yamashiro*, IJN *Fusō*, and IJN *Mogami*. His next contact with the enemy came at about 3 a.m., when he encountered the seven destroyers of Destroyer Squadron 54, commanded by Captain Jesse Coward. Captain Coward had already received notification of an unidentified contact at 2:40 a.m. The contact soon was confirmed to be a column of ships steering due north. Coward ordered his destroyers to attack with only torpedoes since their 5-inch guns would be ineffective against large enemy warships.

The destroyer squadron split into two groups. USS *Melvin*, USS *McGowan*, and USS *Remy* would attack from the east, while USS *Monssen* and USS *McDermut* would make their approach from the west. Captain Coward, aboard USS *Remy*, closed with Nishimura's ships at about 30 knots, making smoke. At 2:58 a.m., he turned his destroyers to the left, bringing torpedo tubes to bear, and gave the order, "Fire when ready." USS *Remy*, USS *Melvin*, and USS *McGowan* began launching their torpedoes, firing twenty-seven in about seventy-five seconds. It would take about eight minutes before they completed their runs of between 8,200 and 9,300 yards. With all torpedoes expended, Coward turned hard to port on a base course of 21°(T), the three destroyers zigzagging individually and made smoke. None of the American destroyers suffered damage.

Behind Coward followed six destroyers from Captain McManes's Destroyer Squadron 24, steaming south in two sections. USS *Hutchens*, USS *Daly*, and USS *Bache* were closest to the Leyte Island shore. HMAS *Arunta*, an Australian destroyer assigned to the squadron, followed by USS *Killen* and USS *Beale*, cruised off their port quarter. Finally, Captain Smoot's nine-ship Destroyer Squadron 56 attacked in three columns. USS *Robinson*, USS *Halford*, and USS *Bryant* would proceed down the eastern side. The *Newcomb*, USS *Richard P. Leary*, and USS *Albert W. Grant* would go down the middle of the strait, head on, firing, then looping back. USS *Heywood L. Edwards*, USS *Leutze*, and USS *Bennion* would attack on the west side of the strait. As Nishimura's force steamed up the center of the strait, the destroyers executed their battle plan firing salvos of torpedoes at ranges of about 4 miles, and then turning and speeding away before the Japanese guns could find them. Nishimura's ships quickly turned on their searchlights and illuminated the destroyers. The destroyers escaped the enemy fire by zigzagging and throwing up smoke screens. The results of the destroyer attacks were devastating to the Japanese. Two of their ships were hit by the first salvo of torpedoes. The attacks continued until the battleship IJN *Fusō* blew up and split in two. Admiral Nishimura's flagship, the battleship IJN *Yamashiro*, took hits, and two of his destroyers were sunk. However, Nishimura continued to advance as Destroyer Squadrons 24 and 56 pulled clear and Admiral Oldendorf prepared to cross the enemy's "T."

Strangely, Admiral Nishimura did not take any evasive action, even though he must have guessed that the American destroyers had fired torpedoes at his column. Several explosions were observed by sailors aboard Coward's destroyers. A few minutes later, a large ship in the column slowed and began turning slowly to starboard. The battleship IJN *Fusō* had been hit by a torpedo from USS *Melvin*, but Admiral Nishimura continued to send orders to IJN *Fusō* as though the ship were still undamaged.

While Captain Coward's division was withdrawing, the destroyers USS *McDermut* and USS *Monssen* were still steaming due south. The destroyer division's commanding officer, Commander Richard H. Phillips, turned to port to get into firing position, swinging his two destroyers back on a southerly course. A moment later, he ordered torpedoes to be fired when ready. USS *McDermut* began firing immediately. USS *Monssen* followed at 3:11 a.m.

This time, Admiral Nishimura did try to take evasive action. He turned 90 degrees to starboard, then 90 degrees to port, but this did not take him away from the torpedoes. At 3:20 a.m., flashes from explosions among Nishimura's ships were observed aboard both destroyers. A searchlight beam, probably from one of the Japanese destroyers, lit up USS *Monssen*. Shell splashes followed almost immediately, and some were so close that columns of water drenched the aft guns of both USS *Monssen* and USS *McDermut*. The destroyers made smoke, changed course, and increased speed. The searchlight beam disappeared along with the bursting shells.

Destroyer Squadron 54 fired a total of forty-seven torpedoes. Captain Coward was positive that they had scored at least three hits. Actually, five of the torpedoes had found targets, resulting in the sinking of three enemy ships. McDermut's torpedo salvo accounted for no fewer than three destroyers, IJN *Yamagumo*, IJN *Michishio*, and IJN *Asagumo*. IJN *Yamagumo* blew up and sank; IJN *Michishio* was badly damaged and drifting and would sink shortly; IJN *Asagumo* had her bow blown off but was able to make headway. USS *Monssen* scored a hit on IJN *Yamashiro*, which continued steaming on course, but USS *Melvin*'s hit on IJN *Fusō* would prove to be fatal.

However, the attack of the destroyers was not over. Destroyer Squadron 24, under Captain K. M. McManes, also came south down the strait in two sections. The first section consisted of USS *Hutchins*, USS *Daly*, and USS *Bache*; the second of USS *Killen*, USS *Beale*, and HMAS *Arunta*. At 3:17 a.m., Commander A. E. Buchanan of the Royal Australian Navy heard Captain McManes's order, "Boil up! Make smoke! Let me know when you have fired." Two minutes later, the destroyer IJN *Yamagumo* blew up, already hit by one of USS *McDermut*'s torpedoes. The light from the explosion was a great help to Commander Buchanan in making his run.

The fire from IJN *Yamagumo*'s burning hulk might have helped the torpedo men see their targets, but it did not help to hit them. HMAS *Arunta* launched four torpedoes at a range of 6,500 yards. All four missed. USS *Beale* fired five torpedoes at 6,800 yards. These missed as well. The *Killen* had better luck, firing five torpedoes at IJN *Yamashiro* and hitting her once. The *Killen*'s captain, Commander H. G. Corey, had been at Pearl Harbor and must have taken pleasure in torpedoing one of the enemy's battleships. The second torpedo hit on IJN *Yamashiro* slowed the ship to five knots, but only for a short time. The tough old battleship still made headway, and steadily regained speed. Captain McManes's three destroyers, USS *Hutchins*, USS *Daly*, and USS *Bache*, were also coming south at 25 knots. At 3:29 a.m., they began launching torpedoes. Admiral Nishimura's neat column had disintegrated by this time. IJN *Yamashiro* still pressed resolutely northward, now at about 15 knots. IJN *Shigure* and IJN *Mogami*, both still undamaged, fanned out on her starboard side. IJN *Fusō* and the remaining destroyers were either drifting with the current or trying to withdraw to the south. This made for much more difficult shooting than Captain Coward had experienced.

McManes's destroyers fired a total of fifteen torpedoes at Nishimura's force, or what was left of it. UAA *Bache* also opened fire with her 5-inch guns at the damaged Japanese destroyers and was joined by USS *Hutchins* and USS *Daly*. The enemy returned an inaccurate fire of its own. While this exchange was taking place, everyone's attention was distracted by what happened to IJN *Fusō*. The hit by USS *Melvin*'s torpedo, or possibly two torpedoes, had apparently caused internal fires that her damage control parties were not able to extinguish. The fires soon spread to one or more of the main magazines. At 3:38 a.m., the battleship exploded with a tremendous concussion and broke in half. Sailors on both sides witnessed the spectacle. The detonation was massive and was made even more spectacular by the moonless night. Both the bow and stern sections continued to float, drifting slowly away from each other. The two sections continued to drift until the forward section went down at 0420. The stern sank less than an hour later.

As McManes's destroyers began to withdraw, USS *Hutchins* launched her five remaining torpedoes at IJN *Asagumo*. All five missed their target, but one hit IJN *Michishio*, which had drifted into the path of the spread. IJN *Michishio* blew up and sank immediately. Admiral Oldendorf's destroyers had completely reversed the Japanese dominance in night torpedo attacks, which had plagued American forces at Guadalcanal two years earlier. The U.S. destroyers suffered no losses during the action.

The battleships and cruisers of Oldendorf's force were steaming across the northern end of Surigao Strait, at the southern entrance to Leyte Gulf, roughly between Hibuson Island and Leyte. On the eastern flank of the disposition, under Oldendorf's direct command, were the heavy cruisers USS *Louisville*,

USS *Portland*, and USS *Minneapolis*, and the light cruisers USS *Denver* and USS *Columbia*. On the right flank, under Rear Admiral Berkey, were the Australian Navy's heavy cruiser HMAS *Shropshire* and the light cruisers USS *Phoenix* and USS *Boise*. In the center of this disposition was a battle line, consisting of six battleships, USS *West Virginia*, USS *Tennessee*, USS *California*, USS *Maryland*, USS *Mississippi*, and USS *Pennsylvania* under the command of Admiral Weyler. The enemy column now reduced to one battleship, one heavy cruiser, and one destroyer, was steaming into a trap. It was a very short vertical to a very broad "T," and Oldendorf was about to cross it, as Admiral Togo had done to Rozhestvensky in 1905 at the Battle of Tsushima Strait, and as naval officers who studied the tactics had since hoped to accomplish.

At 3:23 a.m., radar screens registered the Japanese formation. Ten minutes later, the range then being 33,000 yards, Admiral Weyler signaled the battle line to open fire at 26,000 yards, believing that if he waited any longer his ships would lose their initial advantage of having five salvoes of armor-piercing ammunition immediately available. Admiral Oldendorf ordered all cruisers to open fire at 3:51 a.m. when USS *Louisville*'s range to the nearest target was 15,600 yards. IJN *Yamashiro* slowed to 12 knots at 3:52 a.m. but continued on course firing at visible targets, for she had no fire control radar. Admiral Nishimura was steaming boldly into a terrific concentration of gunfire, supported only by heavy cruiser IJN *Mogami* and destroyer IJN *Shigure* on his starboard quarter. His last message was to IJN *Fusō* at 3:52 a.m. asking her to make top speed. Admiral Nishimura never learned that IJN *Fusō* had been mortally torpedoed by the American destroyers and was no longer in column. There was no reply from that sinking battleship. Busy taking fire, Nishimura never informed Shima of what was happening.

USS *West Virginia*, USS *Tennessee*, and USS *California*, equipped with the latest Mk. 8 fire control radar, had a firing solution in the main battery plot and were ready to shoot long before the enemy came within range. These three were responsible for most of the battle-line action. USS *West Virginia* opened fire at 3:53 a.m. and got off ninety-three rounds of 16-inch armor-piercing shells before checking. USS *Tennessee* and USS *California*, starting at 3:55 a.m., shot sixty-nine and sixty-three rounds of 14-inch respectively, fired in six-gun salvos in order to conserve their limited supply. The other three battleships, equipped with Mk. 3 fire control radar, had difficulty finding a target. USS *Maryland* picked it up by ranging on USS *West Virginia*'s shell splashes and got off forty-eight rounds of 16-inch in six salvos, starting at 3:59 a.m. USS *Mississippi* fired a single salvo, and USS *Pennsylvania* never managed to locate a target and took no part in the action. At 4:08 a.m., the *Mississippi* got on the big target IJN *Yamashiro* and fired a full salvo. Admiral Oldendorf had just ordered cease fire, but she had not yet got the word. Thus, USS *Mississippi* fired the last major-caliber salvo of the battle. While Japanese sailors worked frantically to make temporary repairs, they returned fire, IJN *Mogami* for a few minutes and IJN *Yamashiro* longer. The Japanese battleship directed her main battery fire at the enemy cruisers, while her secondary battery fired at the retiring torpedo squadrons. Neither one had any effect.

While the destroyers were making their torpedo attacks, Admiral Oldendorf's battle line and flanking cruisers waited for Nishimura's group to come within range of their guns. Explosions from the torpedo hits, along with the eruption of IJN *Fusō*, were visible to anyone topside on any of the cruisers or battleships. Radar screens began to pick up the enemy at 3:23 a.m. The battleships and cruisers had been steering back and forth, east and west, across the northern end of Surigao Strait. At 3:30 a.m., they were all near the western side of the strait, steering east. Twenty-one minutes later Oldendorf ordered the cruisers to open fire. Two minutes later the battleships joined in.

The situation was a Naval War College textbook exercise, at least from the American point of view. Admiral Nishimura's force, now down to three ships, one battleship, one heavy cruiser, and one destroyer, continued steaming northward. Oldendorf was about to cross the "T" in the classic naval maneuver, which allowed the ships forming the horizontal stroke to bring all guns to bear, while the ships forming the down stroke could only fire their forward-facing guns at the enemy.

The battle line changed course from 120°(T) to 270°(T) at 4:02 a.m. by simultaneous turns and continued to fire as it steamed west. Since this maneuver closed the battleships' range, the volume of fire became even greater. At 4:09 a.m., Admiral Oldendorf, on receiving word that USS *Grant* and her sisters were being hit by friendly fire, ordered all ships to cease fire to give the destroyers' time to retire. Despite the punishment, IJN *Yamashiro* had been taking, she increased speed to 15 knots, turned 90 degrees left, and began to retire southward. At 4:19 a.m., she capsized and sank, taking down Admiral Nishimura and all but a few members of the crew. The heavy cruiser IJN *Mogami* turned left at 3:53 a.m. when the shooting began, launched torpedoes at 4:01 a.m., and at the same time received gunfire from Captain MacManes's destroyers to the southwestward. She caught fire at 3:56 a.m., turned south to retire, increased speed and made smoke, but received many more hits

At 4:18 a.m., Admiral Weyler ordered USS *Mississippi,* USS *Maryland*, and USS *West Virginia* to turn due north, away from the enemy. Admiral Chandler ordered the other battleships westward. The northward turn took half of battle line out of the fight. When Admiral Oldendorf ordered all ships to resume fire at 4:19 a.m., no target was left on their radar screens. The ten-minute check-fire allowed IJN *Shigure* and IJN *Mogami* to retire south. Even so, by 4:20 a.m. on October 25, with only another twenty minutes to go before the first glimmerings of dawn appeared over Dinagat Island, Admiral Nishimura's force, which had counted on being off Dulag by that time, was done for. Of the two battleships only the burning stern of IJN *Fusō* was still afloat, three destroyers were sunk or stopped by torpedoes in mid-strait, and a badly damaged heavy cruiser and a damaged destroyer were retiring. Of Admiral Oldendorf force, only destroyer USS *Grant* had been hit and that mostly by friendly fire.

Of the American battleships, USS *Tennessee*, USS *West Virginia*, and USS *California* had the advantage of Mk. 8 fire control radar. The radar data, the distance, speed, and course of the enemy were fed into the gunnery computer and produced a firing solution before the enemy ships even came within range. Ammunition was in relatively short supply since the ships had been bombarding enemy shore installations and were carrying relatively few armor-piercing shells. The *Yamashiro* continued on a course of 20°(T) at 12 knots, firing at USS *Denver*, USS *Columbia*, and other left-flank cruisers. The battleship did not have any fire control radar and was limited to shooting at visible targets. The cruisers were closer and easier to see than Oldendorf's battleships. USS *Denver*, USS *Columbia*, and USS *Minneapolis* were straddled by shell splashes. The cruisers and battleships returned a devastating fire of their own. Dwight Weir, a seventeen-year-old sailor aboard USS *Columbia* remembered hundreds of Japanese sailors in the water after their ships were sunk after being attacked by machete-wielding Filipinos in canoes. Many of the sailors drowned themselves. On USS *Columbia*, a gun would be emptied in about twenty-five minutes of fighting, Weir said, and by that time, he and his fellow gunners would be exhausted from the anxiety and accelerated blood pressure of battle.

Every caliber shell, from 6-inch to 16-inch, came cascading down in the immediate vicinity of IJN *Yamashiro* and IJN *Mogami*. "This was modern war at sea," wrote one commentator. "They fired at something they couldn't see, and it fired back." Actually, IJN *Yamashiro* and IJN *Mogami* were firing at the cruisers and withdrawing destroyers and only managed to hit the unfortunate USS *Albert W. Grant*.

Aboard the battleships of both navies, the concussion from the big guns was staggering. Every time a salvo was fired, the recoil rocked the ship and seemed to push it sideways. The blast from the guns squeezed the breath out of the body and popped rivets out of the bulkheads. Shells weighing nearly a ton each rocketed out of muzzles at over 1,600 miles per hour. Thick clouds of cordite smoke burned the eyes and stuck in the throat. Flash-less powder was being used, but the muzzle flashes still lit up each ship on this black night. An easterly breeze blew the smoke clear, a great help for visual spotting and observation.

USS *West Virginia* fired a total of ninety-three rounds of 16-inch armor-piercing shells, while USS *Tennessee* and USS *California* fired sixty-nine and sixty-three rounds, respectively, of 14-inch ammunition. The other three battleships were hindered by their Mk. 3 radar, which was far less effective in finding targets than the Mk. 8 and resulted in dramatically fewer rounds fired. USS *Maryland* fired forty-eight rounds, its fire control managing to find the

Yamashiro by ranging on the splashes from USS *West Virginia*'s shells. USS *Mississippi* fired only one salvo, and USS *Pennsylvania* did not fire a shot all night long.

At midnight, when he received the message that Admiral Nishimura's force was in action with American torpedo boats, Admiral Shima and his Second Striking Force were about 40 miles astern of Nishimura. For three hours, Shima sailed towards Leyte unmolested. Then, at about 3:15 a.m., *PT-134* made a torpedo attack, but missed. Shortly afterwards *PT-137* attacked Shima's force, firing at a destroyer which at the time had reversed course to take station astern of Shima's formation. *PT-137*'s torpedoes missed the destroyer by chance one of them struck the light cruiser IJN *Abukuma*, which fell out of formation. As Shima's group, consisting now of the two heavy cruisers and four destroyers, proceeded northwards, what appeared to be two large burning ships were sighted. Shima took these to be the IJN *Fusō* and IJN *Yamashiro*. In fact, they were the two halves of the torpedoed IJN *Fusō*.

At 4:20 a.m., Admiral Shima still thought he was speeding up to the support of Admiral Nishimura, who had just gone down with his ship. Heavy cruiser IJN *Ashigara* was astern of IJN *Nachi*, and the four destroyers were ranging ahead northwesterly. All six ships were ready to fire torpedoes as soon as they found a target. Shima observed on his radar screen what he supposed to be two enemy ships. At 4:24 a.m., he ordered both cruisers to attack these targets with torpedoes. They turned right to course and fired eight torpedoes each.

This was Second Striking Force's only contribution to the battle. Torpedoes must have run erratically, since at least two of them were recovered from Hibuson Island later. Shima did not know what had happened to Nishimura, but guessed the worst, and the heavy smoke made by American destroyers curtained his view northward. He decided to temporarily retire and await development of events. His destroyers, which had now penetrated farther north than the cruisers without seeing anything to shoot at, were recalled about 4:25 a.m. At the same time, he sent a radio dispatch to Vice Admiral Mikawa and to all Shō-Go forces that his force has concluded its attack and is retiring from the battle area to plan subsequent action.

Off the coast of Leyte, the sailors aboard the U.S. support vessels were too far away to see or hear the battle, but they did see the flashes of gunfire reflected in the clouds. Nobody knew the outcome of the battle until morning, when reports began to filter in that the Japanese had been stopped. The news was not conclusive, mostly bits and pieces based on radio reports, but the word that was going around was certainly reassuring. There was no need to worry. Oldendorf had certainly plugged Surigao Strait, as he had intended. No Japanese ship had come anywhere near Leyte Gulf, and what was left of the enemy fleet was retiring south.

Later in the morning, American Grumman TBF Avengers caught up with IJN *Mogami*. A bomb hit on her engine room left her dead in the water. The destroyer

IJN *Akebono* took off the crew and sank the cruiser with a torpedo at 12:30 p.m. Shima's force proved to be much luckier. All four of its destroyers escaped destruction at Surigao Strait, along with the heavy cruiser IJN *Ashigara*. Two days later, IJN *Abukuma*, which had been struck by a PT torpedo at Surigao Strait, was hit several times by U.S. bombers. One of the bombs touched off the ship's torpedo warheads, and the cruiser went down south of Negros Island. IJN *Nachi* was sunk by dive–bombers from the aircraft carrier USS *Lexington* in Manila Bay on November 5.

On USS *Louisville*, Oldendorf studied the smoke, oil fires, and silence through his binoculars and ordered a cautious pursuit of his beaten enemy. He had no idea if there were more enemy ships out there. Intelligence suggested there might be as many as three battleships, five cruisers, and six to eight destroyers beyond the smoke ready to ambush him with shells and Long Lance torpedoes. And his battle line was increasingly short on ammunition. At 4:37 a.m., USS *Louisville*, USS *Portland*, USS *Minneapolis*, USS *Denver*, and USS *Columbia* headed south. At 4:41 a.m., Shima ordered his ships to follow behind IJN *Nachi*. Hobbling along at 20 knots, they were retreating at a slow speed. On the battered IJN *Mogami*, ammunition started cooking off, hampering repairs and endangering the crew. Arai ordered his men to jettison torpedoes to prevent them from exploding, but four of them exploded, adding to the smoldering fires.

Incredibly, the engines kept turning, and Arai used hand steering to maneuver his ship. The battle still sputtered on. As the Japanese ships retreated, they met up with the PT boats that had not expended their torpedoes earlier in the struggle. Lieutenant Carl T. Gleason's Section 11, consisting of three PT boats, attacked the destroyers IJN *Shigure* and IJN *Asagumo*. The Japanese fire was ragged and off target, but one American torpedo detonated prematurely. Another slithered out of its tube on *PT-326* and clattered to the deck, a defective "hot run." The blazing fish provided the Japanese with a target, and the Japanese hurled 5-inch shells at the PT boats. Shrapnel injured one man before the burning torpedo could be rolled overboard. The Japanese ships continued to withdraw, now hooking up with the IJN *Abukuma*, which had repaired its damage and was ready to attack. Shima declined the offer but was happy to add another escort to his damaged force.

By 5:20 a.m., USS *Louisville* was 8 miles west of Esconchada Point, where IJN *Nachi* and IJN *Mogami* had collided an hour earlier. Oldendorf studied the scene through his binoculars and told his column to turn right and prepare to shell the fleeing Japanese with full broadsides. The open fire gongs rang at 5:29 a.m., and the Americans hurled more shells at the IJN *Mogami*, scoring several direct hits. Yet the cruiser survived this latest bombardment, cranking up to 14 knots. Other American shells rained down from USS *Minneapolis* on IJN *Asagumo*, starting a fire, holing her oil tanks. Barely able to make seven knots, the destroyer was on fire, spreading and menacing its torpedoes. At 6 a.m., IJN *Asagumo*'s skipper, Commander Kazuo Shibayama, ordered his men to abandon ship.

Worried about Japanese torpedoes, Oldendorf ceased fire at 5:39 a.m. and swung back north. Now the American destroyers began nosing into the wreckage in the growing dawn to pursue survivors of the two battleships and two destroyers sunk in Surigao Strait. Oldendorf ordered his ships, "Do not overload your ships with survivors. Search each man well to see that he does not have any weapons. Anyone offering resistance, shoot him. Proceed independently to pick up survivors."

American casualties totaled thirty-nine killed and 114 wounded, most of them aboard USS *Albert W. Grant*. No records of Japanese casualties exist, but they probably total in the thousands. IJN *Fusō* and IJN *Yamashiro* each had complements of 1,400 men, most of whom went down with their ships. Surigao Strait also saw the end of the battle line in naval warfare. The development of the aircraft carrier meant that no line of battleships could withstand a sustained air attack.

By now, Shima's weary collection of ships was heading out of Surigao Strait into the Mindanao Sea, enduring further brushes with PT boats. First up was *PT-491*, which charged IJN *Mogami*, firing torpedoes. IJN *Mogami* hit back with 8-inch shells, and *PT-491* retreated. Back in Surigao Strait, American destroyers slowly steamed into debris-strewn waters filled with Japanese survivors who refused American entreaties to surrender. Other ships pursued the crippled IJN *Asagumo*, whose bows had been torn open. *PT-323* hurled a torpedo into the immobile tin can, throwing men on her weather decks into the water. Hearing word of this target, Oldendorf sent in the cruisers USS *Denver* and USS *Columbia* and six destroyers to polish off IJN *Asagumo*. Oldendorf was beginning to receive frantic messages from his bosses at Seventh Fleet that Kurita's battleships had steamed through the unguarded San Bernardino Strait and were bearing down on the poorly defended escort carriers off Samar. Oldendorf had to steam to the rescue, despite his shortages of ammunition. Nishimura had succeeded in one thing—drawing off Kinkaid's heavy warships to expend ammunition and energy against the attack from the south instead of Kurita's thrust from the north.

Meanwhile, Shima's retreating ships, heading home in the early morning, awaited the one certainty of the day, an American air attack. Shima radioed for fighter cover but instead received an attack of nine Grumman TBF Avenger torpedo bombers and four Grumman F6F Hellcat fighters from the escort carrier USS *Santee* and two Avengers and six Hellcats from USS *Sangamon*, launched at 5:45 a.m. They pounced on Shima's battered vessels and incorrectly reported them as two battleships. That happened often. Japanese heavy cruisers had massive superstructures and looked like battleships to airmen. The Americans swooped in for the attack. Strafing killed nine and wounded twenty-five on

IJN *Shiranuhi*, and the luckless IJN *Mogami* took yet another torpedo hit. Ten Avengers and five Grumman FM-2 Wildcats from USS *Ommaney Bay*'s VC-75 came next, storming down on the smoking IJN *Mogami*, scoring two more hits, starting fires, and bringing the ship to a halt.

The destroyer IJN *Akebono* sprayed hoses on the cruiser. Everyone but the anti-aircraft crews fought the fires. The American bombs smashed into the cruiser's oil tanks, setting them ablaze. Gunnery officer and acting commander Arai ordered the three forward 8-inch magazines flooded to prevent an explosion. But the warped bulkheads meant that the valves for the No. 1 gun room would not open. The cruiser was blazing and could sink at any moment. In tears, Arai ordered his men to abandon ship at 10:30 a.m. With her davits broken, IJN *Mogami* could not use her cutter, so IJN *Akebono* closed IJN *Mogami*'s port quarter to take aboard the cruiser's crew. At 9:33 a.m., Shima faced his last attack of the day: thirteen Curtiss SB2C Helldiver dive bombers, which strafed the Japanese ships, punching holes in the destroyer IJN *Ushio*.

On IJN *Mogami*, the exhausted crew mustered topside on weather decks to abandon ship after three hours of desperate firefighting, shuffling aboard IJN *Akebono*. At 12:56 p.m., IJN *Akebono* fired a Long Lance into IJN *Mogami*'s port side, and the cruiser began to sink, her demise hastened by an explosion in No. 1 magazine. At 1:07 p.m., as her crew stood by on IJN *Akebono* watching and crying, IJN *Mogami* slipped beneath the waves. All but twenty officers, 171 enlisted men, and one civilian of IJN *Mogami*'s 850-man crew were saved by IJN *Akebono*.

At 1:33 p.m., Shima got more bad news—a message from Kurita that the main force was canceling its planned attack on the Leyte anchorage and was retreating, having failed in its mission. Shima's reaction is unrecorded, but he continued his retreat. IJN *Shigure* headed for Brunei and ultimate safety in Japan. But when IJN *Shigure* tied up at Sasebo on November 14, her skipper, Nishino, faced relief of command at the end of the month, accused of lack of aggressiveness in Surigao Strait. The fallout continued. IJN *Abukuma* was caught a day later, on October 26, by U.S. Army Air Forces Consolidated B–24 Liberators of the 33rd Squadron, which hammered her. Japanese anti-aircraft gunners knocked down three B-24s, but flames spread across IJN *Abukuma*'s decks, igniting torpedoes. Her skipper, Captain Takuo Hanada, ordered the ship abandoned. He and twenty-five officers and 257 enlisted men of her 438-man crew survived.

Philip Hollywood was a nineteen-year-old fire control man, second class, manning one of the destroyer USS *Melvin*'s guns. He recalled the battle:

> Our attack took about five minutes. The job was to get as close as we could to the enemy ships, launch torpedoes and get out alive. We were in total darkness inside the fire control director, a fully enclosed box above the bridge. But

> occasionally, through my lens, I could see a salvo of shells coming down. I was hearing a lot on the headphones from fellows at battle stations outside: "They turned on a searchlight!" "Wow, we just got illuminated by a star shell!" "Those guys are on target!"
>
> Nobody in our box was making a sound. Japanese shells started landing on both sides of us, and guys were screaming about how close that one was or this one was. When our torpedoes finally launched, we made a fast turn. We started making smoke from our boiler rooms to camouflage our movement and went around the north end of Dinagat Island. I opened my hatch and watched the show. These huge salvos from our battleships and cruisers at the top of the strait seemed to float down—then, Boom!
>
> I felt sorry for the Japanese. Because our ships were crossing in front of them, we could fire all our guns at once—but the Japanese could fire only their forward batteries—it's a naval tactic called crossing the T. They had steamed into an ambush. I'm proud of my service to my country. It will never happen again, a sea battle like that. I was a part of history.

On October 25, the Japanese force was broken up or in retreat, with Admiral Oldendorf's force in pursuit. The use of the battle tactic of crossing the "T" had been used successfully for the last time. The Battle of Surigao Strait was over with the Americans and Admiral Oldendorf the clear winner.

9

Action Reports at Surigao Strait

USS *Louisville* World War II Cruise Book

Reconquering the Philippines was the beginning of the inevitable end. No one knew this better than the Nips. Goaded by the taunts of "Bull" Halsey, confronted with severance of supply lines to South China and the East Indies, losing face and heart with our every strike, they had to fight back. Like cornered rats, a stand had to be made, and the Philippines had to be the spot. We suspected it. We were prepared. If any of us had any doubts concerning the determination of the Japs to wrest Leyte from our hands, he began changing his mind on the 23rd of October when scuttlebutt raced like wildfire through the ship of the approach of large enemy naval forces. Those reports formed the current that set mighty machines in action. Communicators worked all night decoding dispatches. By early morning the dope was out. The enemy, in an all-out gamble to smash our hold in the Philippines, was deploying his entire fleet. Three powerful task forces, like giant pincers, were closing in for the kill: one from the north moving south from the Empire, one from the west steaming towards San Bernadino Straits, and the other approaching Leyte Gulf from the Mindanao Sea.

Decisions, the kind that win wars or lose them, had to be made. Admiral Halsey, in one of history's boldest, most courageous gambles, ordered his entire Third Fleet to intercept and sink the Jap forces to the north. That order meant that Admiral Kincaid's Seventh Fleet, of which we were part, had to meet the other two forces. On our success hinged the fate of thousands of men ashore and in troop transports in the Gulf.

Officers and men worked shoulder to shoulder loading ammunition in a blazing, unmerciful sun that turned the tar of decks into blistered rivulets. Admirals' barges and captains' gigs skimmed from ship to ship, as hasty conferences were held and hurried, terse briefings made. The Japs were no idlers. Their plan of attack was a skillfully coordinated operation designed to crush with inexorable force our offensive. Mass air attacks greeted us that morning. Relentlessly they pressed their attacks, only to be intercepted and decimated with each attempt by our Lightning and Corsair fighter planes based on the airfields at Dulag and Tacloban.

As the dogfights raged to the north over Luzon, our plans were formulated. Admiral Kincaid was informed that the Jap force approaching San Bernadino Straits had reversed course and was retiring. We were later to discover this report to be in error. Based on this misinformation, Task Group 77.2, under Rear Admiral Oldendorf, consisting of six battleships, four heavy cruisers, four light cruisers; and twenty four destroyers, was ordered to guard the southern entrance of Leyte Gulf; to attack and destroy any enemy forces attempting to enter. The Louisville had reached the pinnacle of her career. With Admiral Oldendorf aboard, she was the flagship that spear-headed the greatest surface engagement of this war. Under cover of darkness, we weighed anchor. Silently, grimly, we steamed in column down the Gulf with the Lou [USS *Louisville*] in the van.

"Now hear this," the calm, deliberate voice of the "old man" broke the stillness of the night. Through the rasping back ground of the loudspeakers, our skipper told us the moment was at hand to decisively defeat the enemy. Clammy sweat moistened the palms of our hands as nervous tension heightened. Many a man standing at his battle station said a silent prayer as the Captain told of the certainty of battle, He concluded by expressing his confidence in his officers and crew. His confidence in us was exceeded only by our confidence in him.

Plucky PT boats, stationed as advance pickets at the mouth of the entrance, reported radar contacts closing in column from the southeast between Camiguin and Bohol Islands at 0100 on the morning of October 25. Our forces were disposed in classic naval form. A battle-line of battleships with right and left flank forces of cruisers to each side and forward some three or four thousand yards. The USS *Louisville* took her station in the left flank. Alert and apprehensive, we steamed back and forth across Surigao Straits waiting our prey.

In two columns, one four miles ahead of the other, the enemy cautiously felt his way forward. As he entered the Straits, the command to attack was given to the PT boats. Valiantly, the mosquito fleet struck. Star shells shattered the black of night. Greenish yellow flares slowly descended, their illumination probing every shadow, exposing the mighty midgets as they attempted to press home their torpedo attack. Tracers laced the dark as the J aps laid a solid curtain of fire before them, and it proved impenetrable. Our boys were beaten back.

Twenty miles away we continued our wait. Tensions electrified the air. What man aboard did not shudder when the report, "No hits claimed," came back from the commander of the PTs? No sooner did the word reach us via inter-ship communication than it was relayed to every battle station over our sound-powered telephone circuits. We had ring-side seats at the greatest show on earth. Soon we were to be in the ring-no longer the spectator. The stakes were high, too high to think about very much.

Over two hours had passed since the first enemy contact. Having fought their way safely through the picket line of our PT boats, the Jap columns closed steadily at eighteen knots. Twenty-four of our destroyers were lurking in the radar shadows of Dinagat Island. When the leading Nip heavyweight crossed the ten-mile range band, the order was relayed to the tin cans to close the enemy and launch their torpedoes. The destroyers, zig-zagging crazily in the night to foil enemy gunners, suddenly knifed into a graceful curve and fired their underwater missiles. One hundred and twenty-seven deadly fish churned away toward Jap ships, their wakes forming a series of expanding fans. A large part of the Emperor's proud battle fleet stood in the path. Hits were scored.

Retiring from a torpedo run is often a more hazardous venture than the attack itself. In this case, the assault had been a surprise to the enemy, but he retaliated with a murderous barrage directed at the destroyers as they raced back to protection under our big guns. One unfortunately, dropped behind the main destroyer formation and being mistaken for an enemy ship was fired upon by our own forces. In night engagements, gunners do not take a chance on questionable targets. However, the USS *Grant* finally identified herself by radio and limped through our formation and returned to Leyte Gulf.

Meanwhile, our own radar has picked up the approaching ships. The ranges and bearings were being continually disseminated. Over the telephone circuits came the ominous report, using code nomenclature, "Skunks—bearing 192—range 28,500." Anticipation made our breathing shorter, quicker. Again the range, "... 25,000." Not long to go now. At 24,000 we expected all hell to break loose, for that was the maximum effective range of our main battery. Unconsciously we sucked in our breath, taut for the expected blast.

The moon had set, leaving a sky blanketed with low, dense clouds, blacker than ink. Only the churning of the propellers, and the throaty rumble of the screws, which ordinarily are imperceptible background noise, broke the deadly silence. "Range 21,000." "For Christ sakes, what the hell are they waiting for," muttered one of the anti-aircraft gunners, anxiety and fright giving a hoarse trembling timber to his voice. For once it was his turn to wait and pray and watch, with his fate in the hands of the men of the main battery.

"Range 18,000." The silence was heavy, unbearable. Why didn't they open up? They should have fifteen minutes ago. Was something wrong? Weren't we crossing the damned Japs' 'T'?

Wasn't that what every Admiral in the world dreamed of doing in naval battle? What the hell was wrong with the old man? Open up! Doubts, curses, misgivings such as these flashed through our minds. Those of us with binoculars thought we could vaguely make out the portentous hulls of the enemy ships. Doubts were giving way to a gnawing, helpless fear when the word was passed, "Stand by for main battery." The range was 17,000 yards, almost close enough for our secondary battery.

It appears that difficulty had been experienced getting ships into position. With further delay impossible, Oldendorf gave the word to open fire. Two rapid warning buzzers alerted us. Bodies stiffened; hands cupped projectingly over the ears. Suppose we missed! The Jap's fire was going to be just as benefited by the closer range as ours.

A blinding spurt of fire billowed into massive, rolling flames, filled with acrid, orange smoke. The Lady lifted a few feet, recoiled to port and shook as her nine-gun salvo hurled over a ton of steel and explosives at the approaching column of ships. At 0350, we had touched off the greatest ship-to-ship battle of World War Two. Lazily, indifferently, the tracers arced through the air. With nothing stationary to serve as a comparison, that was the impression one received as he watched.

Actually those projectiles were traveling over 2,000 feet per second. Other ships opened up at our signal. Night was day as their guns belched flame and fire. Our attention was riveted on the first group of shells fired as they descended toward the target. A hit! Our second salvo drowned the mighty cheers. The lead Jap ship was a mass of flames shooting hundreds of feet into the sky. What an awe-inspiring sight! The enemy never quite knew what happened as salvo after salvo tore into him, ripping ships apart like matchboxes, setting off magazines that scattered the remnants of battered hulls into oblivion.

Time and again, the Lou's guns roared. Shaking· and shuddering from stem to stern with each blast of the turrets, we continued our devastating fire. At 0404 a Jap destroyer closed enough to allow our secondary battery to open up. With both batteries aboard hurling death and destruction, the USS *Louisville* proved her mettle. During that decisive battle she fired more main battery eight-inch shells than the total of all calibers fired by the six battleships added together.

Admiral Oldendorf later paid tribute to her greatness by beaming proudly, "Remember, an eight-inch shell which hits is far better than a sixteen-inch that misses." In utter confusion, the Japs broke formation and retired. By dawn, only the dying and the dead remained. Our left flank made a sweep down the channel to polish off the cripples, sinking a game destroyer whose single remaining after–gun was still firing as she settled, bow first, into the sea. Countless survivors amid miles of debris struggled in the waters turned pink by the reflections of the rising sun. Our attempts at rescuing them were abruptly ended by a pleading, frantic radio message from a group of escort carriers who were under attack by a powerful Japanese force off the east coast of Samar, just above the eastern entrance to Leyte Gulf.

The Jap plan materialized suddenly, tragically. That Jap force in San Bernadino Straits had faked a retirement and then had reversed course, this time heading for the vulnerable, unprotected troop transports and cargo vessels lying off Dulag and Tacloban. Had they not run into the carrier force, they would have been able to inflict heavy damage on the transports, and the consequent loss of life and equipment might have postponed the Philippine operation for months.

Fortune had smiled upon us, but not upon the CVE's and their escorts, who were taking a murderous beating from the Japs. With most of our ammunition spent, we sped north through the Gulf to their assistance. By the time we reached the transport area, the Japs had turned and fled, but were intercepted by the planes of Admiral Halsey's fleet, which had previously trounced the northernmost pincers of the Japs.

By the grace of God, and some phenomenal marksmanship, the enemy's plan went asunder. The Second Battle of the Philippine Sea, of which the Surigao Strait Battle was one phase, made possible the conquest of the Philippines, which clinched the outcome of the war. The Japs were fighting a lost cause.

USS *California* Radio Logs Recorder's Notes

Chronological Account of Action—October 25, 1944

0020: CANFSWPA from USS *Wachapreague* (APG8-MTB Tender): Following received from PT-130. Report contact with 3 enemy destroyers and 2 large ships at 2310(I) 10 miles off southwest tip of Bohol Island headed north.

0027: From Battleline Commander: Execute "One Turn."

0032: From USS *McGowan*: Skunks, several, bearing 193°, 8 miles.

0043: From Screen Commander: Second contact from *PT-127*. He reports second contact bearing 320°, 10 miles from Camiguin Island, now closing in.

0055: Screen Commander, from USS *McGowan*: We have skunks bearing 188°, 7 miles.

0056: USS *McGowan* from Screen Commander: Challenge him.

0105: Screen Commander, from USS *McGowan*: Challenged skunk on M25, received reply one by one but could not make out call, believe him to be friendly.

0108: Officer in Tactical Command from USS *McGowan*: *PT-533* reports seeing three star shells or flares distance 10 miles, bearing 230° off southern tip of Panaon Island.

0136: CANFSWPA from USS *Wachapreague*: *LCI-272* reports surface contact bearing 140°, 18 miles from Taancan Point.

0145: Battleships, DesDiv X from Commander Battleline: Execute "Turn 13."

0200: Officer in Tactical Command from Commander Cruiser Division 15: *PT-134* reports an unidentified target proceeding up the strait and that it was opposite the southern tip of Panaon Island. He made that report about four minutes ago.

0200: Weather summary: For period 0200 to 0600, October 25, 1944. 5 to 6 tenths of low clouds base abound 1,500 feet. Wind at 0230, 075°(T), 12 knots; 0400, 052°(T), 8 knots. Visibility 6 to 8 miles. Half-moon obscured by clouds at times. Calm sea.

0203: CANFSWPA from Screen Commander: We have just received report from a PT that an unidentified ship is proceeding up the strait and is now abeam south tip of Panaon Island.

0207: Officer in Tactical Command from Commander Cruiser Division 15: *PT-134* reports the target was a very large vessel and that he has taken him under attack with undetermined results.

0210: Officer in Tactical Command from Commander Cruiser Division 15: Target being attacked by PTs is trying to drive them off with gunfire.

0222: Commander Battleline from Officer in Tactical Command: Two large ships are standing up Surigao Strait. Have passed initial line of PT boats.

0225: Officer in Tactical Command from Screen Commander: I am going to start down in a few minutes.

0228: Screen Commander from Officer in Tactical Command: Please relay to MTBs that it is desired for them to determine whether other targets are following the two which have started up the Strait.

0229: Officer in Tactical Command from Commander Cruiser Division 15: *PT-134* just reported he hit a heavy object in very deep water, ran over it and his screws hit it and he thought it might be a submarine coming up the channel with whatever targets might be with them.

0233: Went to General Quarters upon signal from Commander Battleline. Set material condition ZEBRA.

0236: All ships from Officer in Tactical Command: Execute on receipt: Take Condition of Readiness ONE

0238: Changed course to 270°(T) upon receipt of signal from Commander Battleline to execute "One Turn."

0240: Remey from USS *McGowan*: Skunk, single, bearing 184°, distance 18.

0245: Changed speed to 12 knots upon signal from Commander Battleline to execute speed two.

0245: Two skunks reported bearing 184°(T), 15 miles, course 000°(T).

0258: Officer in Tactical Command from Screen Commander: There are 5 targets. 2 large ones, 3 small ones. Targets are approximately 4 miles west of Kanihaan. Targets are all in column.

0300: Officer in Tactical Command from Screen Commander: Fish are in water. We are starting retirement.

0301: Heavy gunfire and star shells observed to southward.

0301: Commander Destroyer Squadron from Commander Destroyer Division 15: Proceed to attack. Follow down west shoreline. Follow other groups in, then retire to northward. Make smoke.

0302: Officer in Tactical Command from Screen Commander: Target 4 miles west of Kanihaan, course 340°, speed 20.

0306: Changed course to 090°(T) upon receipt of signal from Commander Battleline to execute "Turn One Eight."

0307: Officer in Tactical Command from Screen Commander: There was just one group, two large and one small. We are being straddled now.

0308: Heavy gunfire bearing 163°(T), distance about 20 miles.

0311: Officer in Tactical Command from Commander Cruiser Division 12: Screen Commander reports two large and one small, all standing north in one column.

0312: Enemy target (Raid ABLE) picked up by forward SG radar. Range 42,200, bearing 162°(T). Target evaluated as three ships in column. After SG picked up target and CIC commenced tracking, using after SG.

0314: Officer in Tactical Command from Screen Commander: Two of them have been hit they are slowing down and dropping behind the rest.

0315: Officer in Tactical Command from USS *West Virginia*: Skunks two, bearing 166° from us, distance 42,000 yards, time 0315.

0317: Officer in Tactical Command from Screen Commander: Did you receive my transmission that there were five targets; that two of them had been hit and were slowing down?

0318: Fire on horizon off starboard beam.

0318: Screen Commander from Officer in Tactical Command: Please report if possible, the type of target.

0319: To Officer in Tactical Command: Commander Destroyer Division 108 reports just seeing a big flare on one of them.

0320: Forward Mark 8 radar picked up targets, having been coached on by CIC at a range of 38,000. Targets on course 010°, speed 16.

0321: Star shells off starboard beam.

0324: Officer in Tactical Command from Commander Cruiser Division 12: Following from Screen Commander: believe two BBs, one or two cruisers, one DD. Believe several hits scored, saw two.

0325: Officer in Tactical Command from Screen Commander: Enemy now bears 326°, distance 6 and ½ miles from Kanihaan Island, slowing down considerably.

0326: Officer in Tactical Command from Screen Commander: There were several fish fired at north group.

0333: All battleships from Commander Battleline: Open fire at 26,000 yards.

0336: Destroyer Squadron 56 from Commander Destroyer Squadron 56: Corpen 9 and work up to speed in making your attack; section 3 attack in sector 270°(T) to 315°(T), section 2 attack in sector 090°(T) to 045°(T), use individual target plan, medium speed setting for fish.

0337: Destroyer Squadron 56 to OTC: Enemy course 010°(T), speed 12.

0337: Commander Cruiser Division 15 from Officer in Tactical Command: Destroyer Squadron 6 is launching his attack.

0338: Destroyer Division X from Commander Battleline: Concentrate your sections van and rear 4,000 from nearest battleship.

0341: Turrets I and II were ordered to load. Range 26,300.

0341: Commander Battleline from Officer in Tactical Command: Enemy seems to be retiring, close battleline.

0341½: Turret I reported broken powder bag, right gun, and jammed powder car. Turret I was ordered to remedy casualty before coming in with any guns on any salvo. Turret III was ordered to load.

0341½: Target commenced evasive maneuvers remaining on a generally northerly course.

0345: Officer in Tactical Command from Commander Cruiser Division 12: *PT-523* reports 5DDs and 1 large ship have just passed bottom of Surigao Strait in a northerly direction up the Strait.

0348: Officer in Tactical Command from Commander Cruiser Division 15: My destroyer leader reports he's been hitting them regularly with 5-inch and one of the enemy appears to be dead in the water.

0349: Cruiser Division 12 opened fire.

0350: Officer in Tactical Command from Commander Battleline: I have a group of small ones followed by a group of large ones. When the large reach 26,000 yards I will open.

0351: All destroyers from OTC: WE are about to open fire.

0352: Large explosion bearing 176°(T).

0353: From Commander Cruiser Division 15: Believe those three little ones out in front are friendly trying to get over to the shore line.

0354: Changed course to 120°(T) to close range upon receipt of signal from Commander Battleline to execute "Turn Three."

0354: Target commenced to turn to the left, making USS *California* target the middle one of the three pips on radar screen (the right hand one of the two larger pips).

0355: Commander Cruiser Division from Officer in Tactical Command: Open fire.

0355: Commenced fire, following lead of Mississippi, turrets II and III firing a six–gun salvo. At commence firing, target bearing was 188°(T), range 20,400, target course 342°, speed 15. Fall of shot was not observed.

0356: Second salvo fired by turrets III and IV. Had misfire in right gun of turret IV. Five rounds fired at a range of 19,750 yards. Fall of shot not observed.

0357: Third salvo fired by turrets III and IV. Six rounds fired at a range of 19,200 yards. Target straddled. The concussion of this salvo caused the Number 2 Mark 8 radar and the Spot I indicator scope to stop functioning. Spotting officer used trainer's 3-inch indicator scope for the remainder of the firing.

0358: Fourth salvo fired by turrets II, III and IV. Eight rounds fired at a range of 18,450 yards. Target straddled.

0359: Fifth salvo fired by turrets II, III and IV. Eight rounds fired at a range of 18,450 yards. Right gun of turret II did not load. Elevating motor kicked out. Target straddled. Observed first definite USS *California* hit on target, having straddled target on at least the two preceding salvos. One of enemy turrets had been observed firing. Two splashes were observed to land 400 to 500 yards off our starboard quarter, and at least one shell was heard passing overhead.

0400: Sixth salvo fired by turrets II, III and IV. Nine rounds fired at a range of 18,200 yards. Target straddled. Enemy observed to have changed course to southward. No further enemy fire was observed.

0401: Battleline from Commander Battleline: Execute to follow, Turn 15.

0401: Checked fire.

0402: Battleline from Commander Battleline: Execute Turn 15. (This signal was improperly reported to the Commanding Officer as a change of course of 15 degrees).

0403: Steadied on course 135°(T), other ships of Battleline turning to course 270°(T).

0403: Target slowed to about four knots on a retiring course.

0403: Resumed fire. Seventh salvo fired by turrets II, III and IV. Nine rounds fired at a range of 18,450 yards. Target straddled.

0405: USS *California* from Commander Battleship Division 2: Did you receive turn signal? From USS *California*: Wilco. Out.

0405: Eighth salvo fired by turrets II, III and IV. Eight rounds fired at a range of 18,200 yards. Range opening. Misfire in left gun of turret II. Target straddled.

0405: Checked fire.

0405: Turning to 270. USS *California* had failed to turn as directed by signal due to error noted above. Due to this error, USS *California* got out of position and briefly blanked fire of USS *Tennessee* and USS *Mississippi*. However, no firing was in progress at the time.

0405: Officer in Tactical Command from USS *Denver*: Splashes dead ahead off starboard bow of *Denver*.

0405: To all ships from Commander Battleship Division 2: Look out for USS *California*. She apparently did not receive the turn signal.

0406: From USS *Minneapolis*: We are being straddled.

0406: From USS *Denver*: USS *Denver* is being straddled.

0407: Target increased speed to about 14 knots.

0407: USS *California* from Commander Battleship Division 2: Fall in astern of USS *Tennessee*.

0408: Steadied on course 270°(T).

0408: Resumed fire, salvo nine, and ceased fire after two rounds from turret II. Target bearing 210°(T), range 18,500. Left gun in turret II misfired again.

0409: Battleline from Commander Battleship Division 2: Cease fire.

0409: Commander Destroyer Squadron 56 from OTC: Get your gang out of channel as soon as possible.

0409: Reprimed left gun of turret II.

0411: Commander Battleline from USS *California*: I have hot loaded guns. Request permission to fire on target.

0412: Commander Battleline: Battleships with hot guns may fire at enemy.

0413: Unloaded left gun of turret II through the muzzle at the target. Expended a total of 63 rounds of 14-inch/50 AP during the action.

0416: Battleship Division 4 plus USS *Mississippi* from Commander Battleline: Execute to follow: Turn 9.

0418: Battleship Division 4 plus USS *Mississippi* from Commander Battleline: Execute Turn 9.

0420: Commander Battleship Division 2 from Commander Battleline: Rejoin battleline when you have your division squared away.

0421: Officer in Tactical Command from Commander Destroyer Division X: Reporting with two divisions, one east and one west of the battleline.

0421: At a range of 21,500 yards lost pip of enemy target simultaneously from the screens of the SG, FH (Mark 8) and FD (Mark 4) radars. It is believed that this target sank.

0422: During firing, using the precision sweep of the Mark 8 radar, all other targets were off the screen. At this time a search was made for the second heavy ship.

0424: Battleship Division 4 and USS *Mississippi* from Commander Battleline: Execute to follow: 9 turn, tackline speed 2.

0425: Battleship Division 4 and USS *Mississippi* from Commander Battleline: Execute 9 turn, tackline speed 2.

0426: Officer in Tactical Command from Commander Cruiser Division 15: Just intercepted from PT boats that they had seen some ships heading south now.

0429: Changed course to 000°(T), upon receipt of signal from Commander Battleship Division 2 to execute "Turn 000."

0435: All targets had either disappeared from screens or were retiring at ranges of 30,000 yards or more on a relative bearing of 180°.

0436: Commander Motor Torpedo Boat Squadron 36, *PT-132*, *PT-127*, and *PT-335* from OTC: Friendly cruisers and destroyers proceeding south. Notify PTs. Acknowledge.

0437: Changed course to 270° and slowed to 10 knots upon receipt of signal from Commander Battleship Division 2.

0440: Battleships from Commander Battleline: Designating Pennsylvania SOPUS.

0441: Commander Allied Naval Forces, Southwest Pacific Area from Officer in Tactical Command: Enemy retiring. Friendly destroyers and cruisers are pursuing for an attack.

0441: Commander Battleline from Commander Battleship Division 2: Battleship Division 2 on course 270° at speed 10. Order of ships USS *Pennsylvania,* USS *Tennessee,* USS *California.*

0450: Officer in Tactical Command from USS *West Virginia*: Plane just passed over us.

0454: Battleship Division 2 rejoined Battleline and resumed patrol in southern area of Leyte Gulf.

0455: Changed course to 090°(T) upon receipt of signal.

0500: "Flash Blue" ordered by Commander Allied Naval Forces, Southwest Pacific Area.

0502: "Flash Red," "Control Yellow," ordered by Commander Allied Naval Forces, Southwest Pacific Area.

0512: Bogies bearing 010°, 11 miles from this ship (SK radar).

0515: Officer in Tactical Command from USS *West Virginia*: Skunk bearing 183°, distance 16 miles from this ship.

0521: Made radar surface contact bearing 127°(T), distance 16 miles from us.

0530: Commander Battleline from USS *Tennessee*: Skunks, few, bearing 129°, distance 16 miles, apparently on reverse course.

0534: Observed gunfire continuing to southward.

0552: Anti-aircraft fire bearing 345°(T).

0559: Changed course to 270°(T) upon receipt of signal from Commander Battleline to execute 18 turn.

0609: Officer in Tactical Command from Commander Destroyer Division 112: We have just passed a large group of survivors.

0609: Commander Destroyer Division 112 from Officer in Tactical Command: Can you identify them?

0610: Officer in Tactical Command from Commander Destroyer Division 112: They appear to be Nipponese survivors.

0610: Commander Destroyer Division 112 from Officer in Tactical Command: Pick them up.

0626: Commander Battleline from Officer in Tactical Command: Dispose battle line between Taytay Point and Homonhon Island.

0648: Received "Flash White" from Commander Allied Naval Forces, Southwest Pacific Area and secured from General Quarters. Set Condition of Readiness II and Material Condition YOKE.

0706: Received "Flash Red," "Control Yellow" from Commander Allied Naval Forces, Southwest Pacific Area and went to General Quarters. Set material condition ZEBRA.

0725: Officer in Tactical Command from Commander Support Aircraft Central Philippines: CVE Group 3 under attack by enemy forces bearing 062—100 miles from Mt. Majuyag.

0730: Commander Allied Naval Forces, Southwest Pacific Area from Officer in Tactical Command: Am sending submarines plus USS *Nashville* to you as reinforcements. Enemy may be attempting to enter Leyte from east.

0735: Course 180°, speed 18 knots.

0749: Course 210°, speed 18 knots.

0750: The following vessels were ordered to proceed and support CVE Group 3 which was reported to be under attack by enemy surface forces: Battleship Division 2, USS *Louisville,* USS *Portland,* USS *Minneapolis,* HMAS *Shropshire* and destroyers of Destroyer Squadron 56. Heavy ships of this group formed in column in the following order: USS *Louisville,* USS *Portland,* USS *Minneapolis,* HMAS *Shropshire,* USS *Tennessee,* USS *California and* USS *Pennsylvania* and proceeded towards the Pacific entrance of Leyte Gulf. Officer in Tactical Command, Rear Admiral J. B. Oldendorf, U.S.N., in USS *Louisville.*

0800: Many bogies reported by USS *Pennsylvania*: 240°, 35 miles from Mt. Majuyag.

0805: Our SK radar indicated bogies, many, bearing 165°, distance 46 miles, course 060°(T) from Mt. Majuyag.

0810: Changed course to 270°(T) and slowed to 10 knots.

0810: Enemy "Vals" [Aichi D3A Type 99 Carrier Bomber] sighted by USS *Pennsylvania* bearing 240°(T).

0811: Observed anti-aircraft fire bearing 225°(T).

0813: Sighted nineteen enemy "Vals" bearing 295°(T).

0814: Enemy planes dived bombed destroyer bearing 335°(T). Bomb appeared to hit close aboard destroyer.

0815: Commenced firing 5-inch/38 on enemy planes passing from aft to forward on port side. Expended 40 rounds 5-inch/38 AAC.

0816: From Officer in Tactical Command to Commander Destroyer Division 112: Screen is formed up well enough to close up for anti-aircraft defense.

0827: Officer in Tactical Command to USS *Wachapreague* for reply to Commander Allied Naval Forces, Southwest Pacific Area: Attack imminent by two cruisers and six destroyers at Sogod Bay.

0830: All battleships from Officer in Tactical Command: Take proper distance.

0845: From Commander Allied Naval Forces, Southwest Pacific Area to Officer in Tactical Command: Proceed with your entire force to point 25 miles west of Point Fin. Be prepared to proceed to Point Mongrel. More later.

0845: Changed course to 270°.
0929: "Flash White," "Control Green," from Commander Allied Naval Forces, Southwest Pacific Area.
1107: Bogey bearing 120°, 14 miles from Mt. Majuyag.
1118: Bogey 345°, 13 miles from Mt. Majuyag.
1118: 5-inch/38 and 40mm anti-aircraft battery opened fire on three enemy planes bearing 015(T). Expended 205 rounds 40mm and 6 rounds of 5-inch/38 AAC. "Zeke" [Mitsubishi A6M Zero] bearing 333°(T) shot down by this disposition.
1240: Secured from General Quarters, set Condition of Readiness II, and Material Condition YOKE.

Ammunition Expended

Total ammunition expended was sixty-three 14-inch/50 armor-piercing projectiles with corresponding service charges.

Effectiveness of Gunnery: Surface

There was a very real problem in this engagement as to proper fire distribution. As the time to commence firing approached, the enemy was in the position to have his "T" crossed. Spot I's pip interpretation identified the enemy as one lighter ship loading with two heavier ships. With this knowledge, the leading heavy ship was chosen as USS *California*'s target. At the time of opening fire, the enemy had already commenced evasive maneuvers as he was under fire from our cruisers and destroyers. It happened that this ship was the right-hand ship at the time of our commencing fire, which supported the belief that he should have been the target of USS *Tennessee*, USS *California*, and USS *Pennsylvania*. Although the target could not be seen, except indistinctly by Spot I, still we were able to observe what we identified as three California hits. These were determined by observing a flash at the target which was distinct from enemy gun fire and could be very accurately gauged as it was simple to follow our tracers all the way.

Enemy Battle Damage

Pattern size appeared to be more than 300 or 400 yards. Consistent straddles were obtained and probable hits. It appears that fire was effective, and that the *California*'s fire was definitely contributory to the destruction of one enemy battleship.

USS *West Virginia* Radio Logs Recorder's Notes

Chronological Account of Action—October 25, 1944

0001: On course 090°(T) in battle disposition, this vessel leading the battleline.

0026: Received report from MTB 127 that 3 enemy DD's 2 large ships were ten miles off the southeast tip of Bobol heading north. That position is 200°, 89 miles from us. Search radars were focused on southern part of straits with negative results.

0041: Received contact report ten miles 310° from Camiguin Island which is 85 miles away.

0108: Flares or star shells were reported by MTB 53, 18 miles southwest of Panaon Island.

0130: Saw three star shells to northwest of us, perhaps over land and fired in connection with troops operation. Wished they would stop as light might silhouette us.

0144: Destroyer Squadron 54 reported contact 10 miles southwest of Panaon Island.

0152: Changed course to 270°(T).

0204: *PT-134* reported contact abeam Panaon Island.

0205: Received report enemy large ships under attack by our PT boats: results undetermined. Saw a light over horizon to southwest.

0206: Saw star shells to southeast far distant.

0208: Gunfire sighted bearing 180°(T).

0209: Same.

0210: PT boats report target they are attacking is trying to drive them off with gunfire.

0232: Went to General Quarters upon signal.

0239: Star shells to northwest. Probably same as 0130 note.

0241: Surface contact reported 184°(T), 18 miles.

0246: DD reported surface contacts, 4 in column 184°, distance 15 miles.

0301: DD's report they had fired torpedoes at enemy.

0303: Observed gunfire to south.

0304: Enemy appeared on scopes of SG radar, 20 mile scale. The pip was visible at extreme edges of the tube on bearing 164°, range 44,000 yards. Several groups of friendly pips appeared on the scopes as our DD's closed to attack from east and west. Two DD's patrolling to north of Dinagat and our cruisers a few thousand yards southwest were showing on the scopes. However, in the dark, and from CIC reports only it was difficult for the Captain to be certain just where our forces were.

0305: Changed course to 090° by turn movement.

0307: Destroyers report two large and one small enemy. Enemy is straddling them.

0310: Main battery plot reported Spot 2's Mark 8 radar had the target.
0311: Saw gunfire to south.
0313: Surface contacts, 2 large 2 small, were in strait heading north at speed 20 knots.
0314: DD reported 5 targets. 2 may be hit slowing down and dropping behind some.
0315: CIC reported two groups about 39,000 yards, one of 3 small pips, the other of a large and medium pip preceded by several smaller pips.
0322: DD report enemy 2 BB 2 cruisers and 1 DD.
0330: CIC reports 1 group 174° 36,00 other group a little closer by about 4,000 yards.
0331: Notified all stations of fighting light code.
0332: Received orders from Commander Battleline to commence firing at 26,000 yards.
0332: DD's report they have attacked.
0333: 4,000 yards to go. Gunnery officer reports range 30,000 and has solution with a large target.
0345: Saw explosion in target area. Talked with gunnery officer to be sure our target was not among our own DD's. Fire control stated he had been on target for some time. CIC stated our DD's were clear.
0349: Star shells in target area. Can't tell if our DD or enemy is firing them. Our range 24,000. Am hesitating to fire until certain target is enemy. Commander Battleship Division 4 directed open fire.
0351: Our cruisers on our right flank opened fire. Our gunnery officer says he has had same big target for a long time, and it is enemy. Commanding Officer ordered commence firing.
0352: Notified Commander Battleline we were opening fire.
0352: First salvo of 8 guns, range 22,800 yards, with AP projectiles.
0353: Could hear gunnery officer chuckle and announce hit first salvo. Watched the second salvo through glasses and saw explosions when it landed. [Note: target later identified as IJN *Yamashiro*.]
0354: Salvos very regular about 40 seconds interval. Other BB's opened after our second or third salvo.
0356: See explosions in target.
0358: Gunnery officer reports target is stopped, and pip is getting small.
0402: BB turn 15 on signal. Ordered cease fire. Have to think about small amount of ammunition on board. (110 AP left). CIC reports targets turned left and reversed course.
0405: CIC reports target speed 0.
0411: Pip reported to "bloom" and then fade.
0412: Target disappeared. Can see ships burning: one is a big fire.

Ammunition Expended

Total ammunition expended was ninety-three 14-inch/50 armor-piercing projectiles with corresponding service charges.

Effectiveness of Gunnery: Surface

Fire was opened with full radar control, with after radar, director 2, range keeper 2, and stable vertical 2 controlling. All spotting was by radar. Turrets were in fully automatic. Rapid salvo fire was used after the second salvo. Computed ballistic plus arbitrary of UP 100 and UP 100 cold gun correction was used. After the first salvo the cold gun correction was removed. Opening range was 22,400 yards. Average gun range was 20,880 yards.

Enemy Battle Damage

At the time of the splash of the sixth salvo, when a distinct flare up was seen, there were three officers and three enlisted men who saw the silhouette as a Japanese battleship by the characteristic construction of its foremast but could not definitely determine her class. Due to the fact that she was heavily pounded with 16-inch projectiles and that she disappeared from all radar screens at 4:12 a.m., it is certain she was sunk. Later reports verified the sinking of one or more battleships.

USS *Maryland* Radio Logs Recorder's Notes

Chronological Account of Action—October 25, 1944

0017: *PT-127* reported three destroyers and two large surface 10 miles off southeast tip of Bohol Island, heading north.

0030: Changed course to 080°(T).

0107: *PT-533* reported seeing flares or star shells 10 miles from south tip of Panaon Island, bearing 230°(T).

0123: The Midas reported contact bearing 140°(T), distance 18 miles from Taancan Point.

0153: Changed course to 280°(T).

0157: *PT-134* reported target proceeding up Strait abeam of southern tip of Panaon Island.

0202: *PT-134* reported previous target to be a large ship which had been attacked with indeterminate results.

0226: Commander Task Group 77.2 announced two heavy ships proceeding up channel.

0235: Set Condition of Readiness I for action, Material Condition ZULU.

0240: Changed course to 270°(T).

0241: USS *McGowan* in station 6, reported contact bearing 184°(T).

0244: USS *McGowan* reported three contacts on course 000°(T), speed 15 knots. Destroyer Squadron 54 proceeded down east and west shore to attack.

0248: Changed speed to 2/3, 10 knots, CIC picked up two contacts at 191°(T), 55,000 yards.

0301: Commander Destroyer Squadron 24 ordered to proceed to attack.

0304: Searchlight illumination and gun flashes observed from tops on port beam.

0307: Changed course to 090°(T).

0308: Commander Task Group 79.11 reported just one group composed of two large and one small headed north in column.

0312: Destroyer Division 108 reported having fired torpedoes and returning.

0313: Commander Task Group 79.11 reported five targets, two of which were slowing down and dropping behind and may have been hit.

0314: CIC reported previous targets now at 43,000 yards.

0316: USS *West Virginia* reported two contacts bearing 166°(T), distance 21 miles.

0320: Lookouts reported explosion on starboard beam.

0320: Commander Task Group 79.11 reported possibly two battleships in enemy force with a large fire burning on one of them.

0321: USS *McGowan* reported six targets of which three or four were small. Commander Task Group 79.11 reported composition of this force as two battleships, one or two cruisers and two destroyers, and that two definite hits had been made on this group.

0322: CIC reported previous targets apparently dead in water at 41,000 yards.

0326: Commander Task Unit 77.2.1 reported three contacts, one small and two large, with fire burning on one of them.

0329: Commander Task Unit 77.2.1 gave permission to Battleline to open fire at 26,000 yards.

0330: Changed speed to standard, 15 knots. Commander Task Group 77.2 ordered Commander Destroyer Squadron 56 to attack and to "get the big boys."

0337: Commander Task Group 77.2 reported estimated enemy course and speed as 010°(T), 12 knots.

0343: CIC picked up two, possibly three, contacts at 28,000 yards. Commander Task Group 77.2 reported that enemy appeared to be retiring and ordered the battle line to close. This transmission was cancelled at once at 0345.

0346: *PT-523* reported five destroyers and one large ship entering the Strait and heading north. Commander Task Group 77.3 reported his destroyers were hitting the target with 5-inch fire and that one target was dead in the water.

0349: Commander Battleship Division 3 reported a small group followed by a large group and that he would open fire at 26,000 yards. Gunfire reported on starboard bow.

0350: Cruisers ordered to open fire.
0352: Commander Task Group 77.3 reported that the little ones out in front were friendly trying to reach the shore line.
0353: USS *West Virginia* reported ready to open fire.
0354: Changed course to 120°(T).
0355: USS *West Virginia* opened fire.
0359: Commenced firing main battery on right hand, closer one of two heavy targets, range 20,800, bearing 210°(T).
0401: Target changed course to left. Top observers reported target to be large ship with heavy superstructure. Another similar ship observed to eastward of target.
0405: Checked fire. Changed course to 270°(T).
0406: USS *Minneapolis* reported being straddled.
0407: Commander Destroyer Squadron 56 reported to Commander Task Group 77.2 that friendly ships were firing on his boys in the center of the channel.
0409: Commander Task Group 77.2 ordered all ships to cease fire. Commander Battleship Division 3 ordered battleships to cease fire.
0411: Commander Task Group 77.2 ordered Commander Destroyer Squadron 56 to clear the channel of his ships as soon as possible.
0413: Commander Task Group 77.2 ordered all ships to unload hot guns toward enemy.
0415: Unloaded guns through the muzzle.
0419: Commander Task Group 77.3 ordered to open fire, since own ships had cleared the channel.
0420: Changed course to 000°(T); changed speed to 2/3, 15 knots. USS *Denver* reported large target at which she had been firing had disappeared bearing 204°(T), distance 11 miles.
0423: Lookouts reported two or three explosions over horizon in direction of cruiser fire.
0424: Left flank cruisers ordered to open fire. Commander Cruiser Division 12 reported four additional contacts bearing 184°(T), distance 17 miles. All reports indicated the enemy to be retreating to the south.
0500: Changed course to 090°(T). CIC reported cruiser divisions heading south down channel.
0500: Changed course to 270°(T).
0635: Set Condition I East. USS *Maryland* operated with Task Group 77.2.1, patrolling the entrance to Surigao Strait remainder of the day.

Ammunition Expended

Total ammunition expended was forty-eight 16-inch/45 armor-piercing projectiles with corresponding service charges.

Effectiveness of Gunnery: Surface

Two large targets were picked up on the Mk. 3 radar. They were separated by about 5 degrees in bearing and by approximately 3,000 yards in range. The target to the right was the closer of the two and was being fired on by the right-flank cruiser force. This target was taken under fire by this ship.

Enemy Battle Damage

The effect of this ship's fire is difficult to judge under the circumstances, especially since several other ships were firing at the target at the same time. However, numerous topside observers report having seen hits on two salvos and the consensus of opinion seems to place them on the second and fourth. Radar spotters are of the opinion that possible straddles were obtained on all salvos after the first.

USS *Mississippi* Radio Logs Recorder's Notes

Chronological Account of Action—October 25, 1944

0000: USS *Mississippi* was steaming as third sip in battle line on course 090°(T), speed 5 knots.

0019: Overheard report that PT boat had at 2310 made contact with two large enemy ships and three destroyers 10 miles southeast of Bohol Island and heading north.

0028: Column turned left to course 080°(T).

0151: Changed course to 280°(T).

0159: Overheard report that PT boat had sighted unidentified target proceeding up Surigao Strait opposite to the south tip of Panaon Island.

0226: Overheard report that two large ships standing up Surigao Strait had passed line of PT boats.

0229: Went to General Quarters.

0235: Changed course to 270°(T).

0243: Changed speed to 10 knots.

0302: Observed gun flashes and star shells bearing about 180(T).

0305: Changed course to 090°(T).

0306: Picked up Raid Able of radar screen, bearing 167°(T), range 43,000 yards. Raid was estimated to consist of two or three large ships on course 327°(T).

0309: Raid Able changed course to 032°(T), speed 25 knots.

0312: Observed search lights and star shells about 180°(T).

0313: Picked up Raid Baker on radar screen, bearing 175°(T), range 36,500 yards. Raid Baker on course 063°(T), speed 17 knots and estimated to consist of one or two small ships.

0317: Raid Able changed speed to 15 knots.

0320: Observed explosion over horizon, bearing about 170°(T). Raid Able changed course to 000°(T).
0327: Changed speed to 15 knots.
0322: Received orders to open fire at 26,000 yards.
0329: Raid Baker merged with Raid Able, bearing 167°(T), range 33,000 yards.
0340: Picked up Raid Charlie on radar screen, bearing 175°(T), range 31,500 yards. Estimated to consist of two or three large ships on course 031°(T), speed 20 knots.
0343: Observed explosions on horizon, bearing about 180°(T).
0345: Raid Charlie changed course to 350°(T).
0351: Observed fire apparently on enemy vessel.
0353: Changed course to 120°(T). Raid Charlie changed course to 185°(T), speed 23 knots.
0354: Picked up Raid Dog on radar screen, bearing 197°(T), range 31,000 yards. Raid Dog estimated to consist of one small vessel on course 307°(T), speed 28 knots.
0358: Raid Dog faded from screen. Up until approximately 0358, USS *Mississippi* had maintained fire control plot on second or third ship of Raid Able, assuming a normal fire distribution. Range was under 26,000 yards, but Raid Charlie was estimated to have two or three large ships and as a warning had been received to "Watch out for ships astern, they may be real target," shifted targets from Raid Able to Raid Charlie. At time of shifting, range was over 26,000 yards and training pips were too weak for s satisfactory fire control solution.
0359: Raid Able changed course to 260°(T), speed 10 knots.
0401: Changed course to 210°(T). Training pips by fire control radar on Raid Charlie were lost completely during the course of the turn.
0409: Having been unable to obtain satisfactory training pips by fire control radar on Raid Charlie, and since range was over 30,000 and increasing, shifted targets to Raid Able.
0411: Fired at second heavy ship of Raid Able, range was 19,790 yards, bearing 205°(T). Ceased firing immediately thereafter on orders from Commander Battleline.
0417: Changed course to 000°(T).
0418: Raid Charlie apparently lost steering control; commenced steering in circles bearing 190°(T), range 36,500 yards.
0420: Raid Able suddenly disappeared from radar screen, bearing 194°(T), range 21,700 yards. Strong echoes were obtained up until 0420; the raid was last seen near the middle of the Strait and clear of other ships.
0430: Changed course to 270°(T); changed speed to 10 knots.
0453: Raid Charlie faded from radar screen, bearing 068°(T), Range 41,000 yards: apparently still out of steering control.

0458: Changed course to 090°(T).
0459: Changed course to 270°(T).
0536: Observed flashes from what was presumed to be hits on enemy vessels beyond horizon.
0551: Observed anti-aircraft fire to the northward.
0633: Changed course to 000°(T); changed speed to 15 knots.
0655: Secured from General Quarters.

Ammunition Expended

Total ammunition expended was twelve 14-inch/50 armor-piercing projectiles with corresponding service charges.

Effectiveness of Gunnery: Surface

The mean radar spot for seven splashes observed on the single twelve-gun salvo fired was down 150 yards, while the observed range pattern was less than 300 yards. It is considered probable that one or more hits were obtained.

Enemy Battle Damage

The only direct evidence of enemy battle damage observed by this vessel is confined to the following:

(a) Raids Able and Charlie were both definitely slowed up in speed after being taken under attack.
(b) Raid Able suddenly disappeared from the radar screen after giving strong echoes up until 4:20 a.m.
(c) Raid Charlie apparently lost steering control.
(d) Fires and explosions observed at 3:20 a.m., 3:43 a.m., 3:51 a.m., and 5:36 a.m. were believed to be on enemy vessels.

USS *Tennessee* Radio Logs Recorder's Notes

Chronological Account of Action—October 25, 1944

0234: Set Condition of Readiness I and Material Condition Zebra. Sip is on course 270°(T), speed 5 knots.
0239: Changed speed to 10 knots.
0302: CIC reports large unidentified surface ship at approximately 170°(T), range 43,900 yards.
0306: Changed course to the right to 090°(T).
0310: Main Battery Director I commenced tracking a large enemy ship with the Mark 8 radar, bearing approximately 165°(T), range 39,000 yards.
0312: Observed gun fire on starboard beam.
0313: Solution of enemy ship: Course 000°(T), speed 16 knots.

0314: Director I picked up second heavy ship, bearing 168°(T), range 39,000 yards. Resumed tracking on leading heavy ship.
0328: Changed speed to 15 knots.
0338: Leading enemy ship changed course to 330°(T), speed 16 knots.
0345: Leading enemy ship changed course to 000°(T), speed 16 knots.
0353: Changed course to the right to 120°(T).
0354: Loaded forward Main Battery guns with AP projectiles and service ammunition.
0355: Commenced firing on leading heavy ship with a three-gun salvo from Turret I. Enemy ship's course 000°(T), speed 16 knots. Opening range was 20,500 yards.
0353:15: Fired a three-gun salvo from Turret II.
0355:35: Fired a six-gun salvo from forward turrets.
0356:15: Fired a five-gun salvo from the after turrets. Left gun on Turret III did not fire.
0357: Fired a four-gun salvo from after turrets. Turret III fired the left gun only.
0357:45: Fired a six-gun salvo from forward turrets.
0358:30: Fired a six-gun salvo from forward turrets.
0359:15: Fired a six-gun salvo from forward turrets.
0400: Fired a six-gun salvo from forward turrets.
0400:45: Fired a six-gun salvo from forward turrets.
0401:30: Fired a six-gun salvo from forward turrets.
0402: Changed course to the right to 270°(T).
0402:20: Fired a six-gun salvo from forward turrets. Checked fire because line of fire was too sharp on the bow.
0403: Held up "resume fire" because the line of sight was fouled by the USS *California*.
0407:50: Line of fire clear. USS *Tennessee* resumed fire with a six-gun salvo from forward turrets, approximate range 19,000 yards.
0408: Ceased fire on order from Officer in Tactical Command with all guns unloaded.
0410: Commander Battleship Division 2 took charge of Battleship Division 2 to reform division.
0426: Heavy ship upon which USS *Tennessee* had been firing disappeared from all radar screens. Last range was approximately 18,000 yards.
0430: Changed course to the right to 000°(T).
0438: Changed course to the left to 270°(T). Changed speed to 10 knots.
0440: Resumed position in battle line and steamed as directed by officer in Tactical Command.

Ammunition Expended

Total ammunition expended was sixty-nine 14-inch/50 armor-piercing projectiles with corresponding service charges.

Effectiveness of Gunnery: Surface

The Mk. 8 radar picked up the designated target from CIC at an initial range of 39,000 yards. A good solution for opening fire was obtained at a range of 37,500 yards. There were two large and three small targets visible on the FH radar screen at the time. The USS *Tennessee* opened fire on the closest heavy ship at a range of 20,500 yards. The performance of the Mk. 8 radar was superlative. Range spots were based primarily on radar. Deflection spots were made by the top spotter from both visual observation and from the radar screen. Direct spots to the target were used. The range pattern was about 400 yards.

Enemy Battle Damage

The target was either hit directly on straddled by twelve salvos. The target was tracked continuously after "cease firing" and was observed to grow smaller on the screen and to finally disappear at about 18,000 yards.

USS *Pennsylvania* Deck Log—October 25, 1044

0004: Steaming in company with Task Group 77.2 in battle disposition. Battle line deployed on course 090°(T), speed 15 knots. Order of ships in battle line: USS *West Virginia*, USS *Maryland*, USS *Mississippi*, USS *Tennessee*, USS *California* and USS *Pennsylvania*. Standard distance 1,000 yards. Prepared to deny entrance of enemy units into Leyte Gulf via Surigao Strait. Material Condition Modified Zebra and Condition of Readiness II-A.
0029: Ships left to 080°(T).
0152: Ships left to 280°(T).
0212: All engines ahead two-thirds.
0224: All engines ahead one-third.
0231: Sounded General Quarters. Enemy surface forces reported entering Surigao Strait.
0238: Ships left to 270°(T).
0242: Set Condition Zebra.
0329: All engines ahead standard.
0356: Officer in Tactical Command ordered ships right to 090°(T).
0329: All engines ahead standard.
0359: Ships right to 120°(T). Weather clear and calm. Sea light.
0402: Ships right to 270°(T).
0409: Ships right to 000°(T).

0436: Ships left to 270°(T).
0437: Battleship Division 2 detached from battle line; continued steaming on course 270°(T).
0457: Ships left to 090270°(T). Battleship Division 2 rejoined battle line.
0523: Set Material Condition Modified Zebra.
0526: Set Condition I-E.
0549: Set Condition I and Material Condition Zebra.
0558: Set Condition Modified Zebra; ships left to 270°(T).
0635: Ships right to 000°(T); all engines ahead standard.
0708: Flash Red. Set Condition Zebra.
0712: Ships right to 090°(T).
0715: Ships right to 180°(T).
0721: All engines ahead full.
0750: Ships right to 220°(T). Weather clear and warm. Sea light.
0800: Ships left to 180°(T).
0807: All engines ahead two-thirds.
0809: Ships right to 270°(T).
0812: Commenced firing secondary battery and anti–aircraft battery to port and starboard at various enemy aircraft.
0817: Ships right to 000°(T).
0818: Ceased firing, having shot down four "Vals."
0820: Ships right to 090°(T).
0845: Ships left to 270°(T).
0902: Set Condition Modified Zebra.
0904: Set Condition I-E.
0910: Ships left to 090°(T).
0919: Column left to 075°(T).
0936: All engines ahead one-third.
0943: All engines ahead standard.
0944: Ships left to 070°(T).
0952: All engines stopped.
0955: All engines ahead one-third.
0956: Ships left to 061°(T).
1001: Ships right to 090°(T). All engines stopped.
1026: All engines ahead one-third. Column left to 075°(T).
1035: All engines ahead two-thirds.
1047: Column right to 110°(T).
1055: Column right to 155°(T).
1105: Column right to 295°(T).
1118: Commenced firing anti-aircraft and secondary batteries at various enemy aircraft. Set Condition Zebra.
1119: Ceased firing.

1134: Set Condition Modified Zebra.
1136: Secured from General Quarters.
1140: Column left to 000°(T).
1152: Column left to 090°(T). Weather warm. Skies overcast. Sea Light.
1206: Increased speed to standard. Battleship Division 3 and 4 detached from battle line. USS *Tennessee*, USS *California* and USS *Pennsylvania* formed in column astern USS *Louisville*, USS *Portland*, USS *Minneapolis* and HMAS *Shropshire* on course 090°(T). Distance 800 yards.
1212: All engines ahead full.
1300: All engines ahead two-thirds.
1301: Ships left to 270°(T).
1307: Secured fires under boiler number 6.
1320: Lit fires under boiler number 6 and cut in on main steam line.
1330: Commenced steaming at ten knots.
1335: Column left to 180°(T).
1338: Unidentified aircraft bearing 085°(T), 32 miles distant, closing.
1343: Sounded Air Defense.
1344: Sounded General Quarters.
1347: Set Material Condition Zebra.
1428: Set Condition Readiness II-A.
1439: Ships left to 000°(T).
1540: Ships right to 090°(T).
1545: Ships right to 180°(T). Weather warm with scattered clouds. Light seas.
1604: Shifted to electric steering.
1619: Changed course left to 090°(T).
1624: Changed course left to 000°(T).
1705: Changed course right to 090°(T).
1719: Changed course to 000°(T).
1745: Changed course to 270°(T).
1754: Changed course right to 000°(T). Weather clear and warm. Smooth sea.
1820: Sounded General Quarters.
1825: Set Condition Zebra.
1841: Changed course to 225°(T). Assumed guide for formation of battle disposition.
1903: Changed speed to 15 knots.
1917: Set Condition Modified Zebra.
1922: Set Condition II-A. Clear and warm weather. Smooth sea.
2007: Column left to course 215°(T).
2013: Flash Red, Control Yellow from Commander Task Force 77.
2055: Ships right to course 035°(T).
2119: Commenced blowing tubes on all steaming boilers and completed at 2124.

2308: Unidentified aircraft bearing 105°(T), distance 15 miles.
2315: Flash Red, Control Yellow from Commander Task Force 77.
2316: Numerous unidentified aircraft reported.

While USS *Pennsylvania* was not able to obtain a firing solution on the enemy surface ships, she did expend the following ammunition firing at enemy aircraft: eighty-one rounds 5-inch/38, thirty-two rounds 5-inch/38 special, 656 rounds 40-mm, and six rounds 20-mm.

Commander of Battleship Division 2 Comments

Commander of Battleship 2 cannot accept USS *Pennsylvania's* statement, "This ship had no opportunity to be in a position to fire" and the reasons given therefore in USS *Pennsylvania's* Action Report.

On the easterly leg (120°T) when the battleline opened fire, USS *Pennsylvania* was the last ship in the column. The battleline remained on this course closing the range to the enemy, for seven minutes after USS *Mississippi* opened fire before reversing course to westward. After reversing course at 0402, USS *Pennsylvania* became leading ship on the battleline.

The Commander of Battleship Division 2 cannot see how failure of USS *California* to reverse course interfered with USS *Pennsylvania* fire in any way. The Commander of Battleship Division 2 is cognizant of the fact that USS *Pennsylvania* is not equipped with Mark 8 radar and was, therefore, handicapped in obtaining an accurate fire control solution.

The Commander of Battleship Division 2 is willing to accept non-participation in the engagement on this basis since ammunition was low and since an accurate fire control solution would probably have endangered our own DD's who were making torpedo attacks and withdrawing from the vicinity of the enemy force.

Commander of Battleship Division 3 Comments

The Commander of the battle line's flagship, USS *Mississippi*, is not equipped with the Mark 8 radar. Full reliance was placed on the SG which USS *Mississippi* CIC was able to present a clear picture of the movements of enemy and own forces throughout the engagement. However, the relative importance of two groups of pips appearing on a SG screen is not evident, nor is it always possible to tell by relative position.

USS *Mississippi's* lateness in opening fire and USS *Pennsylvania's* failure to open fire at all are attributed to both material and personnel. Both ships had difficulty identifying their targets and obtaining an acceptable solution. USS *Mississippi* was able to fire at the end, but USS *Pennsylvania* was not. The Commander of the Battleline believes that if these ships had Mark 8 Fire Control Radar, they would have opened fire with the rest of the Battleline. USS *Maryland* is to be commended for her speed in picking up her target from observation of USS *West Virginia's* fall of shot.

Commander of Battleship Division 4 Comments

The tremendous advantages enjoyed by a vessel equipped with the FH type radar over those equipped with FC were forcibly demonstrated as between USS *Maryland* and USS *West Virginia*. The latter ship had been tracking the target, at which she eventually fired, from a range of about 41,000 yards to 42,000 yards with perfectly definite target indications in range and bearing and there was no hesitation in opening fire. On the other hand the USS *Maryland* with FC radars could, at the time the USS *West Virginia* opened fire, find no identifiable target until the range closed to about 22,000 yards. It appears probable that the leading enemy ship which became the USS *Maryland's* heavy target changed course at about the time the USS *West Virginia* opened fire and therefore presented to the USS *Maryland's* fire control radars a broadside target as it was some minutes after the initial salvo of the USS *West Virginia* that the USS *Maryland* found a target and opened fire.

This same general situation appears to have existed throughout the battleline as intercepted reports indicated that whereas the USS *California* and USS *Tennessee*, both of which were equipped with the FH radars, had fired a large number of salvos, the USS *Mississippi* and USS *Pennsylvania*, which were equipped with FC radars, between them fired but one salvo.

Performance of the ships of the division within the limits of their equipment left little to be desired. The Division Commander is of the opinion that the USS *West Virginia* and the USS *Maryland* fired at separate large targets. The Commanding Officer of the USS *Maryland* has informed the Division Commander that after the West Virginia opened fire and her tracers were seen at the long range an attempt was made to find a target in that vicinity. When one was finally found it bore approximately five degrees to the right of the bearing of the USS *West Virginia's* target, The USS *Maryland* opened fire on this new target. The Division Commander is, therefore, of the opinion that the USS *West Virginia* and the USS *Maryland* each should be given credit for an assist in the destruction of one heavy enemy ship each.

10

Battle Analysis

In the summer of 1944, in order to keep up the rapid pace of operations in the Pacific, Admiral Nimitz developed a second command for the Central Pacific Force, parallel to that of Admiral Spruance. The two flags and their respective staffs would command the same ships, alternately directing an operation and planning their next, thereby allowing less time between offensives and increasing the pressure on the Japanese. Admiral William F. Halsey, commander of the Third Fleet, was selected to be Spruance's counterpart. When under Halsey's command, the ships of the Central Pacific would be the Third Fleet. When Spruance led them, they would once again become the Fifth Fleet. Halsey took Admiral Marc Mitscher and the fast carriers, now TF 38, on a series of raids in September 1944. They struck the Palaus, Mindanao, and the Visayas, covering the invasions of Morotai, the Palaus, and Ulithi. The lack of resistance encountered convinced Halsey that the existing timetable for landings in the Philippines could be accelerated. Within a matter of days, the JCS had approved the new schedule.

The invasion of Leyte, code-named King II, differed from previous large amphibious operations. The unity of command that had existed in previous operations was absent. The Central Pacific and southwestern Pacific offensives met in the southern Philippines, and King II used forces from both theaters. Command was divided between the two, hindering effectiveness and leading to confusion during the naval battles that resulted. Halsey's Third Fleet retained the fast carriers, but the Central Pacific Force's amphibious units, including the old battleships and escort carriers, were transferred to the Seventh Fleet, under command of Vice Admiral Thomas C. Kinkaid, who was subordinate to General MacArthur.

Kinkaid led the amphibious assault. The fast carriers were to suppress Japanese air bases and provide direct air support for the amphibious assault, but Halsey was freed of many of the burdens his predecessor had faced in the Philippine Sea. Without the old battleships and amphibious forces under his command, Halsey was able to develop plans that took full advantage of the mobility of his task forces. He was also free to seek out the Japanese. Admiral Nimitz's plan for the operation stressed that, "in case opportunity for destruction of major portion of enemy fleet offers or can be created, such destruction becomes the primary task." Third Fleet battle plans stressed the importance of this task.

They differed from those of the Fifth Fleet in two important respects. Lacking the old battleships, Halsey ignored them in his tactical planning and envisioned a battle line composed of only fast battleships. This increased his flexibility, because all forces in the battle fleet had sufficient speed to keep up with a carrier formation. Halsey planned to capitalize on this with a well-developed prewar technique. Halsey planned a coordinated attack. He assumed that his four carrier groups, far superior to what the Japanese could muster at this stage of the war, would either win the opening carrier duel or sight the enemy too late in the day for strike operations. In either case, the ensuing plan would be the same. Rather than steaming away at night as Spruance had done, Halsey would approach and, along the way, reorganize the carrier forces. Battleships, cruisers, and supporting destroyers would leave their respective task groups and form TF 34, a battle formation under the command of Admiral Lee, about 70 miles ahead of the carriers.

As morning approached, planes would get ready and launch. The coordinated movements of the fleet were designed to bring the attacking planes and the battleships within range of the enemy at the same time, at dawn. Particular effort was to be made to gain a position from which a predawn carrier strike may be launched concurrently with the release of fast heavy striking force from a favorable attack position. Development of a favorable tactical situation would be effected by dispatching TF 34 and carrier air groups to attack the enemy. The approach would be so conducted as to give TF 34 an opportunity to strike from a favorable position and so coordinate its offensive efforts with those of carrier air groups.

Halsey considered this the optimum plan for decisive action. It would collect nearly all the striking power of TF 38 into one decisive pulse and overwhelm the Japanese. Halsey had revived the prewar coordinated attack. The main landings took place on October 20, with two of Halsey's carrier groups providing direct support. TGs 38.1 and 38.4, with cruisers in support, attacked targets on Leyte and suppressed airfields on Mindanao and the western Visayas. The two other carrier groups, TGs 38.2 and 38.3, remained concentrated farther north, scouting for potential threats from the direction of Japan and Formosa. Halsey kept all the battleships together. TG 38.2 had Battleship Division 7 (USS *Iowa* and USS *New Jersey*), and four battleships were with TG 38.3.

The possibility that the Japanese would commit significant naval forces to defend the Philippines was not seriously considered in Third or Seventh Fleet plans. This was a mistake. In the summer of 1944, the Japanese had created a series of plans, code-named Shō-Go. The southernmost of these, Shō-Go 1, covered the defense of the Philippines. On the basis of preliminary landings around Leyte, the imperial GHQ made the decision to implement Shō-Go 1 on October 18. Two days later, Vice Admiral Ryunosuke Kuasaka, chief of staff to Combined Fleet Commander Admiral Soemu Toyoda, issued the final plans to units of the Combined Fleet.

The Japanese moved toward Leyte in four elements. Vice Admiral Takeo Kurita's First Diversionary Attack Force divided in two, one part comprising his First and Second Sections; led by Kurita himself, it would transit the San Bernardino Strait. Kurita's Third Section, commanded by Vice Admiral Shoji Nishimura, was ordered to pass through Surigao Strait. Kurita planned to reunite with Nishimura in Leyte Gulf early on the morning of October 25 and destroy the invasion forces. The third Japanese element, the Second Diversionary Attack Force, under Vice Admiral Kiyohide Shima, would come through Surigao Strait behind Nishimura and also attack the invasion fleet. Between them, these three attack forces had seven battleships, sixteen cruisers, and twenty-three destroyers. The fourth and last Japanese group, commanded by Vice Admiral Jisaburo Ozawa, was a decoy. Ozawa took the Combined Fleet's remaining carriers south from Japan, hoping with them to draw the Third Fleet's covering forces back north, away from Leyte Gulf. Ozawa had four carriers, two battleship carriers, three cruisers, and nine destroyers. Halsey, still confident that the Japanese would not seek battle, was preoccupied with preparations for the Third Fleet's major follow-on operation, an attack against the Japanese home islands.

On October 22, he sent TGs 38.4 and 38.1 to the fleet base at Ulithi to refuel and rearm. Before detaching them, he took two battleships from TG 38.3 and transferred them to TG 38.4, to go with it to Ulithi. Two task groups and just four fast battleships remained in the area. The same day, Kurita's First and Second Sections left their anchorage at Brunei Bay on the north coast of Borneo. U.S. submarines again provided early warning of Japanese moves. The morning of October 23, while transiting Palawan Passage, the submarines USS *Dace* and USS *Darter* sighted and attacked Kurita's ships, hitting three heavy cruisers. IJN *Atago* and IJN *Maya* were sunk, IJN *Takao* was damaged and forced to retire. Admirals Halsey and Kinkaid received these sightings and additional information from long-range air searches. They became convinced that the Japanese were moving toward the Philippines in force. Halsey quickly realized his dispositions were inadequate and recalled TG 38.4 and its two battleships. He did not recall TG 38.1. That group had more planes available than TG 38.4, but Halsey considered the two battleships more important.

Halsey disposed his forces to allow effective aerial searches to the west and provide warning of the Japanese approach. TG 38.3 was farthest to the north, east of Polillo Island. He placed TG 38.2 in the center, off the San Bernardino Strait, and TG 38.4 in the south, east of Samar. This arrangement dispersed Halsey's battleship strength, each task group had just two battleships, but allowed him to cover the major passages through the archipelago. On October 24, Admirals Kurita and Nishimura were sighted by Halsey's carriers. TG 38.4 subjected Nishimura to a single attack, slightly damaging two of his ships. Since Admiral Kurita posed the greater threat, Halsey left Admiral Nishimura to Kinkaid and moved quickly to consolidate his battleship strength. TG 38.4 was ordered north. All three carrier groups would concentrate off the San Bernardino Strait, launching strikes against Kurita's formation along the way. Over the course of several hours repeated air attacks sank the battleship IJN *Musashi* and damaged several other ships. In the early afternoon Kurita turned back, seeking relief from the onslaught.

In the meantime, Halsey had issued a preparatory battle order in expectation of Admiral Kurita's force exiting the strait. TGs 38.2 and 38.4 were close enough to concentrate. The plan combined Battleship Division 7 with the two battleships from TG 38.4. Four battleships, five cruisers, and ten destroyers would form as a surface striking unit. Admiral Lee would command the resulting formation, designated TF 34. Because TG 38.3 was too distant, its battleships were not included. Halsey planned to make do with the forces immediately on hand. He did not implement the plan. A variety of circumstances convinced him otherwise. Scouting reports indicated that Kurita was heavily damaged and withdrawing. Also, intelligence available to Halsey suggested that Japanese forces in the area of the home islands were stronger than in fact they were, and this led him to the conclusion that the most serious threat would come from the north.

In the afternoon, planes from TG 38.3 found that threat. They sighted Ozawa's main body. Halsey considered his alternatives. The option of leaving TF 34 to block San Bernardino Straits was rejected. The potential strength of the Northern Forces, under Admiral Ozawa, was too great to leave unmolested and requiring TF 34 to engage the Center Force, under Admiral Kurita, while at the same time exposed to attack by land-based and carrier-based air attack was not sound. This alternative spread U.S. strength and risked unprofitable damage in detail.

During the evening of October 24, Admiral Halsey made the decision to move north with all his forces and pursue Ozawa. Along the way, he put his battle plan in motion. The fleet slowed as all six battleships, seven cruisers, and eighteen destroyers separated themselves from the carrier groups and formed TF 34, under Lee. TG 38.2 was designated as the battle-line carrier group, to support Lee's surface forces. Admiral Mitscher expected the surface contact to take place at 4:30 a.m. but estimates of the Japanese position were incorrect. The first air strike from the carriers hit Ozawa long before TF 34 could come into action. Coordinated attacks would have to wait until the battleships were in position. Halsey ran out of time.

As TF 34 approached the Japanese, urgent messages were received from Admiral Kinkaid. Escort carriers on his northern flank were engaged in a running battle with Kurita's First and Second Sections. The remnants of the First Striking Force had reversed course, passed through the San Bernardino Strait and were now moving toward the landing beaches. Halsey sent TF 34, minus four cruisers and nine destroyers, south to assist. TG 38.2 followed in support. The cruisers and destroyers detached from TF 34 filled in and formed a surface striking force. They continued north and attacked Japanese ships damaged by the carrier strikes, finishing off the carrier IJN *Chiyoda* and sinking the destroyer IJN *Hatsuzuki* after a running gun battle. Ozawa's other carriers, IJN *Zuikaku*, IJN *Zuiho*, and IJN *Chitose*, were sunk by planes from TF 38. The submarine USS *Jallao* sank the light cruiser IJN *Tama*, previously damaged by air attack. Demoralized and broken, Ozawa's force retreated. In the meantime, Admiral Nishimura's Third Section had steamed into a trap set by Kinkaid's Seventh Fleet in Surigao Strait and been virtually annihilated.

Although Kinkaid had not anticipated that the Japanese would seek major action, his forces had been well prepared for it. The Seventh Fleet's battle plan called for Rear Admiral Jesse B. Oldendorf's Fire Support Group, designated TG 77.2, and Rear Admiral Russell S. Berkey's Close Covering Group, TG 77.3, to combine in the face of strong enemy opposition. Oldendorf had all six of the old battleships supporting Leyte, along with escorting cruisers and destroyers. He and his ships had been part of the Fifth Fleet's offensives in the Central Pacific. Berkey's group was part of the multinational Seventh Fleet. Depending on the nature of the threat, Kinkaid planned to detach Berkey, Oldendorf, or both. Kinkaid also envisioned combining Berkey's group with units from the Third Fleet if Japanese light forces threatened the invasion fleet. Details were left up to the individual commanders.

By noon on October 24, Kinkaid had realized that the Japanese were seeking major action and ordered Oldendorf to prepare for a night battle in Surigao Strait and to take Berkey's TG 77.3 in support. Oldendorf began to formulate a plan. He called Berkey and his battle-line commander, Rear Admiral George L. Weyler, to his flagship so he could familiarize them with the details. The battleships were loaded mainly with bombardment ammunition. Oldendorf stressed the need to fire at medium ranges, where the effect would be maximized. He also discussed the use of destroyer attacks before the main action; he planned to send them down both sides of the strait. After the conference, Oldendorf signaled his battle plan to the six battleships, eight cruisers, and twenty-one destroyers of his force. The battle plan placed the battle line in the center and light forces at either flank. This was an efficient arrangement for the confined waters at the head of the strait, and it maximized the effectiveness of Oldendorf's gunfire. The plan worked to perfection, including one small, extemporized addition. Picket destroyers from TG 79.11 commanded by Captain Jesse G. Coward were the first to attack. Coward had joined Oldendorf on his own initiative, displaying the aggressiveness inherent in the navy's doctrine. Nishimura's attempt to penetrate into Leyte Gulf failed, disorganized by a series of destroyer torpedo attacks and shattered by battleship and cruiser gunfire. One destroyer and a badly damaged cruiser were all that survived to retreat down the strait. Following in Nishimura's wake, Shima's Second Diversionary Attack Force fired ineffective torpedoes at radar ghosts to the north and quickly withdrew.

Soon thereafter, Kurita's force reappeared off Samar, within visual range of Kinkaid's escort carriers. A desperate fight ensued. Both Halsey and Kinkaid mustered powerful forces to counter the threat. Kinkaid ordered Oldendorf to send a battleship division, a heavy cruiser division, and supporting destroyers to assist the carriers. Oldendorf chose to send the three battleships that had the most armor-piercing ammunition remaining, all four of his heavy cruisers, and twenty destroyers, all of which had at least five torpedoes. Halsey sent TF 34 and TG 38.2 south to support Kinkaid, but they would not find Kurita. Shortly after noon on October 25, he had turned to the north and headed back toward the San Bernardino Strait. When this became apparent, Halsey ordered TG 34.5, a pursuit force formed around Battleship Division 7, to separate from TF 34 and go after the retreating enemy.

The pursuit force contained two battleships, three cruisers, and eight destroyers under the command of Rear Admiral Oscar C. Badger. Halsey's intention was for Badger to concentrate all light forces in the front. TF 34.5 would engage on parallel courses at long range, with light forces on the offensive. Badger arrived too late to engage Kurita but, in the darkness, found destroyer IJN *Nowaki*, which had remained behind to pick up survivors, and sank it. The battle of Leyte Gulf was over. Japanese efforts to contest the landings in the Philippines and Marianas had led to the decisive battle both navies had anticipated before the war. Although the expected clash of battle lines did not occur, the outcome was decisive. The remaining Japanese surface forces lacked the fuel and strength necessary to challenge further offensives and the Japanese Combined Fleet had become a hollow shell.

The operational plan to defend the Philippines against the impending U.S. invasion there occurred in a strategic environment much different from previous plans. First, Operation Shō-Go was conceived at a time when the strength of Japanese forces were at their all-time low. Second, planning for Operation Shō-Go was quite compressed. The Japanese had just suffered a major defeat during the Battle of the Philippine Sea. They had counted on a great victory there, and no plans for future operations were prepared. Lastly, when formulating plans for the Battle of the Coral Sea and the Battle of Midway, the Japanese had to plan to encounter only two to four American carriers. Here they would confront over thirty-two U.S. carriers of all types. The overall operational objective was to prevent U.S. forces from landing on the Philippines in support of the larger strategic goal of defending the Japanese homeland. An additional operational goal was to seek out the U.S. fleet and, once again, meet them in a decisive battle.

Japanese planners were quite encumbered in their planning. They did not believe the Imperial Fleet would be ready for another major engagement until the spring of 1945. However, it was thought that the U.S. Pacific Fleet would be bearing down on the Philippines by the late fall of 1944. The broad operational scheme of the original plan called for the First Striking Force, under Vice Admiral Kurita, to intercept the landing force and annihilate them. Vice Admiral Ozawa's carrier division would come from the northeast to draw the U.S. carrier force away from Leyte and its protection of the U.S. landing force. Kurita was to reach Leyte through San Bernardino Strait via the Sibuyan Sea. A southern force under Rear Admiral Nishimura, with a follow-on force under Rear Admiral Shima would transit the Surigao Strait south of Leyte Gulf. Land-based air would be provided by Vice Admiral Onishi's Fifth Base Air Force in the Philippines and by Vice Admiral Fukudome's Sixth Base Air Force out of Formosa.

A split in doctrine would negatively impact the operational plan. First, was this an offensive or defensive operation? Admiral Toyoda, chief of staff of the naval general staff, had directed that the fleet intercept and destroy the enemy transports before they disassemble. And if this was impossible, to engage and destroy the enemy in their anchorage. In addition, the First and Second Air Fleets were to conduct surprise attacks on the carriers and transports. But Kurita's staff was disturbed by this and asked Combined Fleet HQ for clarification of the intent. They queried that according to the order, the primary targets of the First Striking Force were enemy transport, but if by chance carriers come within range of their force, can they, in cooperation with shore-based aircraft, engage the carrier and then return to annihilate the transport? To this question, Combined Fleet said yes.

Thus, even among the senior staffs, the operational plan did not have a definite direction. Moreover, the plan that resulted required three separate surface forces to transit through two risky and potentially well-defended straits in support of an ill-defined operational objective. In addition, even this late in the war, battleships were still seen as being able to effectively win the decisive naval engagement. However, even though the Japanese had come to appreciate the carrier's role in naval warfare, they nonetheless held steadfast to the belief that their battleships and heavy cruisers could still win a decisive victory. At this point in the war, holding on to his belief may have been born of desperation, as they simply could not match America's carrier force in late 1944.

The operational level tactics envisioned for the plan also created potential difficulties. This essay has analyzed just two of the many Japanese operational plans that relied heavily on operational surprise. However, at Leyte, operational surprise could not be employed by the Japanese. While they were still looking for the decisive battle, for them, Leyte was inherently a defensive operation. They could only strike once they ascertained where and when U.S. forces would land on the Philippines. Even Vice Admiral Ozawa's carrier force, which had some offensive potential was there not to attack, but to be attacked.

Surprise was an integral part of the Japanese operational plans—those plans failed. This suggests that operational surprise was not all that effective. However, where operational surprise may have been an important aspect of the Japanese plans is in building morale and giving the troops a psychological edge. The absence of this element from Operation Shō-Go contributed to the diminished psychological momentum the Japanese experienced at Leyte.

In the plan for Leyte, the Japanese also lost their potential advantage in outranging. Land-based aircraft, if used effectively, could have provided the critical outranging needed to counter the U.S. carrier fleet. However, significant support from shore-based air power was lost because of the limited numbers of planes, poor training, and most significantly, difficulty in coordinating air support between the unit ashore and forces afloat. With this loss, any hope of outranging the U.S. fleet through use of air power vanished.

The Japanese tried desperately to enhance the outranging capability of their surface ships.

While at Hiroshima Bay, both Ozawa's and Kurita's fleets were retrofitted with the first Japanese radar sets. But with only limited training and experience in this new technology, this action proved to be too little, too late. Thus, in the air and on the surface, Japanese forces entered Operation Shō-Go clearly outranged by the U.S. Fleet.

Lastly, the final plan called for four separate forces of varying size, and with specialized strengths and weaknesses, to converge on the enemy fleet. To mass operational fires, flawless synchronization and coordination were vital. But problems with converging these forces were compounded by the local terrain which required they transit through two very narrow and potentially well-defended straits. Complicating this further was the fact that the plan contained no contingencies for delays or diversions. Thus, when Admiral Kuita's fleet was stalled on the morning of October 24 as a result of attack, Admiral Nishimra's force was slowed to 13 knots so as to arrive at Leyte in synch with Kurita. This invited attack from patrol boats and submarines and eventually spelled doom for Nishimura's force.

Several elements related to training also impacted the Japanese plan. While at Lingga Anchorage, an area just across the strait from Singapore, the Imperial Fleet trained furiously. Tomiji Koyanagi, Kurita's chief of staff at the time, believed that overall, training during this period was quite satisfactory. Relentlessly, the officers and sailors trained for, what many believed, would be the last stand of the Imperial Navy. Night surface action was stressed. Their best chance of defeating U.S. forces was to engage them in a night surface battle using the 18.1-inch guns on IJN *Yamato* and IJN *Musashi.*

Another key phase of the Japanese plan, one for which they had practiced and thought about at Lingga, was breaking into the U.S. anchorage during the invasion. Optimally, this should be done while the U.S. fleet was landing personnel and equipment ashore, which they would no doubt do during daylight hours. But if the Japanese attacked during the day, their battleships and cruisers were quite vulnerable to attack from U.S. carrier planes. Conversely, the difficulties of penetrating the anchorage with large ships, at night were tremendous. Thus, the Japanese plan contained one operational task which was almost impossible to effectively accomplish with the operational tactics proposed. This was a serious conceptual flaw in the Japanese plan.

Evidence of the tremendous difficulty in intercepting and attacking during the day can be seen in the action of Kurita's force when they encountered several U.S. carriers in the early morning of October 25. In a dash to close the gap between his forces and the American carriers on the horizon, Kurita's force sped forward without any coordination and were spread out over an area in excess of 15 miles. This, in part, can be attributed to a breakdown in tactical procedures as a result of insufficient training.

Effective land-based air power was essential if the Japanese plan for Leyte had any chance of succeeding. Japan's only offensive resources were her land-based air fleets, whose pilots were pitifully inexperienced. These pilots had virtually no combat experience, and perhaps even more significantly, possessed only minimal flight time. Out of this serious shortfall in training and with the absolute sense of desperation the Japanese felt, the *kamikaze* corps were born. Almost daily, men were killed in practice landing and take-offs from carrier decks. Observing these accidents, the pilots themselves began to feel that if they were going to die on carrier decks, it would be much better to die crashing into the decks of enemy carriers.

Thus, Leyte Gulf was the first time American forces encountered the *kamikaze* pilot. Of the ninety-three fighters and fifty-seven bombers the Japanese used on October 25 in conventional attacks against the U.S. Fleet, none inflicted any damage. However, of the ten special attack planes launched on October 25 five scored direct hits on U.S. ships, causing notable damage as the disbelieving Americans stood by dazed and bewildered. It is safe to say that the *kamikaze* corps represent the most serious and grave response to poor training and inferior numbers in all of military history.

Many historians believe that the critical failure in Japanese leadership was the single most important element leading to their defeat at Leyte Gulf. From the very start of the planning for Leyte, the leadership failed to recognize that the probability of preventing a U.S. landing on the Philippines was near zero. And regardless of how noble and gallant it is to stand up to an overwhelming foe, it is pure folly to do so when there is absolutely no realistic hope of winning. Many of the senior Japanese leaders felt that this would be their final sortie. Vice Admiral Nishimura had severe personal reservations over the chances of the plan working, he was nonetheless committed to the operation. Nishimura had lost his only son, Teiji, at the Philippines, and though the plan for Leyte was near hopeless, he may have welcomed the opportunity to have an assignment which would permit him to die nobly and join his son.

One of the most solemn responsibilities a commander has to his troops is to determine when his forces have had enough and cannot reasonably expect to prevail, and then, to take action to ensure their safety and security. But deceive leadership suffered in another way too. Admiral Toyoda, commander-in-chief, Combined Fleet, was not present at the battle. Many officers felt that he should come from Japan to lead the fleet at this most crucial time. Complicating this was Combined Fleet Staff's indecision during the planning phase of operations, as well as their tendency to try to control the battle from the beach. This was not only fruitless but added confusion to the action and infuriated those fighting the battle at sea.

From its inception, Operation Shō-Go suffered from compressed, unrealistic, and insufficient planning. This coupled with significant shortfalls in training and less-than-optimum leadership, led to the eventual demise of the Imperial Fleet at Leyte—the last real battle they would fight. Asked if the plan for Operation Shō-Go was the best that could have been formulated given the forces available, Vice Admiral Ozawa replied, "I think that was the best plan which we could apply but not the best theoretical plan, but I think it was the best plan under the conditions."

All great nations recognize principles of war and incorporate them in their doctrine. The lists vary from nation to nation. In the western world, the accepted principles are essentially a post-Napoleonic conception, advanced by Clausewitz, the great Prussian philosopher of war in the early nineteenth century, and his contemporary, Jomini, the well-known French general and theorist. These principles are common to ground, as well as, naval operations. The U.S. Army recognizes nine principles and includes them in its *U.S. Army Field Manual (FM) 100-5*. Their proper application, the army holds, is essential to the exercise of effective command and to the successful conduct of military operations. These nine principles are true for naval operations as well and provide an effective model to analyze the Battle of Surigao Strait.

The first of the nine principles is "Objective." *FM 100-5* definition states that every military operation must be directed toward a clearly defined, decisive, and attainable objective. The ultimate military objective of war is the destruction of the enemy's armed forces and his will to fight. The objective of each operation must contribute to this ultimate objective. Each intermediate objective must be such that its attainment will most directly, quickly, and economically contribute to the purpose of the operation. The selection of an objective is based upon consideration of the means available, the enemy, and the area of operations.

Every commander must understand and clearly define his objective and consider each contemplated action in light thereof. Once planes from Admiral Halsey's carriers spotted Admiral Nishimura's fleet making for the Surigao Strait and Admiral Kurita's large fleet coming through the San Bernardino Strait, it was obvious to Admiral Kinkaid that the Japanese planned to converge in Leyte Gulf to attack MacArthur's invasion ships. He immediately sent world to Admiral Oldendorf to take his fleet to the north side of the Surigao Strait and prepare for a night battle. The objective was to engage and destroy the enemy force.

The second principle of war to examine in the context of the Battle of Surigao is "Offensive." Offensive action is defined in *FM 100-5* as action that is necessary to achieve decisive results and to maintain freedom of action. It permits the commander to exercise initiative and impose his will upon the enemy; to set the pace and determine the course of battle; to exploit enemy weaknesses and rapidly changing situations; and to meet unexpected developments. The defensive may be forced on the commander, but it should be deliberately adopted only as a temporary expedient while awaiting an opportunity for offensive action or for the purpose of economizing forces on a front where a decision is not sought. Even on the defensive the commander seeks every opportunity to seize the initiative and achieve decisive results by offensive action.

Admiral Oldendorf formulated an offensive plan that utilized his destroyer's potent hitting power. His PT boats would attack first then withdraw under the cover of darkness, to lurk nearby to report the Japanese positions to. The destroyers would then attack the Japanese fleet in three squadrons, ranging down both the eastern and western sides of the narrow strait to launch torpedoes at the enemy from the flanks. Each destroyer carried ten torpedoes and Oldendorf and his commanders hoped they would be devastating. The results of the destroyer attacks were devastating to the Japanese. Two of their ships were hit by the first salvo of torpedoes. The attacks continued until the battleship IJN *Fusō* blew up and split in two. Nishimura's flagship, the battleship IJN *Yamashiro* took hits, and two of his destroyers were sunk. Clearly, the audacious plan devised by Admiral Oldendorf met the definition of Offensive.

"Mass" is the third principle to be examined. Superior combat power must be concentrated at the critical time and place for a decisive purpose. Superiority results from the proper combination of the elements of combat power. Proper application of the principle of mass, in conjunction with the other principles of war, may permit numerically inferior forces to achieve decisive combat superiority. Oldendorf's plan for massing fire power involved his six battleships, under the tactical control of Rear Admiral Weyler, cruising single file across a 15-nautical-mile stretch of water at the northern outlet of the strait.

Steaming parallel to them, 5 miles to their south, would be eight cruisers under Rear Admiral Berkey, three to Weyler's right and three to his left. Straddling the exit of the strait, the battle line would be poised to finish off any of Nishimura's ships that survived the destroyer attacks. Salvages from the wreckage of Pearl Harbor most of the battleships were equipped with modern fire-control systems. They would, as the Naval War College textbooks dictated, cross the "T" of the enemy fleet, thereby bringing more guns to bear. With overwhelming force, Oldendorf's classic maneuver clearly satisfied the principle of "Mass."

The fourth of the nine principles is "Economy of Force." *FM 100-5* defines it as, "Skillful and prudent use of combat power will enable the commander to accomplish the mission with minimum expenditure of resources. This principle is the corollary of the principle of mass. It does not imply husbanding but rather the measured allocation of available combat power to the primary task as well as secondary tasks such as limited attacks, the defense, deception, or even retrograde action in order to insure sufficient combat power at the point of decision." When Oldendorf's destroyers executed their battle plan firing salvos of torpedoes at ranges of about 4 miles, and then turning and speeding away before the Japanese guns could find them, they minimized the risk to themselves. The destroyers escaped the enemy fire by zigzagging and throwing up smoke screens. Executing this principle permitted them to be able to continue attacking the Japanese formation while protecting and economizing their force.

"Maneuver" is defined as an essential ingredient of combat power. It contributes materially in exploiting successes and in preserving freedom of action and reducing vulnerability. The object of maneuver is to dispose a force in such a manner as to place the enemy at a relative disadvantage and thus achieve results which would otherwise be more costly in men and materiel. Successful maneuver requires flexibility in organization, administrative support, and command and control. It is the antithesis of permanence of location and implies avoidance of stereotyped patterns of operation. The very essence of Oldendorf's plan was "Maneuver." From the PT boat attacks to attacks by his destroyers and finally the damaging fire brought by his battleships and cruisers, the plan clearly exploited successes, preserving freedom of action, reduced vulnerability, and denied the enemy freedom of action.

"Unity of Command" is the decisive application of full combat power requires unity of command. Unity of command obtains unity of effort by the coordinated action of all forces toward a common goal. While coordination may be attained by cooperation, it is best achieved by vesting a single commander with the requisite authority. Admiral Oldendorf's conference with his principle commanders aboard his flagship insured that all of his commanders understood their parts. While each was in tactical control of his own force, each knew the intent of the overall plan.

The seventh principle of war is "Security." According to *FM 100-5*, security is essential to the preservation of combat power. Security is achieved by measures taken to prevent surprise, reserve freedom of action, and deny the enemy information of friendly forces. Since risk is inherent in war, application of the principle of security does not imply undue caution and the avoidance of calculated risk. Security frequently is enhanced by bold seizure and retention of the initiative, which denies the enemy the opportunity to interfere. Based on the sightings by aircraft from the Third Fleet carriers *Enterprise* and *Franklin* of Rear Admiral Davison's task group Oldendorf knew the position Nishimura's Force and Shima's Second Striking Force. After Halsey ordered the carriers north, Oldendorf stationed his PT boats along the south entrance to the strait. While they attacked the Japanese force, more importantly, they were able to provide an early warning net, reporting the Japanese position as they steamed north up the strait.

"Surprise" is the eight principle of war and *FM 100-5* states that surprise can decisively shift the balance of combat power. By surprise, success out of proportion to the effort expended may be obtained. Surprise results from striking an enemy at a time, place, and in a manner for which he is not prepared. It is not essential that the enemy be taken unaware but only that he becomes aware too late to react effectively. Factors contributing to surprise include speed, deception, application of unexpected combat power, effective intelligence and counterintelligences, to include communication and electronic security, and variations in tactics and methods of operation. The PT boats were the first to surprise the Japanese fleet. They were able to fire their torpedoes and escape into the darkness before the Japanese could do much damage. The destroyers attacked and withdrew behind smoke screens. They could emerge from the smoke and attack again without being detected. Finally, the array of Oldendorf's battleships and cruisers was the last surprise for Admiral Nishimura's fleet.

The ninth and final principle of war is "Simplicity." It is described as contributing to successful operations. Direct, simple plans and clear, concise orders minimize misunderstanding and confusion. If other factors are equal, the simplest plan is preferred. Admiral Oldendorf's plan for defeating the Japanese in the Surigao Strait was not complicated. It did not require the near-impossible precision of the Japanese plan. The plan was simply to attack Admiral Nishimura's fleet until they were destroyed and in doing so it marked the last time the "T" was crossed in an engagement between battleships, and in fact was also the last occasion ever on which one battleship fired its main armament at another.

Admiral Oldendorf ability to take full advantage of both the geography of the battle area and his foreknowledge of the enemy's route of advance enabled PT squadrons to be deployed at the entrance to Surigao Strait at a place where the Japanese would have to reform in column to negotiate the narrow passage. Behind the torpedo boats, covering the northern part of the strait, were posted the destroyer squadrons, cruisers, and battleships to form the horizontal bar to a "T" of vast fire power, which the enemy would be forced to approach vertically as he moved forward. With overwhelming force, Oldendorf created an impenetrable gauntlet that defeated the Japanese at Surigao Strait and played a significant in winning the Battle of Leyte Gulf and in so helping to secure the beachheads of the U.S. Sixth Army on Leyte against Japanese attack from the sea.

Performance of U.S. Battleships at Surigao Strait

At Surigao Strait, three battleships did the majority of the shooting—USS *West Virginia*, USS *California*, and USS *Tennessee*. All three ships had received total reconstructions during the war and installation of Mk. 8 fire control radar. A fourth battleship, USS *Maryland*, contributed meaningfully. It was refitted before the war and fitted with Mk. 3 fire control radar during the war. Also present were USS *Mississippi* and USS *Pennsylvania*. USS *Mississippi* received a total reconstruction before the war and was fitted with Mk. 3 fire control radar during the war. USS *Pennsylvania* received an extensive refit during the war and was fitted with Mk. 3 fire control radar. USS *Mississippi* managed only one salvo during the engagement. USS *Pennsylvania* failed to fire.

That the Mk. 8 fire control radar was superior to the Mk. 3 is neither a mystery, in contention, nor a surprise. That USS *Maryland* was able to get on target and fire six salvos while her Mk. 3 fitted compatriots did not is more interesting. Why was the *Maryland* able to do this? A simple explanation is crew proficiency. It is entirely possible the *Maryland* simply had a more experienced and/or talented radar and gunnery team than the other two Mk. 3 battleships. But there is probably more to it than that. A clue lies in the explanation commonly given for USS *Maryland*'s achievement—she ranged off USS *West Virginia*'s shell splashes. Another clue lies in the geometry of the engagement.

The battle line started the action at 3:48 a.m., steaming course 090 at 15 knots in the following order at 1,000-yard intervals: USS *West Virginia*, USS *Maryland*, USS *Mississippi*, USS *Tennessee*, USS *California*, and USS *Pennsylvania*. Length of the line was 5,000 yards. At 3:55 a.m., all six ships simultaneously turned right to course 120°(T), proceeding in parallel to the southeast. At 4:02 a.m., all six ships again simultaneously turned right, this time to course 270°(T). By 4:06 a.m., they completed this turn and were proceeding in reverse of their original heading and in reverse order: USS *Pennsylvania*, USS *California*, USS *Tennessee*, USS *Mississippi*, USS *Maryland*, and USS *West Virginia*.

Roughly 6,500 yards south of the battle line was the eastern cruiser line steaming course 092°(T) at 10 knots in the following order at 500-yard intervals: USS *Louisville*, USS *Portland*, USS *Minneapolis*, USS *Denver*, and USS *Columbia*. Length of the line was 2,000 yards. From 3:48 a.m. to 4:09 a.m., the eastern cruiser line maintained its course and speed, executing a simultaneous turn to port (north) at 4:09 a.m. Thus, at the start of the action, the rears of both lines were almost abeam each other, meaning the cruisers masked USS *Tennessee*, USS *California*, and USS *Pennsylvania*, but not USS *West Virginia*, USS *Maryland*, and USS *Mississippi*. As the two lines moved to the east on roughly parallel courses, the battle line began to pull ahead of the cruiser line until 3:55 a.m. when the battle line turned to 120°(T). The difference in speed roughly maintained the relative positions of the last three battleships, the five cruisers and the target battleship, IJN *Yamashiro*. Thus, USS *Pennsylvania* was masked throughout this period, but neither USS *Mississippi* nor USS *Maryland* was masked. However, none of these ships fired during this period.

At 3:55 a.m., the turn to 120°(T) caused the battle line to stop running away from the cruiser line and the relative position of the cruiser line began to move up the battle line. However, the cruisers did not clear the range for USS *Pennsylvania* (the last battleship) until roughly 4:02 a.m., when the battle line commenced its turn to 270. As the battleships progressively turned to the rough reciprocal of the cruisers' course, the cruisers steadily unmasked more of the battle line. By roughly 4:05–4:06 a.m., the USS *Mississippi*, USS *Tennessee*, USS *California*, and USS *Pennsylvania* all enjoyed a clear range and only USS *West Virginia* and USS *Maryland* were masked. By the time cease fire was ordered at 4:09 a.m., the entire battle line was unmasked. Based on this motion analysis the USS *Maryland*, USS *Mississippi*, and USS *Pennsylvania* probably enjoyed the following range conditions: USS *Maryland*—unmasked 3:48–4 a.m., masked 4–4:08 a.m., unmasked 4:08–4:09 a.m.; USS *Mississippi*—unmasked 3:48–3:56 a.m., masked 3:56–4:06 a.m., unmasked 4:06–4:09 a.m.; USS *Pennsylvania*—masked 3:48–4:02 a.m., unmasked 4:02–4:09 a.m.

From 3:48 a.m. to 3:51 a.m., neither the cruiser line nor the battle line fired. During this period, both USS *Maryland* and USS *Mississippi* should have had an unobstructed visual and radar line of sight to IJN *Yamashiro*. USS *Pennsylvania* would have had to contend with the cruisers' visual silhouettes, but proper employment of the radar should have eliminated any spurious returns from the cruisers. At 3:51 a.m., the cruiser line opened fire and maintained fire until cease fire at 4:09 a.m. Throughout this period, the flash of the cruisers' firing could foul the visual range of any masked ships. At 3:53 a.m., the USS *West Virginia* opened fire, followed by USS *Tennessee* and USS *California* at 3:55 a.m. and USS *Maryland* at 3:59 a.m. USS *Mississippi* fired her sole salvo at cease fire at 4:09 a.m.

USS *West Virginia* opened fire two minutes prior to a simultaneous turn right 30 degrees to course 120°(T). USS *Tennessee* and USS *California* opened fire while executing that turn. USS *Maryland* opened fire while on course 120°(T). USS *Mississippi* fired her single salvo on course 270°(T). At the other end of the engagement, the IJN *Yamashiro* was roughly on course 020°(T) from 3:53 a.m. to 3:56 a.m. At 3:56 a.m., she came left to roughly course 265°(T), steadying up briefly at 4 a.m. and then gradually arcing more southerly until 4:09 a.m., at which time she executed a roughly 90-degree left turn to course 170°(T) on which she staggered until she capsized at 4:19 a.m.

Throughout most of the period from 3:53 a.m. to 3:59 a.m., the American battleships were within an arc from 10 degrees right of IJN *Yamashiro's* bow to about 5 degrees left. Thus, IJN *Yamashiro* was presenting a very narrow visual and radar target to the battle line. From 3:59 a.m. to 4:09 a.m., the IJN *Yamashiro*'s left turn gradually expanded the visual and radar target to maximum (when IJN *Yamashiro* was beam-on in her turn) until the American ships were placed roughly 30 degrees abaft IJN *Yamashiro*'s starboard beam, still a very good visual and radar target with IJN *Yamashiro* presenting three large areas of vertical development to vision and radar (foremast, funnel, and mainmast).

What all this means is that for twelve minutes, USS *Maryland* had an unobstructed visual and radar line of sight to the target at the start of the engagement. However, USS *Maryland* did not open fire until eleven of those minutes had passed and only one minute before being masked. USS *Mississippi* had eight minutes of unobstructed line of sight to the target but did not open fire. USS *Pennsylvania* was still masked. Why did USS *Maryland* wait so long to fire and why did USS *Mississippi* not fire? Probably for two reasons: 1) At over 22,000 yards at night, the *Yamashiro* was probably largely invisible from head on to the eye; 2) Beginning at 3:53 a.m., the *Yamashiro* was probably localized by, but obscured within, shell splashes. From 3:53 a.m. to 3:56 a.m., USS *Mississippi* had an opportunity to localize and acquire Yamashiro by spotting the fall of shells from the three Mk. 8 battleships, but she failed to do so. Why? Probably because during this period she was almost directly ahead of Yamashiro and so presented with IJN *Yamashiro*'s narrowest profile.

Meanwhile, USS *Maryland* enjoyed an extra three minutes and a better vantage point farther to the east presenting more of Yamashiro's profile, but not much. Thus from 3:53 a.m. to about 3:55 a.m., USS *Maryland*'s radar operators probably took note of the transients of USS *West Virginia*'s shell splashes and began to prepare to shoot. But at 3:55 a.m., I suspect they lost any potential hard return in the increased clutter of splashes as USS *Tennessee* and USS *California* joined in. This probably blinded USS *Maryland*'s operators for a minute until IJN *Yamashiro* started turning at 3:56 a.m. The shell splashes told her radar operators where to look but obscured the radar target IJN *Yamashiro* was presenting.

As IJN *Yamashiro* began turning, she progressively presented a larger and more distinct radar target to Maryland and her operators were probably then able to pick out the hard return off IJN *Yamashiro* amidst the transients of the splashes. At 3:59 a.m., IJN *Yamashiro* was probably headed roughly 300, USS *Maryland*'s reciprocal, and presenting her full broadside to USS *Maryland*. As USS *Maryland* was not yet visually masked, quick confirmation was probably sought from the directors. Broadside on and afire, IJN *Yamashiro* was probably easily identified, and fire was commenced. USS *Maryland* probably held a solid radar target for the next three to five minutes and then probably lost the target briefly (4:04–4:05 a.m.?) in her turn to 270°(T) as the superstructure masked the Mk. 3 radar on the after director and it slewed around to reacquire on a port bearing. With the broad target angle presented by IJN *Yamashiro* at this time, reacquisition was probably not difficult. Throughout, USS *Maryland*'s forward director should have been able to remain visually on target.

At some time around 4:02–4:03 a.m., the cruiser line finally unmasked USS *Pennsylvania*. By this time she would have been presented with a beautiful visual and radar target as IJN *Yamashiro* opened her profile coming to 265°(T). However, USS *Pennsylvania* was also in a turn to 270°(T) and her Mk. 3 on her after director was probably masked at least until about 4:05 a.m. at which point it could commence establishing a lock. This gave USS *Pennsylvania* four minutes without obstruction to engage IJN *Yamashiro*. Meanwhile USS *Mississippi* was getting her second chance. Unmasked later than USS *Pennsylvania* and at about the time the turn to 270°(T) was complete (4:05–4:06 a.m.), USS *Mississippi*'s Mk. 3 would not be masked (assuming she had both fore and aft installations). This gave USS *Mississippi* three minutes without obstruction to engage IJN *Yamashiro*, at the end of which she successfully got off one salvo.

There were probably several important factors in USS *Maryland*'s success and the failure of her fellow Mk. 3 ships:

1. USS *Maryland* enjoyed the most time unmasked.
2. USS *Maryland* enjoyed the best geometry to gain a solid radar contact soonest.
3. USS *Maryland* enjoyed the best geometry to gain a visual contact soonest.
4. USS *Maryland*'s radar operators were probably somewhat more proficient.
5. USS *Maryland*'s gunnery officer was probably somewhat more certain of his target and/or more decisive about engaging it.

Given the Mk. 3 FCR's good range discrimination and poor azimuth discrimination, USS *Maryland*, USS *Mississippi*, and USS *Pennsylvania* should all have had solid range information on IJN *Yamashiro* prior to 3:53 a.m.

Between 3:53 a.m. and 3:55 a.m., their radar contact would have suffered some clutter from the transients of USS *West Virginia*'s shell splashes. During this period, both USS *Maryland* and USS *Mississippi* should also have had a clear visual to the target as well and should have picked out its rough azimuth, however, they were presented with a very narrow visual target and might have perceived nothing more than the transient visual images of the shell splashes.

Between 3:55 a.m. and 3:59 a.m., the IJN *Yamashiro* was probably badly obscured on radar due to the profusion of shell splashes as a result of the fire from USS *West Virginia*, USS *Tennessee*, and USS *California*. By 3:59 a.m., IJN *Yamashiro*'s turn to port presented a larger radar target that became distinctly hard within the soft returns of shell splashes, reestablishing the ship's range. At the same time, afire and broadside on, IJN *Yamashiro* probably became a distinctive visual target, and was therefore discernable in azimuth. At this time, USS *Maryland* was the only unmasked Mk. 3 ship and she opened fire. USS *Mississippi* and USS *Pennsylvania* may not have clearly perceived IJN *Yamashiro* visually past the flashes of the cruiser line's fire.

Apparently, having found the target, USS *Maryland* held it and continued to fire as she was masked. USS *Pennsylvania* remained masked until 4:05 a.m. and USS *Mississippi* until 4:06 a.m. This presented both USS *Pennsylvania* and USS *Mississippi* an opportunity in which they would have had solid range information from the Mk. 3 and visual azimuth information on the burning IJN *Yamashiro* to establish a fire control solution. USS *Mississippi* accomplished this in three minutes and fired her salvo as Oldendorf ordered cease fire for fear he was shooting at a friendly destroyer. USS *Pennsylvania* did not.

Why did USS *Mississippi* obtain a solution, but not USS *Pennsylvania*, particularly given that *Pennsylvania* had an extra minute? The explanation may be that USS *Pennsylvania*'s Mk. 3, positioned aft, was still partly masked by her superstructure as she completed the turn to 270°(T), while USS *Mississippi*, with dual (fore and aft) Mk. 3 installations was able to track IJN *Yamashiro* with her forward Mk. 3. However, from 4 a.m. until 4:09 a.m., IJN *Yamashiro* presented a very broad and strong radar profile to the Mk. 3 sets, so at any time during that period, USS *Mississippi* should have held a solid target in range. From 4–4:02 a.m., while on course 120°(T) USS *Pennsylvania* should also have been able to hold a solid target, and again from 4:06–4:09 a.m. Quite probably the gap was less than four minutes and more like one minute that the Mk. 3 aft was completely masked.

So why did USS *Mississippi* not open fire at 4:06 a.m., the moment she was unmasked? And why did USS *Pennsylvania* not open fire at the same time, assuming she had to complete her turn to unmask the aft radar? This is where the situation might be one of radar operator and gunnery officer proficiency. It might be that USS *Maryland*'s operators were slightly more proficient with their equipment, her maintainers groomed it for action better, and/or her gunnery officer was more proficient and/or confident.

An aside, to lay to rest one false explanation that has absurdly (given even a brief glance at a track chart of the engagement) persisted for years: The issue was never one of firing over the cruiser line. USS *West Virginia* commenced fire at 21,300 yards with the cruiser line anywhere from 6,700 to 4,200 yards to the south. USS *Tennessee* and USS *California* commenced fire at 20,400 yards with the cruiser line anywhere from 6,200 to 4,000 yards to the south. USS *Maryland* commenced fire at 19,300 yards with the cruiser line anywhere from 6,000 to

4,200 yards to the south. None of these ships had any compunctions about firing over the cruisers of the eastern cruiser line as these ships progressively crossed their line of fire. Thus, the physical positioning of the cruisers did not preclude USS *Mississippi* or USS *Pennsylvania* from firing over them.

A final aside, explaining the difference between the Mk. 8 and Mk. 3 FCRs: The Mk. 3 FCR had a small pulse width and a broad beam width. As a result, it achieved extremely good range discrimination, but poor azimuth resolution. Thus when Washington engaged Karishma at Second Guadalcanal with such equipment, it was using radar range inputs and visual azimuth inputs to the fire control computer. The later Mk. 8 FCR was a centimetric radar with a more refined wavelength and beam width as well as the small pulse width of the earlier set. This permitted the Mk. 8 to establish both range and azimuth very precisely. It also permitted the Mk. 8 to generate a much harder return off of a much narrower target, and to better discriminate targets in close proximity. By extension, with such refined radiation parameters, the Mk. 8 was less likely to have its display cluttered by transient soft returns such as shell splashes. This explains the ability of the Mk. 8 ships at Surigao to initiate and maintain fire on the *Yamashiro* regardless of the target angle and visual masking from the cruiser line during the engagement.

Ship	Capacity	Total On-Board	AP	HC	Rounds Expended
USS *West Virginia*	800	375	200	175	93
USS *Maryland*	800	685	240	445	48
USS *California*	1,200	318	240	78	63
USS *Tennessee*	1,200	664	396	268	69
USS *Mississippi*	1,200	744	201	543	12
USS *Pennsylvania*	1,200	453	360	93	Did not fire

Epilogue

What had happened was simple enough. Admiral Nishimura and Admiral Shima had steamed into a gauntlet of gunfire and had been defeated in one of the most one-sided naval actions in history. The Japanese could not count their dead, but they numbered in the thousands, including Admiral Nishimura. Two battleships, a heavy cruiser, and three destroyers were lost in the action, and the light cruiser IJN *Abukuma* was lost shortly after. The Americans lost exactly thirty-nine killed and 114 wounded, most of them on USS *Albert W. Grant* due to friendly fire, and a single PT boat.

More importantly, the southern portion of the Japanese plan to smash the American invasion fleet with a double pincer movement had failed completely. The northern pincer nearly defeated a much weaker American force off Samar, mostly due to Vice Admiral Halsey's controversial decision to leave the San Bernardino Strait unguarded. But Rear Admiral Oldendorf's cool, meticulous planning and courageous men had crushed the southern pincer.

The answer to why the Japanese attack failed was easy. The Japanese underestimated American power and resilience, as they had all through the war, and overestimated their own resolve. The *bushido* code was not enough against American technology and determination. Japanese gunnery and torpedo efficiency was far below the glorious standards of 1942. Even Japanese seamanship, as evidenced by the collision of IJN *Nachi* and IJN *Mogami*, was faulty. Admiral Nishimura and Admiral Shima did not coordinate their forces. They did not even seem to know where their own ships were. Probably the single most intelligent Japanese decision in the entire battle was Shima's decision to withdraw.

The surviving Japanese blamed their late boss, Admiral Nishimura. Hiroshi Tanaka of IJN *Yamashiro* described survivors as saying that Nishimura's strategy was that of a warrant officer, not an admiral. Still, it was difficult to see what else Nishimura could have done. His orders were clear and specific: steam into Surigao Strait, punch through the American defenses, and savage the American transports. He had tried to do so with every ship at his command and fiber of his being, paying the price with his own life. The very cause was hopeless, but Admiral Nishimura and his sailors did their best to carry out their orders with full and hopeless valor.

It was also the end for a style of warfare that dated back to the Battle of Lissa in 1866. It had translated from the age of sail to that of steam. Now the battle line had been rendered obsolete by the development of air power, the brawling night surface actions of Guadalcanal, and the unsporting but deadly submarine. The even more deadly power of guided missiles and atomic weaponry were yet to come. Such thoughts probably did not occur to the victorious American sailors as the sun rose over the smoking wreckage, fuming muzzles, and oil fires in Surigao Strait. Aboard USS *Louisville*, Rear Admiral Oldendorf assessed the desperate messages from Samar and ordered his officers to start plotting courses and formations to support the endangered escort carriers.

As a result of the combined battles of Leyte Gulf, the Imperial Japanese Navy suffered its greatest loss of ships and crew ever—twenty-six out of sixty front-line warships. The Americans had eight fleet carriers and eight light carriers with 1,500 planes against the Japanese single fleet carrier, IJN *Zuikaku*—the only surviving carrier from the Pearl Harbor attack, which was sunk—and three light carriers. The U.S. lost the USS *Saint Lo*, a light carrier. American casualties were about 3,000 dead to about 10,500 sailors and pilots for the Japanese. During the Battle of Surigao Strait, the American casualties were thirty-nine dead and 114 wounded. Of nine Japanese battleships, three were sunk, with a loss of no American battleship. The Imperial Japanese Navy's failure to dislodge the Allied invaders from their beachheads in Leyte meant the inevitable loss of the Philippines. Leyte was not completely in Allied hands until the end of December 1944. This in turn meant that resource-poor Japan would soon be all but cut off from the Pacific and Southeast Asian territories still in Japanese hands. These overseas territories had been using a wide variety of maritime vessels, diminished by the month, to deliver resources of oil, rubber, tin, and bauxite ore that were vital to Japan's wartime economy. Finally, the loss of Leyte opened the way for the 1945 invasion of the Ryukyu Islands, the chain of Japanese islands lying south of the Home Island of Kyūshū, and which included Okinawa.

On the American battleships, the young sailors marveled that despite a night of sound and fury their battleships had suffered nothing. They were all alive to greet the new day. The loudspeakers blared, "Now hear this. Secure from general quarters. Set torpedo defense watch." A sailor from the USS *Louisville* captured the essence of the battle at Surigao Strait with a poem:

The battleship's bark was heard through the dark,
As they belched their heavy shell.
Let the enemy feel our hot white steel,
And hope they fry in hell.

Our salvos straddled them time on time,
And their counters were slow with no force.
We were crossing their "T" and they tried to flee.
But the shoal water held them in course.

How bright was the sky? Like the fourth of July,
Or midway at a fair.
And the awesome sound that was all around,
I cannot begin to compare.

They closed the range till they cleared the strait,
Then they turned to run it past.
But the damage we'd done left few to run,
For we'd given them to much too fast.

Next day the water was slick with oil,
Still echo's, that awful sight.
And scraps of debris all around in the sea,
From their ships sunk there in the night.

The Japs had come down looking to squeeze,
Us out of the Philippines base.
But we caught 'em close and gave 'em a dose,
So they will have quite a time to save face.

Now I'm not so wise as these columnist guys,
Nor a pro at covering a fight.
But it 'twas Navy, all Navy, that night.

Now these are the simple details for the show,
And though Tokyo Rose won't agree.
'Twas a sizeable sample the Japs found it ample,
Compliments of the U.S. Navy.

APPENDIX I

American Fleet at the Surigao Strait

Task Force 79 (Vice Admiral T. S. Wilkinson)

USS Mount Olympus

USS *Mount Olympus* (AGC-8) was a *Mount McKinley*-class amphibious force command ship, named for the highest peak in the Olympic Mountains of the State of Washington. She was designed to be an amphibious forces flagship—a floating command post with advanced communications equipment and extensive combat information spaces to be used by the amphibious force's commander and landing force commander during large-scale operations.

USS *Mount Olympus* departed from the East Coast in early July, arriving at Hawaii via the Panama Canal on July 23. With the commander, 3rd Amphibious Force, embarked, she was underway from Hawaii on August 29. She arrived Leyte Gulf October 20, there to serve as the floating headquarters for the huge U.S. Army invasion force. The landing force was subjected to continual air attacks, but its survival was assured by the American naval victory in the Battle of Leyte Gulf, which destroyed the Japanese Navy as an effective combat force.

Shipyard:	North Carolina Shipbuilding Company, Wilmington, North Carolina
Laid down:	August 3, 1943
Launched:	October 3, 1943
Commissioned:	May 24, 1944
Decommissioned:	April 4, 1956
Class and type:	*Mount McKinley*-class command ship
Displacement:	12,142 tons
Length:	459 feet 2 inches
Beam:	63 feet

Draft:	25 feet
Speed:	15 knots
Complement:	729
Armament:	2 × 5-inch guns
	8 × 40-mm guns
	20 × 20-mm guns

Battle Line (Rear Admiral George L. Weyler)

USS Mississippi (Captain Herman J. Redfield)

Entering service in 1917, *USS Mississippi* (BB-41) was the second ship of the *New Mexico*-class. After seeing brief service in World War I, the battleship later spent the majority of its career in the Pacific. During World War II, USS *Mississippi* took part in the U.S. Navy's island-hopping campaign across the Pacific and repeatedly clashed with Japanese forces.

On June 12, 1924, USS *Mississippi* found herself off the coast of California conducting gun trials. The 14-inch/50-caliber gun was plagued with technical issues, a major problem considering it was the primary armament on the majority of serving U.S. Navy battleships. On the eighth salvo, turret two, gun two suffered a rare "flare back." The four powder bags inserted into the breech, totaling 470 pounds of explosive powder, caught fire and ignited other bags waiting to be loaded. Forty-eight sailors were killed, and only one of the sailors manning the turret survived. Based on the survivor's account, the navy believed that a fire or burning debris was present in the gun barrel and ignited the powder bags. Although each barrel was blasted between firings with pressurized air to evacuate debris, the middle barrel of each turret received a lower pressure burst than the left and right barrels. This could have led to dangerous debris remaining in the breech when the gun crew assumed it was safe to load.

A bizarre accident occurred afterward while the USS *Mississippi* was anchored in San Pedro Bay. The hand of a dead crewman in the number two turret accidentally hit the firing switch for the port gun, firing it. The shell flew harmlessly out to sea. Nearly twenty years—and a major refit—later, the USS *Mississippi* went to war in the Pacific. In 1943, the big battleship was off the coast of Makin Island, providing naval gunfire support to a landing force preparing to secure the island. After an extensive preliminary bombardment, the marine assault force headed towards the beach and USS *Mississippi* and the other ships increased their rate of fire.

Suddenly, in the midst of the barrage, smoke and gas erupted from the rangefinders on either side of the number two turret. Incredibly it had happened again: in their haste to lay down a rain of shells on the Japanese, the gunners of number two turret had apparently experienced yet another flare back.

Debris from firing the big guns had again ignited powder bags, causing the same accident and the same damage. Forty-two sailors were killed and another sixteen wounded. The battleship's three remaining turrets continued firing until the naval support phase of the invasion had ended. Retained for several years after the war, the battleship found a second life as a test platform for the U.S. Navy's early missile systems.

Shipyard:	Newport News Shipbuilding, Newport News, Virginia
Laid down:	April 5, 1915
Launched:	January 25, 1917
Commissioned:	December 16, 1917
Decommissioned:	September 17, 1956
Class and type:	*New Mexico*-class battleship
Displacement:	33,000 tons
Length:	624 feet
Beam:	97 feet 5 inches
Draft:	30 feet
Propulsion:	9 × Babcock and Wilcox boilers, 4 screws, turbo-electric drives
Speed:	21 knots
Range:	8,000 nautical miles
Complement:	55 officers, 1,026 enlisted
Armament:	12 × 14-inch/50 Mark 4 guns
	14 × 5-inch guns
	4 × 3-inch guns
	2 × Mark 8, 21-inch torpedo tubes
Armor:	Belt: 8–13.5 inches
	Turret face: 18 inches
	Conning tower: 16 inches
	Decks: 3.5 inches

USS California (Captain Harry B. Burnett)

Entering service in 1921, USS *California* (BB-44) served the U.S. Navy for over a quarter-century and saw combat operations during World War II. Dubbed "The Prune Barge" due to the large volume of the fruit exported by California in the early part of the twentieth century, the battleship was the second vessel of the *Tennessee*-class. USS *California* was moored in Pearl Harbor on 7 December 1941 when the Japanese attacked the port, bringing the U.S. into World War II. The ship was moderately damaged by a pair of torpedoes and a bomb, but a fire disabled the ship's electrical system, preventing the pumps from being used to keep the ship afloat. USS *California* slowly filled with water over the following three days and eventually sank. Her crew suffered heavy casualties in the attack and four men were awarded the Medal of Honor for their actions during the attack. She was raised in April 1942, repaired and heavily rebuilt, and returned to service in January 1944.

The ship thereafter supported the amphibious operations conducted during the Pacific War, including the Mariana and Palau Islands campaign (though she was damaged in a collision with USS *Tennessee* and thus missed the Battle of Peleliu) and the Philippines campaign, during which she took part in the Battle of Surigao Strait. She was hit by a *kamikaze* during the invasion of Lingayen Gulf in January 1945, after repairs, joined the fleet supporting troops fighting on Okinawa during the Battle of Okinawa. Her crew took part in the occupation of Japan after the end of the war, and after returning to the U.S. via the Indian and Atlantic Oceans, was laid up in Philadelphia in 1946. She remained in the fleet's inventory until 1959, when she was broken up for scrap.

Shipyard:	Mare Island Naval Shipyard, Vallejo, California
Laid down:	October 25, 1916
Launched:	November 20, 1919
Commissioned:	August 10, 1921
Decommissioned:	February 14, 1947
Class and type:	*Tennessee*-class battleship
Displacement:	40,992 tons
Length:	624 feet
Beam:	97 feet 5 inches
Draft:	30 feet 2 inches
Propulsion:	8 × Babcock and Wilcox boilers, 4 screws, turbo-electric drives
Speed:	21 knots
Range:	8,000 nautical miles
Complement:	114 officers, 2,129 enlisted
Armament:	4 × triple 14-inch guns
	8 × twin 5-inch guns
	11 × quadruple, 6 x twin 40-mm anti-aircraft guns
	43 × single 20-mm anti-aircraft guns
	2 × Mk. 8, 21-inch torpedo tubes
	Aircraft carried: 3 x floatplanes
	Aviation facilities: 2 x catapults
Armor:	Belt: 8–13.5 inches
	Barbettes: 13 inches
	Turret face: 18 inches
	Conning tower: 16 inches
	Decks: 3.5 inches

USS Tennessee (Captain John B. Heffernan)

The lead ship of the *Tennessee*-class of battleship, USS *Tennessee* (BB-43), was laid down shortly after the U.S.'s entry into World War I (1914–1918). The first class to take advantage of the lessons learned in the conflict, the battleship was not completed until two years after the fighting had ended. Entering the peacetime U.S. Navy, USS *Tennessee* spent almost the entirety of its career in the Pacific. USS *Tennessee* was moored in Battleship Row when the Japanese attacked Pearl Harbor on 7 December 1941, which brought the U.S. into World War II. She was not seriously damaged, and after being repaired she operated off the West Coast of the U.S. in 1942. In 1943, USS *Tennessee* and many of the older battleships were thoroughly rebuilt to prepare them for operations in the Pacific War and in June–August, she took part in the Aleutian Islands Campaign, providing gunfire support to troops fighting to retake the islands. The Gilbert and Marshall Islands campaign followed from November 1943 to February 1944, including the Battles of Tarawa, Kwajalein, and Eniwetok. In March, she raided Kavieng to distract Japanese forces during the landing on Emirau, and from June through September, she fought in the Mariana and Palau Islands campaign, bombarding Japanese forces during the Battles of Saipan, Guam, Tinian, and Anguar.

The Philippines campaign followed in September, during which the ship operated as part of the bombardment group at the Battle of Leyte. The Japanese launched a major naval counterattack that resulted in the Battle of Leyte Gulf, a series of four naval engagements. During the Battle of Surigao Strait, USS *Tennessee* formed part of the U.S. line of battle that defeated a Japanese squadron; this was the last battleship engagement in history. USS *Tennessee* shelled Japanese forces during the Battle of Iwo Jima in February 1945 and the Battle of Okinawa from March to June. During the latter action, she was hit by a *kamikaze* but was not seriously damaged. In the final months of the war, she operated primarily in the East China Sea, and after Japan's surrender in August, she participated in the occupation of Japan before returning to the U.S. late in the year. In the postwar draw down of naval forces, USS *Tennessee* was placed in the reserve fleet in 1946 and retained, out of service, until 1959, when the navy decided to discard her. The ship was sold to Bethlehem Steel in July and broken up for scrap.

Shipyard:	New York Navy Yard, New York, New York
Laid down:	May 14, 1917
Launched:	April 30, 1919
Commissioned:	June 3, 1920
Decommissioned:	February 14, 1947
Class and type:	*Tennessee*-class battleship
Displacement:	33,723 tons

Length:	624 feet
Beam:	97 feet 5 inches
Draft:	30 feet 2 inches
Propulsion:	8 × Babcock and Wilcox boilers, 4 screws, turbo-electric drives
Speed:	21 knots
Range:	8,000 nautical miles
Complement:	57 officers, 1,026 enlisted
Armament:	4 × triple 14-inch guns 14 × single 5-inch guns 4 × single 3-inch guns 2 × Mk. 8, 21-inch torpedo tubes
Armor:	Belt: 8–13.5-inch Barbettes: 13-inch Turret face: 18-inch Conning tower: 16-inch Decks: 3.5-inch

USS Pennsylvania (Captain Charles F. Martin)

Commissioned in 1916, USS *Pennsylvania* (BB-38) proved to be a workhorse for the U.S. Navy's surface fleet for over thirty years. USS *Pennsylvania* was not sent to European waters during World War I, since the necessary fuel oil was not as readily available as coal. Instead, she remained in American waters and took part in training exercises; in 1918, she escorted President Woodrow Wilson to France to take part in peace negotiations.

During the 1920s and 1930s, USS *Pennsylvania* served as the flagship of first the Atlantic Fleet, and after it was merged with the Pacific Fleet in 1921, the Battle Fleet. For the majority of this period, the ship was stationed in California, based in San Pedro. USS *Pennsylvania* was occupied with a peacetime routine of training exercises (including the annual Fleet Problems), port visits, and foreign cruises, including a visit to Australia in 1925. The ship was modernized in 1929–1931. The ship was present in Pearl Harbor on the morning of December 7, 1941; she was in dry-dock with a pair of destroyers when the Japanese launched their surprise attack on the port. She suffered relatively minor damage in the attack, being protected from torpedoes by the dry-dock. While repairs were effected, the ship received a modernized anti-aircraft battery to prepare her for operations in the Pacific War.

USS *Pennsylvania* joined the fleet in a series of amphibious operations, primarily tasked with providing gunfire support. The first of these, the Aleutian Islands Campaign, took place in mid-1943, and was followed by an attack on Makin later that year. During 1944, she supported the landings on Kwajalein and Eniwetok in the Marshall Islands and the Mariana and Palau

Islands campaign, including the Battles of Saipan, Guam, Peleliu, and Battle of Angaur. During the Philippines campaign, in addition to her typical shore bombardment duties, she took part in the Battle of Surigao Strait, though due to her inadequate radar, she was unable to locate a target and did not fire. During the Battle of Okinawa, she was torpedoed by a Japanese torpedo bomber and badly damaged, forcing her to withdraw for repairs days before the end of the war.

Allocated to the target fleet for the Operation Crossroads nuclear tests in 1946, USS *Pennsylvania* was repaired only enough to allow her to make the voyage to the test site, Bikini Atoll. She survived both blasts but was badly contaminated with radioactive fallout from the second test, and so was towed to Kwajalein, where she was studied for the next year and a half. The ship was ultimately scuttled in deep water off the atoll in February 1948.

Shipyard:	Newport News Shipbuilding & Drydock Company, Newport News, Virginia
Laid down:	October 27, 1913
Launched:	March 16, 1915
Commissioned:	June 12, 1916
Decommissioned:	August 29, 1946
Class and type:	*Pennsylvania*-class battleship
Displacement:	32,429 tons
Length:	608 feet
Beam:	97.1 feet
Draft:	28.9 feet
Propulsion:	12 Babcock and Wilcox boilers, 4 screws, turbo-electric drives
Speed:	21 knots
Range:	8,691 nautical miles
Complement:	56 officers, 1,031 enlisted
Armament:	12 × 14-inch guns 16 × 5-inch guns 40 × 40-mm anti-aircraft guns 51 × 20-mm anti-aircraft guns 2 × Mk. 8, 21-inch torpedo tubes Aircraft carried: 2 × floatplanes Aviation facilities: 2 × catapults
Armor:	Belt: 13.5 inches Deck: 3 inches Turrets: 18 inches Conning Tower: 16 inches

USS Maryland (Captain Herbert J. Ray)

USS *Maryland* (BB-46) was the second ship of the U.S. Navy's *Colorado*-class of battleship. Entering service in 1921, the battleship briefly served in the Atlantic before spending the majority of its career in the Pacific. On the morning of December 7, 1941, USS *Maryland* was moored along Ford Island, with USS *Oklahoma* to port, connected by lines and a gangway. To her fore was USS *California*, while USS *Tennessee* and USS *West Virginia* were astern. Further aft were USS *Nevada* and USS *Arizona*. The seven battleships, in what is now known as Battleship Row, had recently returned from maneuvers. Many of USS *Maryland*'s crew were preparing for shore leave at 9 a.m. or eating breakfast when the Japanese attack began. As the first Japanese aircraft appeared and explosions rocked the outboard battleships, USS *Maryland*'s bugler blew general quarters.

USS *Maryland* was struck by two armor-piercing bombs which detonated low on her hull. The first struck the forecastle awning and made a hole about 12 feet by 20 feet. The second exploded after entering the hull at the 22-foot water level at Frame 10. The latter hit caused flooding and increased the draft forward by 5 feet. USS *Maryland* continued to fire and, after the attack, sent firefighting parties to assist her compatriots, especially attempting to rescue survivors from the capsized USS *Oklahoma*. The men continued to muster the AA defenses in case the Japanese returned to attack. In all, two officers and two men were killed in the attack.

The Japanese erroneously announced that USS *Maryland* had been sunk, but on December 30, the damaged ship entered Puget Sound Navy Yard for repairs just behind USS *Tennessee*. Two of the original twelve 5-inch/51-caliber guns were removed and the 5-inch/25-caliber guns were replaced by an equal number of 5-inch/38-caliber dual-purpose guns. Over the course of the next two months, she was repaired and overhauled, receiving new fighting equipment. Repairs were complete on February 26, 1942. She then underwent a series of shakedown cruises to West Coast ports and the Christmas Islands. She was sent back into action in June 1942, the first ship damaged at Pearl Harbor to return to duty.

USS *Maryland* steamed for Seeadler Harbor, Manus, where she was assigned to the Seventh Fleet under Admiral Kinkaid. The fleet sortied October 12, and USS *Maryland* joined Task Group 77.2, which was the gunfire and covering force for the invasion of Leyte. She, along with four other battleships and numerous cruisers and destroyers, steamed into Leyte Gulf on the morning of October 18. USS *Maryland* took position between Red and White Beaches and began bombarding them ahead of the invasion, which began at 10 a.m. on October 20. Securing the beaches quickly, USS *Maryland* then took up a sentinel position in Leyte Gulf to guard the beaches against Japanese counterattack by sea.

For the next several days, Japanese forces launched air raids to counter the incursion. These included the first widespread use of the *kamikaze* suicide attack.

Several days later, U.S. submarines in the South China Sea spotted two Japanese forces on approach: five battleships steaming toward San Bernardino Strait, and another force of four Japanese carriers in northern Luzon. On October 24, USS *Maryland* sailed to the southern end of Leyte Gulf to protect Surigao Strait. Following the victory, USS *Maryland* patrolled the southern approaches to Surigao Strait until October 29.

She then steamed for the Admiralty Isles for brief replenishment and resumed patrol duty around Leyte on November 16, protecting the landing forces from continued Japanese air attacks. On November 29, during another Japanese air attack, a *kamikaze* aircraft surprised and struck USS *Maryland*. The aircraft crashed into USS *Maryland* between turrets Nos. 1 and 2, piercing the forecastle, main, and armored decks and blowing a hole in the 4-inch steel, causing extensive damage and starting fires. In all, thirty-one men were killed and thirty wounded in the attack, and the medical department was destroyed but still functional.

She was decommissioned at Bremerton on April 3, 1947 and remained there as a unit of the Pacific Reserve Fleet. USS *Maryland* was sold for scrapping to Learner Company of Oakland, California, on July 8, 1959.

Shipyard:	Newport News Shipbuilding, Newport News, Virginia
Laid down:	April 24, 1917
Launched:	March 20, 1920
Commissioned:	July 21, 1921
Decommissioned:	April 3, 1947
Class and type:	*Colorado*-class battleship
Displacement:	33,100 tons
Length:	624 feet
Beam:	97 feet 6 inches
Draft:	30 feet 6 inches
Propulsion:	12 Babcock and Wilcox boilers, 4 screws, turbo-electric drives
Speed:	21.17 knots
Range:	8,000 nautical miles
Complement:	58 officers and 1,022 enlisted
Armament:	8 × 16-inch guns
	12 × 5-inch guns
	4 × 3-inch guns
	2 × Mk. 8, 21-inch torpedo tubes
Armor:	Belt: 8–13.5 inches
	Barbettes: 13 inches
	Turret face: 18 inches
	Turret sides: 9–10 inches
	Turret top: 5 inches

Turret rear: 9 inches
Conning tower: 11.5 inches
Decks: 3.5 inches
Aircraft carried: 4 × floatplanes
Aviation facilities: 2 × aircraft catapults

USS West Virginia (Captain Herbert V. Wiley)

The final ship of the *Colorado*-class of battleship, USS *West Virginia* (BB-48), entered service in 1923. Though built at Newport News, VA, it became a fixture in the Pacific for the majority of its career. USS *West Virginia* was moored in Battleship Row on the morning of December 7, 1941 when Japan attacked Pearl Harbor, bringing the U.S. into World War II. Badly damaged by torpedoes, the ship sank in the shallow water but was later refloated and extensively rebuilt over the course of 1943 and into mid-1944. She returned to service in time for the Philippines Campaign, where she led the American line of battle at the Battle of Surigao Strait on the night of October 24–25. There, she was one of the few American battleships to use her radar to acquire a target in the darkness, allowing her to engage a Japanese squadron in what was the final action between battleships in naval history.

After Surigao Strait, the ship remained in the Philippines to support troops fighting during the Battle of Leyte in 1944 and then supported the invasion of Lingayen Gulf in early 1945. The ship also took part in the Battles of Iwo Jima and Okinawa later that year, providing extensive fire support to the ground forces invading those islands. During the latter operation, she was hit by a *kamikaze* that did little damage. Following the surrender of Japan, USS *West Virginia* took part in the initial occupation and thereafter participated in Operation Magic Carpet, carrying soldiers and sailors from Hawaii to the mainland U.S. before being deactivated in 1946. She was decommissioned in 1947 and assigned to the Pacific Reserve Fleet, where she remained until 1959 when she was sold to ship breakers and dismantled.

Shipyard:	Newport News Shipbuilding Corporation, Newport News, Virginia
Laid down:	April 12, 1920
Launched:	November 19, 1921
Commissioned:	December 1, 1923
Decommissioned:	January 9, 1947
Class and type:	*Colorado*-class battleship
Displacement:	34,130 tons
Length:	624 feet
Beam:	97 feet 6 inches
Draft:	30 feet 6 inches
Propulsion:	8 Babcock and Wilcox boilers, 4 screws,

	turbo-electric drives
Speed:	21 knots
Range:	8,000 nautical miles
Complement:	64 officers, 1,241 enlisted
Armament:	8 × 16–45-inch guns
	16 × 5-inch guns
	40 × 40-mm anti-aircraft guns
	43 × 20-mm anti-aircraft guns
	2 × Mk. 8, 21-inch torpedo tubes
Armor:	Belt: 8–13.5 inches
	Barbettes: 13 inches
	Turret face: 18 inches
	Conning tower: 16 inches
	Decks: 3.5 inches
	Sensors and processing systems: CXAM-1 radar

USS Sigourney (Lieutenant Commander Fletcher Hale)

USS *Sigourney* (DD-643) was a *Fletcher*-class destroyer, the second ship of the U.S. Navy to be named for James Sigourney, an officer during the War of 1812. The destroyer underwent shakedown training in Casco Bay, Maine, and in the Bermuda operating area. After post-shakedown repairs, Sigourney sailed, on September 14, 1943, from Norfolk with cruiser USS *Baltimore* (CA-68) *en route* to the west coast. They arrived at San Diego on October 3, and the DD departed the next day for Pearl Harbor. She was routed onward to Espiritu Santo, New Hebrides. The ship arrived October 24 and was assigned to Destroyer Squadron 22, Destroyer Division 44.

Shipyard:	Bath Iron Works, Bath, Maine
Laid down:	December 7, 1942
Launched:	April 24, 1943
Commissioned:	June 29, 1943
Decommissioned:	May 1, 1960
Class and type:	*Fletcher*-class destroyer
Displacement:	2,050 tons
Length:	376 feet 6 inches
Beam:	39 feet 8 inches
Draft:	17 feet 9 inches
Propulsion:	2 propellers
Speed:	35 knots
Range:	6,500 nautical miles
Complement:	329
Armament:	5 × 5-inch guns

	4 × 40-mm anti-aircraft guns
	4 × 20-mm anti-aircraft guns
	10 × 21-inch torpedo tubes
	6 × depth-charge projectors
	2 × depth-charge tracks

USS Claxton (Commander Miles H. Hubbard)

USS *Claxton* (DD-571), a *Fletcher*-class destroyer, was the second ship of the U.S. Navy to be named for Thomas Claxton, born in Baltimore, Maryland. On February 4, 1944, while bombarding Sarime Plantation on Bougainville, USS *Claxton* was seriously damaged by an explosion aft, probably of two medium caliber shells. Despite her damage and fifteen wounded, USS *Claxton* completed her mission with her three forward guns, then sailed for temporary aid at Purvis Bay and permanent repairs on the west coast. She returned to action in August 1944, and assigned to screen escort carriers, took part in the invasion of the Palaus in September. Sailing north for the invasion of the Philippines, the destroyer covered the operations of underwater demolition teams preparing the beaches, then gave screening and fire support during the landings on October 20. In the phase of the Battle for Leyte Gulf known as the Battle of Surigao Strait on October 24–25, USS *Claxton* screened the battle line in the surface action which virtually destroyed the Japanese southern force.

Shipyard:	Consolidated Steel Corporation, Orange, Texas
Laid down:	June 25, 1941
Launched:	April 1, 1942
Commissioned:	December 8, 1942
Decommissioned:	April 18, 1946
Class and type:	*Fletcher*-class destroyer
Displacement:	2,080 tons
Length:	376 feet 6 inches
Beam:	39 feet 8 inches
Draft:	17 feet 9 inches
Propulsion:	2 propellers
Speed:	35 knots
Range:	6,500 nautical miles
Complement:	329
Armament:	5 × 5-inch guns
	10 × 40-mm anti-aircraft guns
	7 × 20-mm anti-aircraft guns
	10 × 21-inch torpedo tubes
	6 × depth-charge projectors
	2 × depth-charge tracks

USS Aulick (Commander John B. Andrew)

USS *Aulick* (DD-569) was an American *Fletcher*-class destroyer, was the second ship of the U.S. Navy to be named for Commodore John H. Aulick (1787–1873). On October 25, USS *Aulick* was part of the screen that was protecting American battleships and cruisers guarding the waters approaching Surigao Strait. The guns of these warships defeated the first of the Japanese southern forces so decisively that the second force turned back before really getting into action. As the Japanese retreated, the American ships, including USS *Aulick*, joined in sinking a Japanese destroyer of the *Akitsuki*-class. Before the Americans could finish off any more ships, they were ordered to return to Leyte Gulf.

Shipyard:	Consolidated Steel Corporation, Orange, Texas
Laid down:	May 14, 1941
Launched:	March 2, 1942
Class and type:	*Fletcher*-class destroyer
Displacement:	2,050 tons
Length:	376 feet 6 inches
Beam:	39 feet 8 inches
Draft:	17 feet 9 inches (5.41 meters)
Propulsion:	2 propellers
Speed:	35 knots
Range:	6,500 nautical miles
Complement:	329
Armament:	5 x 5-inch guns
	4 × 40-mm anti-aircraft guns
	4 × 20-mm anti-aircraft guns
	10 × 21-inch torpedo tubes
	6 × depth-charge projectors
	2 × depth-charge tracks

USS Cony (Commander Allen W. Moore)

USS *Cony* (DD/DDE-508), a *Fletcher*-class destroyer, was a ship of the U.S. Navy named for Joseph S. Cony (1834–1867), a naval officer during the Civil War. As Japanese forces entered Leyte Gulf on October 24 to begin the Battle of Surigao Strait phase of the epic Battle for Leyte Gulf, USS *Cony* took her station with the battleships and cruisers in the battle line, joining in the furious firing of the night action, and pursuing and constantly dueling with Japanese destroyer IJN *Asagumo*, finally sunk in the morning of October 25 with the aid of fire from another destroyer and two cruisers.

Shipyard:	Bath Iron Works, Bath, Maine
Laid down:	December 24, 1941
Launched:	August 16, 1942

Commissioned:	October 30, 1942
Decommissioned:	July 2, 1969
Class and type:	*Fletcher*-class destroyer
Displacement:	2,050 tons
Length:	376 feet 6 inches
Beam:	39 feet 8 inches
Draft:	17 feet 9 inches
Propulsion:	2 propellers
Speed:	35 knots
Range:	6,500 nautical miles
Complement:	336
Armament:	5 × 5-inch guns
	10 × 40-mm anti-aircraft guns
	7 × 20-mm anti-aircraft guns
	10 × 21-inch torpedo tubes
	6 × depth-charge projectors
	2 × depth-charge tracks

USS Thorn (Lieutenant Commander Frederick H. Schneider Jr.)

USS *Thorn* (DD-647), a *Gleaves*-class destroyer, was the first ship of the U.S. Navy to be named for Jonathan Thorn. During the fierce night action at Surigao Strait, USS *Thorn* screened the American battleships as they mauled the Japanese force coming through the strait. Originally ordered to conduct a torpedo attack on the Japanese battle line, USS *Thorn* and her mates were recalled as the Japanese retreated back south through Surigao Strait. She then formed up with the left-hand flank of cruisers and destroyers and headed south to polish off the cripples from the Japanese force. The American ships came across one Japanese destroyer and smothered it with fire which summarily dispatched it to the depths. During her seventeen salvoes, USS *Thorn* observed twelve hits.

Shipyard:	Federal Shipbuilding and Drydock Company, Kearny, New Jersey
Laid down:	November 15, 1942
Launched:	February 28, 1943
Commissioned:	April 1, 1943
Decommissioned:	May 6, 1946
Class and type:	*Gleaves*-class destroyer
Displacement:	1,630 tons
Length:	348 feet 3 inches
Beam:	36 feet 1 inch
Draft:	11 feet 10 inches
Propulsion:	4 boilers, 2 propellers

U.S. battleships heading for the Surigao Strait. (*U.S. Navy Archives*)

U.S. cruisers firing on the night of October 24, 1944. (*U.S. Navy Archives*)

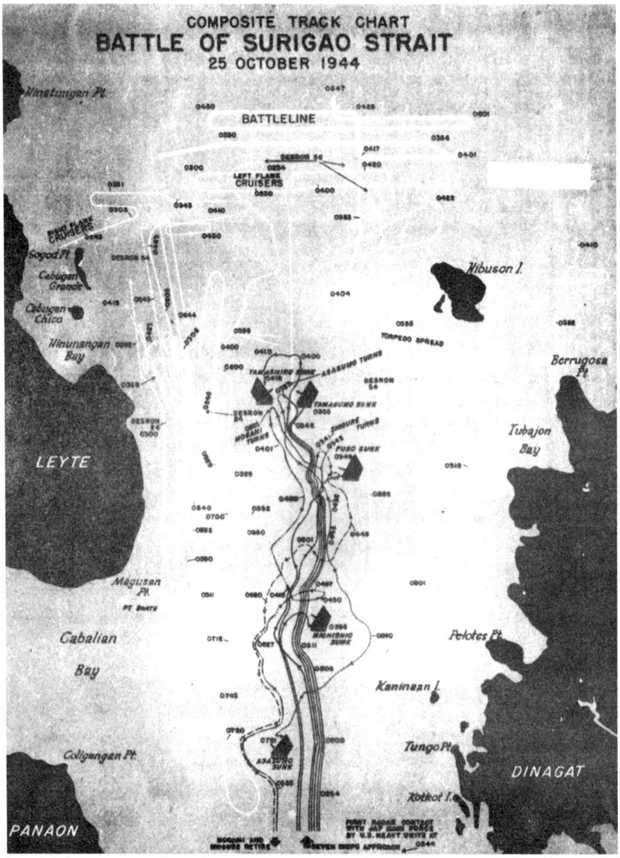

Left: Composite track chart of the Surigao Strait battle. (*Hyper War Foundation*)

Below: *PT-131* before the Battle of Surigao Strait, 1944. (*U.S. Navy Naval History and Heritage Command*)

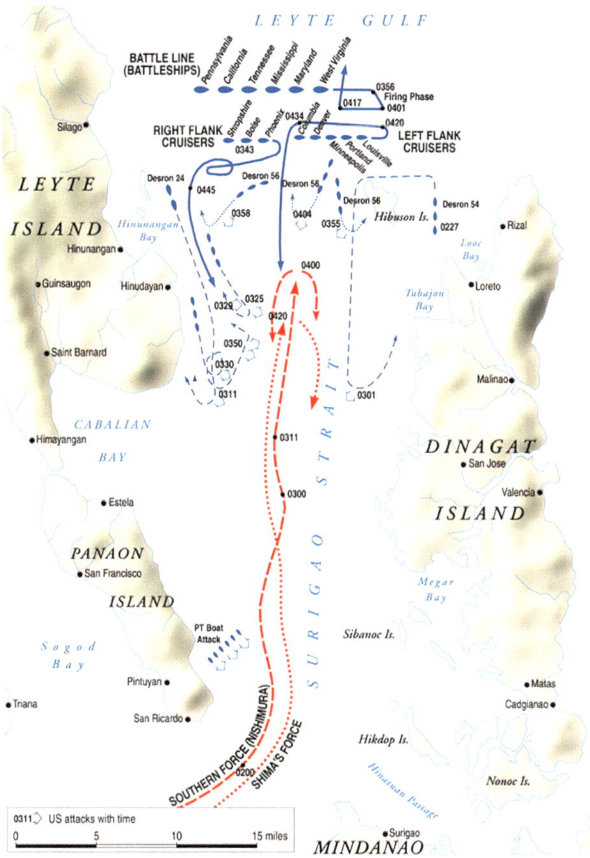

Right: Map of the Battle of Surigao Strait. (*U.S. Navy Archives*)

Below: Rear Admiral Jesse B. Oldendorf (left) and Vice Admiral Shoji Nishimura (right). (*U.S. Naval Institute Photo Archive*)

USS *West Virginia*. (*U.S. Navy Archives*)

USS *Maryland*. (*U.S. Navy Archives*)

Above: USS *California*. (*U.S. Navy Archives*)

Below: USS *Tennessee*. (*U.S. Navy Archives*)

Left: USS *Mississippi*. (*U.S. Navy Archives*)

Below: USS *Pennsylvania*. (*U.S. Navy Archives*)

IJN *Yamashiro*. (Imperial Japanese Navy Archives)

IJN *Fusō*. (*Imperial Japanese Navy Archives*)

IJN *Mogami*. (*Imperial Japanese Navy Archives*)

U.S. PT boat picks up a Japanese survivor. (*U.S. Navy Archives*)

Explosion aboard the USS *St. Louis* after she was hit be a *kamikaze* off the coast of Samar Island, on October 25, 1944. (*File photo by U.S. Navy/UPI*)

USS *West Virginia* firing during the Battle of Surigao Strait. (*File photo by U.S. Navy/UPI*)

Crewmen on USS *Birmingham* (CL-62) play fire hoses on the burning USS *Princeton* (CVL-23), as their ship comes alongside to assist in damage control measures, October 24, 1944. (*File photo by U.S. Navy/UPI*)

U.S. troops landing on Leyte in the Philippines. (*National Archives*)

General Douglas MacArthur (center) and others arriving ashore during the initial U.S. landings at Leyte, Philippines, October 20, 1944. (*National Archives*)

Unknown Japanese warship illuminated by search lights during the Battle of Surigao Strait. (*U.S. Navy Archives*)

A casemate gun crew services its 5-inch weapon while a line of sailors passes ammunition forward. (*U.S. Navy Archives*)

The Japanese Centre Force leaves Brunei Bay, Borneo, on October 22, 1944, *en route* to the Philippines. (*U.S. Navy Archives*)

Right: The battleship USS *Pennsylvania* fires its guns during shore bombardment in the Pacific. (*File photo by U.S. Navy/UPI*)

Below: The battleship USS *Pennsylvania* is silhouetted against the darkened sky by the gun flashes of her cohorts on the American battle line at Surigao Strait. (*File photo by U.S. Navy/UPI*)

Left: Able Seaman W. Thompson aboard HMAS *Warramunga* manning an Oerlikon anti-aircraft gun. (*State Library of Victoria*)

Below: The 5-inch/25 (12.7-cm) AA guns on USS *New Mexico* (BB-44) in June 1944. (*U.S. Naval Historical Center*)

Sailors firing Bofors 40-mm anti-aircraft guns on a Mk. 12 quadruple mount. (*File photo by U.S. Navy/UPI*)

Forward 14-inch guns of USS *California*. (*File photo by U.S. Navy/UPI*)

USS *Tennessee* underway on May 12, 1943. (*U.S. Naval Historical Center*)

Speed: 37.4 knots
Range: 6,500 nautical miles
Complement: 16 officers, 260 enlisted
Armament: 4 × 5-inch dual-purpose guns
4 × 40-mm anti-aircraft guns
5 × 20-mm anti-aircraft guns
5 × 21-inch Mk. 15 torpedo tubes
6 × depth-charge projectors
2 × depth-charge tracks

USS Welles (Lieutenant Commander John S. Slaughter)

USS *Welles* (DD-628), a *Gleaves*-class destroyer, was the second ship of the U.S. Navy to be named for Gideon Welles. She moved into Leyte Gulf on October 18, two days before the actual landings, to cover pre-invasion minesweeping and underwater demolition team operations. Her 5-inch shells also contributed to the pre-invasion bombardment of the objective. USS *Welles* joined the screen of Vice Admiral Jesse B. Oldendorf's line of old battleships which virtually annihilated the enemy force which attempted to push through the Surigao Strait south of Leyte on the night of October 24–25.

Shipyard: Seattle-Tacoma Shipbuilding Corporation, Seattle, Washington
Laid down: September 27, 1941
Launched: September 7, 1942
Commissioned: August 16, 1943
Decommissioned: February 4, 1946
Class and type: *Gleaves*-class destroyer
Displacement: 1,630 tons
Length: 348 feet 3 inches
Beam: 36 feet 1 inches
Draft: 11 feet 10 inches
Propulsion: 4 boilers, 2 propellers
Speed: 37.4 knots
Range: 6,500 nautical miles
Complement: 16 officers, 260 enlisted
Armament: 4 × 5-inch dual-purpose guns
4 × 40-mm anti-aircraft guns
7 × 20-mm anti-aircraft guns
5 × 21-inch Mk. 15 torpedo tubes
6 × depth-charge projectors
2 × depth-charge tracks

Left Flank (Rear Admiral J. B. Oldendorf)

USS Louisville (Captain Samuel H. Hurt)

USS *Louisville* (CA-28) was a *Northampton*-class heavy cruiser that fought at Guadalcanal, in the Aleutians, the invasion of the Marshall Islands, the Pelau Islands, the Battle of Leyte Gulf, and the invasion of Okinawa. She was Rear Admiral Oldendorf's flagship during the Battle of Surigao Strait. She was awarded thirteen battle stars for her actions during World War II.

Shipyard:	Puget Sound Naval Yard, Bremerton, Washington
Laid down:	July 4, 1928
Launched:	September 1, 1930
Commissioned:	January 15, 1931
Decommissioned:	June 17, 1946
Class and type:	*Northampton*-class cruiser
Displacement:	14,500 tons
Length:	600 feet 3 inches
Beam:	66 feet 1 inch
Draft:	23 feet
Propulsion:	8 White-Forster boilers, 4 screws, Parsons reduction steam turbines, Curtis cruising gears
Speed:	32.7 knots
Range:	10,000 nautical miles
Complement:	90 officers 601 enlisted
Armament:	9 × 8-inch guns
	8 × 5-inch dual-purpose anti-aircraft guns
	2 × 47-mm saluting guns
	5 × quad 40-mm anti-aircraft guns
	4 × twin 40-mm anti-aircraft guns
	27 × twin 20-mm anti-aircraft guns
	Aircraft carried: 2 × Seaplanes Curtiss SC Seahawk
	Aviation facilities: 1 × catapult and Seaplane hangar.
Armor:	Belt: 3–3¾ inches
	Deck: 1–2 inches
	Barbettes: 1½ inches
	Turrets: ¾–2½ inches
	Conning Tower: 1¼ inches

USS Portland (Captain Thomas G. W. Settle)

USS *Portland* was the lead ship of the third class of treaty cruisers to be constructed by the U.S. Navy following the Washington Naval Treaty of 1922, following the two vessels of the *Pensacola*-class ordered in 1926 and the six vessels of the *Northampton*-class ordered in 1927. Ordered for the U.S. Navy in Fiscal Year 1930. USS *Portland* was originally designated as a light cruiser, because of her thin armor, and given the hull classification symbol CL-33. She was reclassified a heavy cruiser, because of her 8-inch guns, with the symbol CA-33 on July 1, 1931, in accordance with the London Naval Treaty.

Shipyard:	Bethlehem Shipbuilding Corporation's Fore River Shipyard, Quincy, Massachusetts
Laid down:	February 17, 1930
Launched:	May 21, 1932
Commissioned:	February 23, 1933
Decommissioned:	July 12, 1946
Class and type:	*Portland*-class cruiser
Displacement:	10,000 tons
Length:	610 feet 3 inches
Beam:	66 feet 1 inch
Draft:	24 feet
Propulsion:	8 Yarrow boilers, 4 screws, Parsons reduction steam turbines
Speed:	32.7 knots
Range:	10,000 nautical miles
Complement:	91 officers 757 enlisted men
Armament:	9 × 8-inch guns
	8 × 5-inch anti-aircraft guns
	2 × 47-mm saluting guns
	4 × quad 40-mm anti-aircraft guns
	4 × twin 40-mm anti-aircraft guns
	17 × single 20-mm anti-aircraft guns
	Aircraft carried: 4 × floatplanes
	Aviation facilities: 2 × catapults
Armor:	Belt: 3¼–5 inches
	Deck: 2½ inches
	Barbettes: 1½ inches
	Turrets: 1½–2½ inches
	Conning Tower: 1¼ inches

USS Minneapolis (Captain Harry B. Slocum)

The *New Orleans*-class cruisers were the last U.S. cruisers built to the specifications and standards of the Washington Naval Treaty of 1922. Such ships, with a limit of 10,000 tons standard displacement and 8-inch main guns may be referred to as treaty cruisers. Originally classified a light cruiser, because of her thin armor, she was reclassified, soon after being laid down, a heavy cruiser, because of her 8-inch guns. The term heavy cruiser was not defined until the London Naval Treaty in 1930.

Shipyard:	Philadelphia Naval Shipyard, Philadelphia, Pennsylvania
Laid down:	June 27, 1931
Launched:	September 6, 1933
Commissioned:	May 19, 1934
Decommissioned:	February 10, 1947
Class and type:	*New Orleans*-class cruiser
Displacement:	10,110 tons
Length:	588 feet
Beam:	61 feet 9 inches
Draft:	23 feet 6 inches
Propulsion:	8 × Babcock & Wilcox boilers, 4 screws, Westinghouse geared turbines
Speed:	32.7 knots
Range:	2,000 nautical miles
Complement:	102 officers, 817 enlisted
Armament:	9 × 8-inch guns
	8 × 5-inch anti-aircraft guns
	2 × 47-mm saluting guns
	7 × quad 40-mm anti-aircraft guns
	9 × dual anti-aircraft guns
	Aircraft carried: 4 × floatplanes
	Aviation facilities: 2 × catapults
Armor:	Belt: 3–5 inches
	Deck: 1¼–2¼ inches
	Barbettes: 5 inches
	Turrets: 1½–8 inches
	Conning Tower: 5 inches

USS Denver (Captain Albert M. Bledsoe)

USS *Denver* (CL-58) was a *Cleveland*-class light cruiser. The *Denver* launched on April 4, 1942 by New York Shipbuilding Corp., Camden, New Jersey; sponsored by Miss L. J. Stapleton, daughter of the mayor of Denver; and commissioned on October 15, 1942, Captain Robert Carney in command. It was the second ship named for the city of Denver, Colorado.

Shipyard:	New York Shipbuilding Corporation, Camden, New Jersey
Laid down:	December 26, 1940

Launched:	April 4, 1942
Commissioned:	October 15, 1942
Decommissioned:	February 7, 1947
Class and type:	*Cleveland*-class light cruiser
Displacement:	14,358 tons
Length:	610 feet 1 inch
Beam:	66 feet 4 inch
Draft:	25 feet 6 inch
Propulsion:	4 634-psi steam boilers, 4 screws, 4 geared turbines
Speed:	32.5 knots
Range:	11,000 nautical miles
Complement:	1,255
Armament:	4 × triple 6-inch Mk. 16 guns
	6 × dual 5-inch anti-aircraft guns
	4 × quad 40-mm anti-aircraft guns
	8 × dual 40-mm anti-aircraft guns
	17 × single 20-mm Oerlikon anti-aircraft guns
Armor:	Belt: 3½–5 inches
	Deck: 2 inches
	Barbettes: 6 inches
	Turrets: 1½–6 inches
	Conning Tower: 2¼–5 inches
	Aircraft carried: 4 × floatplanes
	Aviation facilities: 2 × stern catapults

USS Columbia (Captain Maurice E. Curts)

USS *Columbia* (CL-56) was one of twenty-six U.S. Navy *Cleveland*-class light cruisers completed during or shortly after World War II. The ship, the sixth U.S. Navy ship to bear the name, was named for the city of Columbia, South Carolina. USS *Columbia* was commissioned in July 1942 and saw service in several campaigns in the Pacific. Like almost all her sister ships, she was decommissioned shortly after the end of the war, and never saw active service again.

Shipyard:	New York Shipbuilding Corporation, Camden, New Jersey
Laid down:	August 18, 1940
Launched:	December 17, 1941
Commissioned:	July 29, 1942
Decommissioned:	November 30, 1946
Class and type:	*Cleveland*-class light cruiser
Displacement:	14,358 tons
Length:	610 feet 1 inch
Beam:	66 feet 4 inch

Draft:	25 feet 6 inch
Propulsion:	4 × 634-psi Steam boilers, 4 screws, 4 geared turbines
Speed:	32.5 knots
Range:	11,000 nautical miles
Complement:	1,255
Armament:	4 × triple 6-inch Mk. 16 guns
	6 × dual 5-inch anti-aircraft guns
	8 × dual 40-mm anti-aircraft guns
	13 × single 20-mm Oerlikon anti-aircraft guns
Armor:	Belt: 3½–5 inches
	Deck: 2 inches
	Barbettes: 6 inches
	Turrets: 1½–6 inches
	Conning Tower: 2¼–5 inches
	Aircraft carried: 4 × floatplanes
	Aviation facilities: 2 × stern catapults

USS Newcomb (Commander Lawrence B. Cook)

USS *Newcomb* (DD-586) was a *Fletcher*-class destroyer in the U.S. Navy during World War II. She was the only ship named for Commodore Frank H. Newcomb of the U.S. Revenue Cutter Service, Congressional Gold Medal recipient from the Spanish American War. USS *Newcomb* was laid down on March 19, 1943 by Boston Navy Yard and launched on July 4, 1943, sponsored by Mrs. C. C. Baughman.

Shipyard:	Boston Navy Yard, Boston, Massachusetts
Laid down:	March 19, 1943
Launched:	July 4, 1943
Commissioned:	November 10, 1943
Decommissioned:	November 20, 1945
Class and type:	*Fletcher*-class destroyer
Displacement:	2,050 tons
Length:	376 feet 6 inches
Beam:	39 feet 8 inches
Draft:	17 feet 9 inches
Propulsion:	2 propellers
Speed:	35 knots
Range:	6,500 nautical miles
Complement:	336
Armament:	5 × 5-inch guns
	10 × 40-mm anti-aircraft guns
	7 × 20-mm anti-aircraft guns

10 × 21-inch torpedo tubes
6 × depth-charge projectors
2 × depth-charge tracks

USS Richard P. Leary (Commander Frederic S. Habecker)

USS *Richard P. Leary* (DD-664) was a *Fletcher*-class destroyer of the U.S. Navy, named for Rear Admiral Richard P. Leary (1842–1901). Following shakedown off Bermuda, USS *Richard P. Leary* sailed via the Panama Canal for Pearl Harbor. After escort duty to Eniwetok and Saipan in July, she supported the landings at Peleliu September 15, 1944, and at Leyte October 20. During the Battle of Surigao Strait on October 25, she launched torpedoes at the Japanese battleship IJN *Yamashiro*, splashed one enemy plane, and guarded the damaged destroyer USS *Albert W. Grant*.

Shipyard:	Boston Navy Yard, Boston, Massachusetts
Laid down:	July 4, 1943
Launched:	October 6, 1943
Commissioned:	February 23, 1944
Decommissioned:	December 10, 1946
Class and type:	*Fletcher*-class destroyer
Displacement:	2,083 tons
Length:	376 feet 5 inches
Beam:	39 feet 7 inches
Draft:	13 feet 9 inches
Propulsion:	2 propellers
Speed:	35 knots
Range:	6,500 nautical miles
Complement:	329
Armament:	5 × 5-inch guns
	10 × 40-mm anti-aircraft guns
	7 × 20-mm anti-aircraft guns
	10 × 21-inch torpedo tubes
	6 × depth-charge projectors
	2 × depth-charge tracks

USS Albert W. Grant (Commander Terrell A. Nisewaner)

USS *Albert W. Grant* (DD-649) was a *Fletcher*-class destroyer in the U.S. Navy during World War II. She was the only ship named for Vice Admiral Albert W. Grant (1856–1930), an admiral during World War I. USS *Albert W. Grant* was laid down on December 30, 1942 at North Charleston, South Carolina, by the Charleston Navy Yard; launched on May 29, 1943, sponsored by Miss Nell Preston Grant, granddaughter of Admiral Grant; and commissioned on

November 24, 1943, Commander T. A. Nisewaner in command. That day, the destroyer departed Charleston Navy Yard for a shakedown cruise to Bermuda and returned to Charleston Navy Yard on January 29, 1944 for minor alterations.

Shipyard:	Charleston Navy Yard, Charleston, South Carolina
Laid down:	December 30, 1942
Launched:	May 29, 1943
Commissioned:	November 24, 1943
Decommissioned:	July 16, 1946
Class and type:	*Fletcher*-class destroyer
Displacement:	2,050 tons
Length:	376 feet 5 inches
Beam:	39 feet 7 inches
Draft:	13 feet 9 inches
Propulsion:	geared turbines, 2 propellers
Speed:	35.2 knots
Range:	6,500 nautical miles
Complement:	329
Armament:	5 × 5-inch dual-purpose guns
	10 × 40-mm guns anti-aircraft
	7 × Oerlikon 20-mm guns
	10 × 21-inch torpedo tubes
	6 × depth-charge projectors
	2 × depth-charge tracks

USS *Robinson* (Commander Elonzo B. Grantham, Jr.)

USS *Robinson* (DD-562), a *Fletcher*-class destroyer, was the second ship of the U.S. Navy to be named for Captain Isaiah Robinson (died *c.* 1781), who served in the Continental Navy. After shakedown out of San Diego, USS *Robinson* departed Seattle on April 12 for Hawaii. Arriving at Pearl Harbor on April 21, 1944, she trained until getting underway on May 29 with Task Force 52 (TF 52), headed for Eniwetok and the Marianas.

Shipyard:	Seattle-Tacoma Shipbuilding Corporation, Seattle, Washington
Laid down:	August 12, 1942
Launched:	August 28, 1943
Commissioned:	January 31, 1944
Decommissioned:	April 1, 1964
Class and type:	*Fletcher*-class destroyer
Displacement:	2,050 tons
Length:	376 feet 6 inches

Beam:	39 feet 8 inches
Draft:	17 feet 9 inches
Propulsion:	2 propellers
Speed:	35 knots
Range:	6,500 nautical miles
Complement:	273
Armament:	5 × 5-inch guns
	4 × 40-mm anti-aircraft guns
	4 × 20-mm anti-aircraft guns
	10 × 21-inch torpedo tubes
	6 × depth-charge projectors
	2 × depth-charge tracks

USS Halford (Commander Robert J. Hardy)

USS *Halford* (DD-480), a *Fletcher*-class destroyer, was a ship of the U.S. Navy named for Lieutenant William Halford (1841–1919), a recipient of the Medal of Honor. USS *Halford* was one of the three *Fletcher*-class destroyers to be completed, out of six planned, with a catapult for a floatplane, the others being the *Pringle* and *Stevens*. The catapult and an aircraft crane were located just aft of the No. 2 smokestack, in place of the aft-torpedo tube mount, 5-inch mount No. 3, and the second deck of the aft-deck house which normally carried a twin 40-mm anti-aircraft gun on most ships of the class. The twin 40-mm mount was moved to the fantail, just forward of the depth charge racks, where most ships of the class carried 20-mm mounts. It was intended that the floatplane be used for scouting for the destroyer flotilla, which the ship was attached to. It would be launched by the catapult, land on the water next to the ship, and be recovered by the aircraft crane. It turned out to be not operationally suitable for the intended purpose, and the three ships were ultimately converted to the standard *Fletcher*-class configuration.

Shipyard:	Puget Sound Naval Shipyard, Bremerton, Washington
Laid down:	June 3, 1941
Launched:	October 29, 1942
Commissioned:	April 10, 1943
Decommissioned:	May 15, 1946
Class and type:	*Fletcher*-class destroyer
Displacement:	2,050 tons
Length:	376 feet 6 inches
Beam:	39 feet 8 inches
Draft:	17 feet 9 inches
Propulsion:	2 propellers
Speed:	35 knots
Range:	6,500 nautical miles

Complement:	273
Armament:	5 × 5-inch guns
	6 × 40-mm anti-aircraft guns
	11 × Oerlikon 20-mm anti-aircraft guns
	10 × 21-inch torpedo tubes
	6 × depth-charge projectors
	2 × depth-charge tracks

USS Bryant (Commander Paul L. High)

After fitting out at the Charleston Navy Yard, USS *Bryant* conducted a month-long shakedown cruise near Bermuda before returning to the Charleston Navy Yard on February 28, 1944 for a ten-day, post-shakedown availability. The destroyer then set sail for the Boston Navy Yard and arrived there on the 13th. Two days later, she and USS *McNair* got underway for the Pacific as escorts for USS *Wasp*. The trio transited the Panama Canal on the 20th and then steamed north for a one-day replenishment stop at San Diego before heading on toward Hawaii. On April 3, USS *Bryant* entered Pearl Harbor and, following three days of exercises there, devoted the remainder of April and the beginning of May to a yard availability to repair leaks in her reduction gear and fireroom hull. On the 21st, she joined TG 77.2 and readied herself to meet a Japanese attempt to force through Surigao Strait and destroy the American transports in Surigao Strait.

Shipyard:	Charleston Navy Yard, Charleston, South Carolina
Laid down:	December 30, 1942
Launched:	May 29, 1943
Commissioned:	December 4, 1943
Decommissioned:	January 15, 1947
Class and type:	*Fletcher*-class destroyer
Displacement:	2,050 tons
Length:	376 feet 5 inches
Beam:	39 feet 7 inches
Draft:	17 feet 9 inches
Propulsion:	2 propellers, geared turbines
Speed:	35 knots
Range:	6,500 nautical miles
Complement:	329
Armament:	5 × 5-inch guns
	4 × 40-mm anti-aircraft guns
	4 × 20-mm guns anti-aircraft guns
	10 × 21-inch torpedo tubes
	6 × depth-charge projectors
	2 × depth-charge tracks

USS *Heywood L. Edwards* (Commander Joe W. Boulware)

USS *Heywood L. Edwards* (DD-663) was a *Fletcher*-class destroyer of the U.S. Navy, named for Lieutenant Cdr. Heywood L. Edwards (1905–1941), captain of the destroyer USS *Reuben James*, the first U.S. Navy ship sunk in World War II. USS *Heywood L. Edwards* proceeded to Manus Island, Admiralty Islands, where she arrived on October 1. There she joined with Rear Admiral Jesse B. Oldendorf's fire support and bombardment group for the historic return to the Philippines, departing for Leyte October 12, 1944. She conducted pre-invasion bombardment on October 18–20 and provided gunfire support for the landings on October 20. This work continued for four days under frequent enemy air attack. Then USS *Heywood L. Edwards* joined once more with Rear Admiral Oldendorf's force for the impending Battle of Surigao Strait, as the Japanese made a desperate attempt to destroy the landing force.

Shipyard:	Boston Navy Yard, Boston, Massachusetts
Laid down:	July 4, 1943
Launched:	October 6, 1943
Commissioned:	January 26, 1944
Decommissioned:	July 1, 1946
Class and type:	*Fletcher*-class destroyer
Displacement:	2,083 tons
Length:	376 feet 6 inches
Beam:	39 feet 8 inches
Draft:	13 feet 9 inches
Propulsion:	2 propellers
Speed:	35 knots
Range:	6,500 nautical miles
Complement:	319
Armament:	5 × 5-inch guns
	4 × 40-mm anti-aircraft guns
	4 × 20-mm anti-aircraft guns
	10 × 21-inch torpedo tubes
	6 × depth-charge projectors
	2 × depth-charge tracks

USS *Bennion* (Commander Joshua W. Cooper)

USS *Bennion* (DD-662) was a *Fletcher*-class destroyer of the U.S. Navy. The ship was named for Captain Mervyn S. Bennion who was killed in action during the Japanese attack on Pearl Harbor, while in command of USS *West Virginia*. Captain Bennion was posthumously awarded the Medal of Honor. During the Battle of Surigao Strait, in October 1944, USS *Bennion* assisted in sinking the Japanese battleship IJN *Yamashiro* with torpedoes.

Shipyard:	Boston Navy Yard, Boston, Massachusetts
Laid down:	March 19, 1943
Launched:	July 4, 1943
Commissioned:	December 14, 1943
Decommissioned:	June 20, 1946
Class and type:	*Fletcher*-class destroyer
Displacement:	2,050 tons
Length:	376 feet 6 inches
Beam:	39 feet 8 inches
Draft:	17 feet 9 inches
Propulsion:	2 propellers
Speed:	35 knots
Range:	6,500 nautical miles
Complement:	329
Armament:	5 × 5-inch guns
	4 × 40-mm anti-aircraft guns
	4 × 20-mm anti-aircraft guns
	10 × 21-inch torpedo tubes
	6 × depth-charge projectors
	2 × depth-charge tracks

USS Leutze (Commander Barton A. Robbins, Jr.)

USS *Leutze* (DD-481) was a *Fletcher*-class destroyer in the U.S. Navy during World War II. She was named for Admiral Eugene H. C. Leutze (1847–1931). USS *Leutze* completed the necessary performance trials and continued the training of her crew on escort missions to Pearl Harbor and Eniwetok during June and July 1944. On August 2, she departed Seattle for the war zone a sleek new destroyer and returned one year and one day later a battered veteran about to be scrapped. In this short interval, she had played a part in five invasions and a major naval battle before a *kamikaze* ended her fighting days.

Shipyard:	Puget Sound Naval Shipyard, Bremerton, Washington
Laid down:	June 3, 1941
Launched:	October 29, 1942
Commissioned:	March 4, 1944
Decommissioned:	December 6, 1945
Class and type:	*Fletcher*-class destroyer
Displacement:	2,050 tons
Length:	376 feet 6 inches
Beam:	39 feet
Draft:	17 feet 9 inches
Propulsion:	2 propellers, geared turbines

Speed:	38 knots
Range:	6,500 nautical miles
Complement:	329
Armament:	5 × 5-inch guns
	10 × 40-mm anti-aircraft guns
	7 × 20-mm anti-aircraft guns
	10 × 21-in torpedo tubes
	6 × depth-charge projectors
	2 × depth-charge tracks

Right Flank (Rear Admiral R. S. Berkey)

HMAS Shropshire (Captain H. A. Showers)

HMS *Shropshire* was a Royal Navy heavy cruiser of the London subclass of *County*-class cruisers. She is the only warship to have been named after Shropshire, England. Completed in 1929, HMAS *Shropshire* served with the Royal Navy until 1942, when she was transferred to the Royal Australian Navy following the loss of sister ship HMAS *Canberra*. Commissioned as HMAS *Shropshire*, the ship remained in Royal Australian Navy service until 1949 and was sold for scrap in 1954.

Shipyard:	William Beardmore and Company, Dalmuir, Scotland
Laid down:	February 24, 1927
Launched:	July 5, 1928
Completed:	September 12, 1929
Commissioned:	September 24, 1929
Decommissioned:	December 23, 1942
Fate:	Transferred to Royal Australian Navy
Commissioned:	April 20, 1943
Decommissioned:	November 10, 1949
Class and type:	*County*-class heavy cruiser
Displacement:	13,315 tons
Length:	633 feet
Beam:	66 feet
Draft:	21 feet
Propulsion:	8 Admiralty 3-drum boilers, 4-shaft Parsons geared turbines
Speed:	32 knots
Range:	2,546 nautical miles
Complement:	1,000
Armament:	8 × 8-inch Mk. VIII dual guns
	4 × QF 4-inch Mk. XVI dual anti-aircraft guns

	2 × 40-mm eight-barrel anti-aircraft guns
	6 × 20-mm single anti-aircraft guns
	7 × 20-mm dual anti-aircraft guns
	2 × 0.5-inch quadruple Vickers machine guns
	2 × quadruple 21-inch torpedo tubes
Aircraft carried:	One aircraft, one catapult. Three planes used during service; Fairey III, Hawker Osprey, Supermarine Walrus
Armor:	1–4-inch magazine box protection
	1.375-inch deck
	1-inch side-plating, turrets, and bulkheads
	4.5-inch belt
	4-inch internal boiler room sides

USS Phoenix (Captain Jack H. Duncan)

USS *Phoenix* (CL-46) was a light cruiser of the *Brooklyn*-class cruiser family. She was the third *Phoenix* of the U.S. Navy. In the Battle of Leyte Gulf, USS *Phoenix* was a unit of Rear Admiral Jesse Oldendorf's group which annihilated the Japanese Southern Force in the Battle of Surigao Strait. USS *Phoenix* fired four spotting salvoes, and when the fourth hit, opened-up with all of her 6-inch batteries. The target later proved to be IJN *Yamashiro*, which sank after twenty-seven minutes of concentrated fire from the American fleet.

Shipyard:	New York Shipbuilding Corporation, Camden, New Jersey
Laid down:	April 25, 1935
Launched:	March 19, 1938
Commissioned:	October 3, 1938
Decommissioned:	July 3, 1946
Class and type:	*Brooklyn*-class cruiser
Displacement:	12,403 tons
Length:	608 feet 4 inches
Beam:	61 feet 7 inch (18.77 meters)
Draft:	24 feet
Propulsion:	8 steam boilers, 4 screws, 4 geared turbines
Speed:	32.5 knots
Complement:	868
Armament:	15 × 6-inch guns
	8 × 5-inch anti-aircraft guns
	8 × 0.50-inch machine guns
Armor:	Belt: 3¼–5 inches
	Deck: 2 inches
	Barbettes: 6 inches
	Turrets: 1¼–6 inches

Conning Tower: 2¼–5 inches
Aircraft carried: 4 × SOC Seagull floatplanes
Aviation facilities: 2 × stern catapults

USS Boise (Captain John S. Roberts)

USS *Boise* (CL-47) was a light cruiser of the *Brooklyn*-class in the U.S. Navy. The cruiser was named for Boise, the capital city of the state of Idaho. Commissioned in 1938, she saw extensive service during World War II, taking part in fighting in the Mediterranean and Pacific theaters. As the battle front advanced into the Philippines, taking part in the Leyte invasion on October 20–24 and Battle of Surigao Strait on October 25.

Shipyard:	Newport News Shipbuilding and Drydock Company, Newport News, Virginia
Laid down:	April 1, 1935
Launched:	December 3, 1936
Commissioned:	August 12, 1938
Decommissioned:	July 1, 1946
Class and type:	*Brooklyn*-class cruiser
Displacement:	12,403 tons
Length:	608 feet 4 inches
Beam:	61 feet 7 inches
Draft:	24 feet
Propulsion:	8 steam boilers, 4 screws, 4 geared turbines
Speed:	32.5 knots
Complement:	868
Armament:	15 × 6-inch Mk. 16 guns 8 × 5-inch anti-aircraft guns 8 × 0.50-inch machine guns
Armor:	Belt: 3¼–5 inches Deck: 2 inches Barbettes: 6 inches Turrets: 1¼–6 inches Conning Tower: 2¼–5 inches Aircraft carried: 4 × SOC Seagull floatplanes Aviation facilities: 2 × stern catapults

USS Hutchins (Commander Caleb B. Laning)

USS *Hutchins* (DD-476), a *Fletcher*-class destroyer, was a ship of the U.S. Navy named for Lieutenant Carlton B. Hutchins (1904–1938), a naval aviator who was posthumously awarded the Medal of Honor. Built by Boston Navy Yard, the destroyer entered service in 1942 and was assigned to the Pacific fleet in

March 1943. USS *Hutchins* took part in campaigns in the Aleutian Islands, amphibious landings at Cape Gloucester, the Wakde–Sarmi operation and Iwo Jima. USS *Hutchins* joined Admiral Jesse Oldendorf's surface forces waiting in Surigao Strait for Admiral Shōji Nishimura's Southern Force.

Shipyard:	Boston Navy Yard, Boston, Massachusetts
Laid down:	September 27, 1941
Launched:	February 20, 1942
Commissioned:	November 17, 1942
Decommissioned:	November 30, 1945
Class and type:	*Fletcher*-class destroyer
Displacement:	2,050 tons
Length:	376 feet 6 inches
Beam:	39 feet 8 inches
Draft:	17 feet 9 inches
Propulsion:	2 propellers
Speed:	35 knots
Range:	6,500 nautical miles
Complement:	336
Armament:	5 × 5-inch guns
	10 × 40-mm anti-aircraft guns
	7 × 20-mm anti-aircraft guns
	10 × 21-inch torpedo tubes
	6 × depth-charge projectors
	2 × depth-charge tracks

USS Bache (Commander Robert C. Morton)

USS *Bache* (DD/DDE-470), a *Fletcher*-class destroyer, was the second ship of the U.S. Navy of that name. The destroyer was named for Commander George M. Bache. Until October 29, 1944, USS *Bache* operated with the Seventh Fleet taking part in the bombardment of New Britain Islands (December 26, 1943), Los Negros, Admiralty Islands, landings (February 29, 1944); bombardment of Ndrillo and Karunia Islands in the Admiralties (March 4–7); bombardment of various assault beaches and targets of opportunity on New Guinea and adjacent islands (April 10–September 15); bombardment of Leyte Island Philippine Islands (October 20); and finally, October 25, 1944, as a unit of Task Group 77.3 she took part in the overwhelming victory of Battle of Surigao Strait.

Shipyard:	Bethlehem Shipbuilding Corporation, Staten Island, New York
Laid down:	November 19, 1941
Launched:	July 7, 1942

Commissioned:	November 14, 1942
Decommissioned:	March 1, 1968
Class and type:	*Fletcher*-class destroyer
Displacement:	2,050 tons
Length:	376 feet 6 inches
Beam:	39 feet 8 inches
Draft:	17 feet 9 inches
Propulsion:	2 propellers
Speed:	35 knots
Range:	6,500 nautical miles
Complement:	329
Armament:	5 × 5-inch guns
	10 × 40-mm anti-aircraft guns
	7 × 20-mm anti-aircraft guns
	10 × 21-inch torpedo tubes
	6 × depth-charge projectors
	2 × depth-charge tracks

USS Beale (Commander Doyle M. Coffee)

USS *Beale* (DD/DDE-471), a *Fletcher*-class destroyer, was the second ship of the U.S. Navy to be named for Lieutenant Edward Fitzgerald Beale (1822–1893). On the October 13, 1944, USS *Beale*'s close covering group, TG 77.3, stood out of the bay in company with the Northern LST Group whose landings on Leyte near Tacloban at the head of San Pedro Bay it was to support. The warship and her colleagues escorted the Northern Attack Force into Leyte Gulf during the night of October 19–20, and together they made their way toward the northwestern corner of the gulf. While the amphibious forces approached their stations and took up their positions, the battleships of the fire support unit, north, subjected the target area to a withering barrage. At the conclusion of that overture, USS *Beale* and her compatriots in TG 77.3 moved in to play their supporting roles in the opening act of the performance.

Shipyard:	Bethlehem Mariners Harbor, Staten Island, New York
Laid down:	December 19, 1941
Launched:	August 24, 1942
Commissioned:	December 23, 1942
Decommissioned:	September 30, 1968
Class and type:	*Fletcher*-class destroyer
Displacement:	2,050 tons
Length:	376 feet 6 inches
Beam:	39 feet 8 inches
Draft:	17 feet 9 inches

Propulsion:	2 propellers
Speed:	35 knots
Range:	6,500 nautical miles
Complement:	329
Armament:	5 × 5-inch guns
	10 × 40-mm anti-aircraft guns
	7 × 20-mm anti-aircraft guns
	10 × 21-inch torpedo tubes
	6 × depth-charge projectors
	2 × depth-charge tracks

USS Daly (Commander Richard G. Visser)

USS *Daly* (DD-519), a *Fletcher*-class destroyer, was a ship of the U.S. Navy named for Marine Sergeant Major Daniel Daly (1873–1937), one of the very few people to be twice awarded the Medal of Honor. From May 15 to August 5, 1944, USS *Daly* served in the Western New Guinea operations. She provided fire support and bombardment in the Toem–Wakde–Sarmi area, off Biak, Noemfoor, and Mios Woendi Islands, and acted as radar guard and linking ship between the landing and covering forces off Cape Sansapor. After a brief overhaul at Sydney, Australia, she sortied from Humboldt Bay on September 11 for the invasion of Morotai, providing patrol and fire support before returning to Manus on September 29. She got underway on October 11 to render fire support to the troops invading Leyte and joined in the surface action with Japanese ships during the Battle of Surigao Strait phase of the decisive Battle for Leyte Gulf on October 25 and 26.

Shipyard:	Bethlehem Mariners Harbor, Staten Island, New York
Laid down:	April 29, 1942
Launched:	October 24, 1942
Commissioned:	March 10, 1943
Decommissioned:	April 18, 1946
Class and type:	*Fletcher*-class destroyer
Displacement:	2,050 tons
Length:	376 feet 6 inches
Beam:	39 feet 8 inches
Draft:	17 feet 9 inches
Propulsion:	2 propellers
Speed:	35 knots
Range:	6,500 nautical miles
Complement:	336
Armament:	5 × 5-inch guns
	10 × 40-mm anti-aircraft guns

7 × 20-mm anti-aircraft guns
10 × 21-inch torpedo tubes
6 × depth-charge projectors
2 × depth-charge tracks

USS Killen (Commander Edward G. Corey)

USS *Killen* (DD-593), a *Fletcher*-class destroyer, was a ship of the U.S. Navy named for Edward Killen, who served in the First Barbary War. Killen volunteered for Lieutenant Stephen Decatur's daring 1804 expedition into Tripoli Harbor to destroy Philadelphia, a U.S. frigate captured by Tripolitan pirates. When the Japanese Navy decided to contest the landings in the Battle of Leyte Gulf, USS *Killen*'s squadron engaged the enemy at Surigao Strait. On the morning of October 25, at 3:25 a.m., she launched five torpedoes toward battleship IJN *Yamashiro*. One hit, slowing her to 5 knots, enabled other American destroyers to maneuver for the kill.

Shipyard:	Puget Sound Naval Shipyard, Bremerton, Washington
Laid down:	November 26, 1941
Launched:	January 10, 1943
Commissioned:	May 4, 1944
Decommissioned:	July 9, 1946
Class and type:	*Fletcher*-class destroyer
Displacement:	2,050 tons
Length:	376 feet 6 inches
Beam:	39 feet 8 inches
Draft:	17 feet 9 inches
Propulsion:	2 propellers
Speed:	35 knots
Range:	6,500 nautical miles
Complement:	329
Armament:	5 × 5-inch guns 4 × 40-mm anti-aircraft guns 4 × 20-mm anti-aircraft guns 10 × 21-inch torpedo tubes 6 × depth-charge projector

HMAS Arunta (Commander A. E. Buchanan)

HMAS *Arunta* (I30/D5/D130) was a *Tribal*-class destroyer of the Royal Australian Navy. Named for the Arrernte Aboriginal peoples, the destroyer was laid down in 1939 and commissioned into the Royal Australian Navy in 1942. On October 13, HMAS *Arunta* formed part of the Allied fleet bound for Leyte Gulf in the Philippines and was part of the Allied ambush of a Japanese fleet during the Battle of Surigao Strait on October 25.

Shipyard:	Cockatoo Docks and Engineering Company, Sydney, Australia
Laid down:	November 15, 1939
Launched:	December 1, 1940
Commissioned:	March 30, 1942
Decommissioned:	December 21, 1956
Class and type:	*Tribal*-class destroyer
Displacement:	1,990 tons
Length:	377 feet 1 inch
Beam:	36 feet 4.75 inches
Draft:	9 feet
Propulsion:	Parsons geared turbines, twin screws.
Speed:	36.5 knots
Complement:	13 officers, 247 enlisted
Armament:	6 × 4.7-inch QF Mk. XII guns 2 × 4-inch QF Mk. XVI anti-aircraft guns 6 × 20-mm Oerlikon anti-aircraft guns 1 × 40-mm quadruple pom-pom gun 1 × 4-tube 21-inch torpedo launcher 2 × depth-charge throwers (46 charges)
Sensors and processing systems:	Radar: SG1, SG4, 285P4, 253P

USS Remey (Lieutenant Commander Reid P. Fiala)

USS *Remey* (DD-688) was a *Fletcher*-class destroyer of the U.S. Navy, named for Rear Admiral George C. Remey (1841–1928). Departing for Leyte on October 11, 1944, USS *Remey* passed the northern tip of Dinagat Island on the night of October 19–20. In the morning, she screened her charges, landing craft, to the assault area, then took up station in lower Surigao Strait. Through the 24th, she continued her anti-small boat and anti-aircraft patrols, then prepared to meet an enemy surface force reported standing toward the southern entrance to Surigao Strait.

Shipyard:	Bath Iron Works, Bath, Maine
Laid down:	March 22, 1943
Launched:	July 25, 1943
Commissioned:	September 30, 1943
Decommissioned:	December 30, 1963
Class and type:	*Fletcher*-class destroyer
Displacement:	2,050 tons
Length:	376.4 feet
Beam:	39.6 feet
Draft:	13.8 feet

Propulsion:	2 propellers, geared turbines
Speed:	38 knots
Range:	6,500 nautical miles
Complement:	329
Armament:	5 × 5-inch guns
	10 × 40-mm anti-aircraft guns
	7 × 20-mm anti-aircraft guns
	10 × 21-inch torpedo tubes
	6 × depth-charge projectors
	2 × depth-charge tracks

USS McGowan (Commander William R. Cox)

USS *McGowan* (DD-678) was a *Fletcher*-class destroyer of the U.S. Navy, named for Rear Admiral Samuel McGowan (1870–1934). At the end of July, USS *McGowan* sailed to Guadalcanal to prepare for the amphibious assault on the Palaus. Her TG 32.2 sortied on September 8, arriving in the transport area east of the Palaus on the 15th. The *McGowan* remained in that area until the 17th when, with her transport group, she moved toward Angaur Island. There she took position in the anti-submarine screen, remaining through the 22nd. The destroyer then cruised south to Manus Island, the staging area for the upcoming Leyte operation. On October 11, she got underway, screening LSTs and LCIs of the 7th Fleet to Leyte. During the assault on Dulag, on October 20 she served as fighter-director for aircraft covering the landings. In the early hours of the 25th, she participated in the attack on the Japanese fleet in the Surigao Strait.

Shipyard:	Federal Shipbuilding & Dry Dock Co., Kearny, New Jersey
Laid down:	June 30, 1943
Launched:	November 14, 1943
Commissioned:	December 20, 1943
Decommissioned:	November 30, 1960
Class and type:	*Fletcher*-class destroyer
Displacement:	2,050 tons
Length:	376 feet 6 inches
Beam:	39 feet 8 inches
Draft:	17 feet 9 inches
Propulsion:	2 propellers, geared turbines
Speed:	38 knots
Range:	6,500 nautical miles
Complement:	319
Armament:	5 × 5-inch guns
	10 × 40-mm anti-aircraft guns

7 × 20-mm anti-aircraft guns
10 × 21-inch torpedo tubes
6 × depth-charge projectors
2 × depth-charge tracks

USS Melvin (Commander Barry K. Atkins)

USS *Melvin* (DD-680), a *Fletcher*-class destroyer, was the second ship of the U.S. Navy to be named for Lieutenant, junior grade, John T. Melvin (1887–1917). With TG 79.11, USS *Melvin* sailed on October 11 toward the Philippines in the screen of the landing craft to be used in the assault on Dulag. Soon after midnight on October 20, she entered Leyte Gulf and took up her assigned screening station between Dinagat and Hibuson Islands, carrying out similar screening patrols for the next four days. In the early hours of the 25th, she joined in the torpedo attack by Destroyer Squadron 54, which opened the Battle of Surigao Strait.

Shipyard:	Federal Shipbuilding & Dry Dock Company, Kearny, New Jersey
Laid down:	July 6, 1943
Launched:	October 17, 1943
Commissioned:	November 24, 1943
Decommissioned:	January 13, 1954
Class and type:	*Fletcher*-class destroyer
Displacement:	2,050 tons
Length:	376 feet 6 inches
Beam:	39 feet 9 inches
Draft:	17 feet 9 inches
Propulsion:	2 propellers
Speed:	38 knots
Range:	6,500 nautical miles
Complement:	273
Armament:	5 × 5-inch guns 10 × 40-mm anti-aircraft guns 7 × 20-mm anti-aircraft guns 10 × 21-inch torpedo tubes 6 × depth-charge projectors 2 × depth-charge tracks

USS Mertz (Commander W. S. Estabrook, Jr.)

USS *Mertz* (DD-691) was a World War II-era *Fletcher*-class destroyer in the service of the U.S. Navy, named after Rear Admiral Albert Mertz. On October 20, D-Day for the Leyte landing forces, USS *Mertz* escorted landing craft through air attacks to the beach and later in the day patrolled off Dinagat Island at the entrance to Leyte Gulf. Early in the morning of October 25 as the Japanese Southern Force approached Leyte Gulf through the Mindanao Sea, USS *Mertz* and USS *McNair* patrolled between Desolation Point and Homonhon Island, lest the enemy fleet choose to steam north along the east coast of Dinagat Island to attack the Allied beachhead. When the Japanese entered Surigao Strait, Rear Admiral Jesse B. Oldendorf's force met and destroyed the enemy armada in the classic "crossing of the T" maneuver known as the Battle of Surigao Strait, part of the overall Battle of Leyte Gulf. Later that same day USS *Mertz* splashed a Zero at several hundred yards with heavy machine-gun fire.

Shipyard:	Bath Iron Works, Bath, Maine
Laid down:	May 10, 1943
Launched:	September 11, 1943
Commissioned:	November 19, 1943
Decommissioned:	April 23, 1946
Class and type:	*Fletcher*-class destroyer
Displacement:	2,050 tons
Length:	376 feet 6 inches
Beam:	39 feet 8 inches
Draft:	17 feet 9 inches
Propulsion:	2 propellers
Speed:	35 knots
Range:	6,500 nautical miles
Complement:	336
Armament:	5 × 5-inch guns
	10 × 40-mm anti-aircraft guns
	7 × 20-mm anti-aircraft guns
	10 × 21-inch torpedo tubes
	6 × depth-charge projectors
	2 × depth-charge tracks

USS McDermut (Commander Carter B. Jennings)

USS *McDermut* (DD-677) was a *Fletcher*-class destroyer of the U.S. Navy, the second navy ship named for Lieutenant Cdr. David A. McDermut. On October 24, 1944, USS *McDermut* was assigned to the Western Group with the *Monssen* and positioned close to the Leyte shore. Soon after midnight the enemy was reported entering the strait. Between 3 a.m. and 3:01 a.m., the Eastern Group commenced launching torpedoes, firing twenty-seven in less than two minutes. At 3:10 a.m., USS *McDermut* and USS *Monssen* launched their attack. At 3:20 a.m. explosions flashed, USS *McDermut*'s torpedoes hitting three destroyers. IJN *Yamagumo* sank immediately, while IJN *Michishio* and IJN *Asagumo* were disabled and drifting, the latter having lost her bow.

Shipyard:	Federal Shipbuilding & Dry Dock Co., Kearny, New Jersey
Laid down:	June 14, 1943
Launched:	October 17, 1943
Commissioned:	November 19, 1943
Decommissioned:	December 16, 1963
Class and type:	*Fletcher*-class destroyer
Displacement:	2,050 tons
Length:	376 feet 6 inches
Beam:	39 feet 8 inches
Draft:	17 feet 9 inches
Propulsion:	2 propellers, geared turbines
Speed:	35 knots
Range:	6,500 nautical miles
Complement:	319
Armament:	5 × 5-inch dual-purpose guns 10 × 40-mm anti-aircraft guns 7 × 20-mm anti-aircraft guns 10 × 21-inch torpedo tubes 6 × depth-charge projectors 2 × depth-charge tracks

USS Monssen (Commander Charles K. Bergin)

USS *Monssen* (DD-798) was a *Fletcher*-class destroyer of the U.S. Navy, the second navy ship named for Lieutenant Mons Monssen (1867–1930), who was awarded the Medal of Honor for putting out a fire in a magazine on USS *Missouri*. In the screen of TG 79.11 (landing craft), USS *Monssen* arrived in Leyte Gulf and delivered her charges to the Dulag beaches on the 20th and then proceeded to take up her screening station, with Destroyer Squadron 54, across Surigao Strait. Through the 24th, the squadron encountered only sporadic air attacks. In the early morning of the 25th, however, an enemy surface force attempted to force into the Leyte Gulf transportation area through Surigao Strait.

Shipyard:	Bethlehem Shipbuilding, Staten Island, New York
Laid down:	June 1, 1943
Launched:	October 30, 1943
Commissioned:	February 14, 1944
Decommissioned:	April 30, 1946
Class and type:	*Fletcher*-class destroyer
Displacement:	2,971 tons
Length:	376 feet 5 inches
Beam:	39 feet 8 inches

Draft: 13 feet 9 inches
Propulsion: 2 screws, geared turbines
Speed: 35 knots
Range: 6,500 nautical miles
Complement: 319
Armament: 5 × dual 5-inch dual-purpose guns
10 × 40-mm anti-aircraft guns
7 × 20-mm Oerlikon anti-aircraft guns
10 × 21-inch torpedo tubes
6 × depth-charge projectors
2 × depth-charge tracks

USS *McNair* (Commander M. L. McCullough, Jr.)

USS *McNair* (DD-679) was a *Fletcher*-class destroyer of the U.S. Navy, named for Rear Admiral Frederick V. McNair, Sr. (1839–1900). Arriving in the Leyte Gulf transport area on October 20, USS *McNair* took up antisubmarine patrol duty to protect ships and troops as the latter began to storm the shore at Dulag. In the first hours of the 25th, she remained at her station to cover the entrance to Leyte Gulf as her sister ships of Destroyer Squadron 54 conducted their much-heralded night torpedo attack on Japanese men-of-war steaming toward the northern end of Surigao Strait and defeat under the guns of Rear Admiral Jesse B. Oldendorf's battle line.

Shipyard: Federal Shipbuilding & Dry Dock Co., Kearny, New Jersey
Laid down: June 30, 1943
Launched: November 14, 1943
Commissioned: December 30, 1943
Decommissioned: December 30, 1963
Class and type: *Fletcher*-class destroyer
Displacement: 2,050 tons
Length: 376 feet 6 inches
Beam: 39 feet 8 inches
Draft: 17 feet 9 inches
Propulsion: 2 propellers, geared turbines
Speed: 38 knots
Range: 6,500 nautical miles
Complement: 319
Armament: 5 × 5-inch guns
10 × 40-mm anti-aircraft guns

7 × 20-mm anti-aircraft guns
10 × 21-inch torpedo tubes
6 × depth-charge projectors
2 × depth-charge racks

80-foot Elco Motor Torpedo Boat

The typical PT boat that participated in the Battle of the Surigao Strait was the 80-foot Elco model. Motor torpedo boat development had its beginning in the early 1900s, culminating with actual combat use in World War I. It was the British, French, and Italian navies who led the way in development and deployment of this specialized craft. However, it was not until the late 1930s that the U.S. Navy seriously took on the challenge to create their own patrol torpedo boat program. The U.S. originally developed three designs, two from distinguished naval architects and one from the navy. Eight boats (*PT-1* through *PT-8*) were built from these designs. Unfortunately, by the time most of these boats were built and readied for testing, their design and performance was found to be inadequate.

In the meantime, the Electric Boat Company (ELCO) purchased a British 70-foot boat, designed by Hubert Scott-Paine. This boat was subsequently shipped to the U.S. and numbered *PT-9* by the navy. During preliminary testing, the navy was impressed enough to award ELCO a contract to build ten PT boats (*PT-10* through *PT-19*) based on the *PT-9* design. The contract specified some minor to moderate changes, however, which included changes to upper deck structures and replacing the engines with the newly designed 1,200-horsepower Packard Marine engines.

Upon completion of these boats, navy test trials revealed that these new boats were too lightly constructed to withstand the rigors of open seas. It was also realized that the boat's designed length was not sufficient to utilize the longer U.S. torpedo *versus* the shorter British torpedo. Notwithstanding the short comings of these initial 70-foot boats, the navy was convinced that they had a real need for this type of small attack craft. It was recommended that the overall length be increased to accommodate the standard U.S. torpedo and the hull structure be re-engineered to strengthen it for heavier seas.

ELCO was again awarded a contract to build twenty-four new boats (*PT-20* through *PT-44*) with the recommended modifications which increased the length to 77 feet. Unbeknown to anyone at that time, some of these new PT boats would actually become the first U.S. PT boats to see action in World War II (Pearl Harbor and the Philippines).

During the time ELCO was building the new boats, two other companies involved in boat building were developing PT boats at their own expense, to compete with ELCO. These two companies were Higgins Industries and Huckins Yacht Works. Higgins was working on a 76-foot design (*PT-70*) and

Huckins was developing a 72-foot boat (*PT-69*). Eventually all three companies would build PT boats for the war effort. However, just prior to the start of the war, the Navy Department held competition trials known as the "Plywood Derby." This was a shakedown to see which company would be contracted to build the navy PT boats. At the completion of the trials, the navy was impressed with all three designs, with the ELCO 77-footer coming out on top, followed by the Higgins 76-footer and Huckins 72-footer. Although ELCO came in first, the navy saw the merits of the other two boats and decided to offer all three companies' contracts. ELCO received the lion share (385 boats by the end of the war), Higgins was second (199 boats by the end of the war), and Huckins with the smallest contract (eighteen boats by the end of the war).

With contracts awarded, the U.S. Navy's PT boat program was in full swing. However, Higgins increased its boat length to 78 feet and Huckins added 6 feet to its boat length also resulting in a 78-footer. ELCO would build another twenty-four boats at 77 feet, and by navy request designed a larger boat of 80 feet in length with a larger capacity to carry more armament. Thus, the ELCO 80-foot PT boat was born and destined to become the most numerous in service.

Throughout World War II, the PT boats would see many transformations enabling the original designs to be modified to fit the mission they would be called upon to perform. It appears most of the ELCO designed boats served in the Pacific theater, with a small number used in the English Channel and Mediterranean Sea. The typical specifications:

Displacement:	56 tons
Length:	80 feet
Beam:	20 feet 8 inches
Draft:	5 feet
Propulsion:	Three 1,500-hp Packard W-14 M2500 gasoline engines, 3 shafts
Speed:	41 knots
Complement:	17
Armament:	1 × 40-mm gun 1 × 37-mm gun 2 × 20-mm guns 4 × 21-inch torpedoes 2 × .50-caliber twin machine guns

APPENDIX II

Allied Naval Weapons at the Surigao Strait

16-inch/45 Mk. 5 and Mk. 8

Used only on the *Colorado*-class battleships, these guns were reconstructed from the original 16-inch/45 Mk. 1 weapons during the 1930s modernization of the battle fleet. The major difference from the Mk. 1 gun was the redesign of the chamber to permit larger charges, a new liner with heavier taper carbon steel, liner-locking ring, and locking collar. A later version, the Mk. 8, was similar except that rifling was uniform and the bore was chromium plated for increased life. These ships could not fire the super-heavy 2,700-pound AP Mk. 8 projectile, as that shell was too heavy and too long for their handling equipment. However, in the late 1930s, they were given the 2,240-pound AP Mk. 5, which was a heavier projectile with better armor piercing capability than the 2,110-pound AP Mk. 3 that was originally issued. By 1942, these ships were also issued an HC projectile.

Gun Characteristics

Ship class used on:	*Colorado*-class
Date in service:	1938
Gun weight:	235,796 pounds (including breech)
Gun length:	736.0 inches (overall)
Bore length:	720.0 inches
Rifling length:	616.9 inches
Grooves:	96
Rate of fire:	about 1.50 rpm

Ammunition

Projectile types and weights:	AP Mk. 5 Mods 1 to 6—2,240 pounds; HC Mk. 13 Mods 0 to 6—1,900 pounds; HC Mk. 14 Mod 0—1,900 pounds
Projectile length:	64 inches
Propellant charge:	Full charge—545 pounds SPD; reduced charge—295 pounds SPDN; reduced flashless charge—315 pounds SPCG
Muzzle velocity:	Full charge—new gun; AP—2,520 fps; HC—2,635 fps
Approximate barrel life:	Mk. 5—320 rounds; Mk. 8—395 rounds

Range

6,000 yards at 2.9 degrees to 40,180 yards at 45.0 degrees.

14-inch/50 Mk. 7, Mk. 11 Gun

The Mk. 7 was a remanufactured 14-inch/50 Mk. 4 with a smaller chamber, a shell-centering cone, a single-slope band seat, uniform rifling, and a tube-locking ring. The Mk. 11 was the Mk. 7 with the addition of chromium plating to the bore. During the battleship modernization program of the 1930s, the 14-inch/50 Mk. 11 was used to rearm the *New Mexico* and *Tennessee*-class battleships, although the battleship USS *Tennessee* did not receive updated guns until 1942. The problems with dispersion experienced with the 14-inch/50 Mk. 4 guns seem to have been corrected with these rebuilt weapons. At Surigao Strait, USS *Tennessee* and USS *California* reported pattern sizes of 300 to 400 yards for six- and nine-gun salvos at 20,000 yards, which was not appreciably different than that achieved by the newer battleships during the war.

Gun Characteristics

Ship class used on:	Mks. 7 and 11, *New Mexico* and *Tennessee* classes
Date in service:	Mk. 7—about 1935; Mk. 11—about 1940
Gun weight:	179,614 pounds (including breech)
Gun length:	714.0 inches (overall)
Bore length:	700 inches
Rifling length:	607.4 inches
Grooves:	92
Rate of fire:	Mk. 7 and Mk. 11—about 1.75 rpm

Ammunition

Projectile types and weights:	AP Mk. 16 Mods 1 to 11—1,500 pounds; HC Mk. 19 Mods 2 to 6—1,275 pounds; HC Mk. 22 Mod 0—1,275 pounds
Projectile length:	56 inches
Propellant charge:	Full charge—420 pounds SPD; reduced charge—195 pounds SPDN; reduced flashless charge—200 pounds SPCG
Muzzle velocity:	Full charge—new gun; AP—2,700 fps; HC—2,825 fps
Approximate barrel life:	Mk. 7—175 to 200 rounds; Mk. 11—200 to 250 rounds

Range

6,000 yards at 2.8 degrees to 43,000 yards at 45.0 degrees.

14-inch/45 Mks. 8, 9, 10, and 12

During the modernizations of the battleships during the 1930s, the construction of old 14-inch/45 guns were upgraded and their chamber volumes enlarged to allow larger charges to give an increased muzzle velocity. Mks. 1, 3, and 5 became Mks. 8, 9, and 10, respectively. The Mk. 12 was a further conversion that added chromium plating to increase barrel life. Guns had either a horizontal or a down opening Welin breech block and used a Smith-Asbury mechanism. These guns were interchangeable, and most battleships had a combination of mark numbers. The USS *Nevada* and USS *Pennsylvania* battleship classes were further upgraded during the 1930s to increase their maximum turret elevations to 30 degrees. These ships were also now supplied with a heavier AP projectile and by 1942 with a HC projectile. The enlarged propellant charges allowed the heavier AP shell to be used without significant muzzle velocity losses. USS *New York* and USS *Texas* were not modernized, and their existing shell hoists could not handle the new, longer AP and HC projectiles, so modified versions with shorter windshields were produced for these ships.

Gun Characteristics

Ship class used on:	*New York*, *Nevada*, and *Pennsylvania* classes
Date in service:	As Modernized: 1933
Gun weight:	124,000 pounds (including breech)
Gun length:	642.5 inches (overall)
Bore length:	630 inches
Rifling length:	542.7 inches

Grooves:	84
Rate of fire:	about 1.25–1.75 rpm

Ammunition

Projectile types and weights:	AP Mk. 16 Mods 1 to 11—1,500 pounds; AP Mk. 20 Mod 1—1,500 pounds; HC Mk. 19 Mods 1 to 6—1,275 pounds; HC Mk. 22 Mod 0—1,275 pounds; bombardment Mk. 9 Mod 4—1,410 pounds
Projectile length:	56 inches
Propellant charge:	Full charge—425 pounds SPD; reduced charge—205 pounds SPDN; reduced flashless charge—210 pounds SPCG
Muzzle velocity:	Full charge—new gun; AP—2,600 fps; HC—2,735 fps
Approximate barrel life:	Mk. 8, 9, and 10—175 to 200 rounds; Mk. 12—250 rounds

Range

23,000 yards at 15 degrees to 40,000 yards at 45.0 degrees.

8-inch/55 Mks. 9, 10, 11, 13, and 14

This weapon was used on most U.S. Treaty cruisers and the *Lexington*-class carriers. None of these ships ever carried the super-heavy AP projectiles as their ammunition hoists could not accommodate the longer, heavier round. As commissioned, the early cruisers had poor dispersion patterns, sometimes as large as 2,000 yards for a full salvo. Some of these problems were due to the guns having a very high muzzle velocity and poor shot seating. Extensive testing to determine the cause of the problems was performed in 1933 at Manila Bay with the assistance of the Coast Artillery. Corrections included reducing the muzzle velocity and relining the barrels.

These guns and mountings were removed from USS *Lexington* and USS *Saratoga* in 1942 and then reused as coastal artillery on the island of Oahu, Hawaii. It had been planned to rearm these carriers with 5-inch/38 guns, but only USS *Saratoga* actually received her new guns as USS *Lexington* was sunk before the work could be carried out. This series of 8-inch guns were very heavy when compared to most other 8-inch guns for reasons that are not readily apparent. Mk. 9 was the original design and was used on ships built in the 1920s. This gun consisted of liner, "A" tube, jacket, five hoops, three locking rings, and a screw box liner. The Mk. 10, which was never built, was a lighter gun constructed of only three hoops. The Mk. 11 had only one hoop and was autofretted. The Mk. 13 was the Mk. 9 relined with a partially chrome-plated bore. The Mk. 14 was a relined Mk. 9 with a fully chrome-plated bore and a smaller chamber. The Mk. 14 was used for most re-gunning during World War II.

Gun Characteristics

Ship class used on:	*Lexington*, *Pensacola*, *Northampton*, *New Orleans*, and *Indianapolis* classes
Date in service:	1927
Gun weight:	60,000 pounds (including breech)
Gun length:	449.0 inches (overall)
Bore length:	440.1 inches
Rifling length:	373.65 inches
Grooves:	64
Rate of fire:	about 3–4 rpm

Ammunition

Projectile types and weights:	AP Mk. 19 Mods 1 to 6—260 pounds; SP Common Mk. 17 Mods 1 to 4—260 pounds; common Mk. 14 Mod 1—260 pounds; common Mk. 15 Mod 1—260 pounds; HC Mk. 25 Mod 1—260 pounds
Projectile length:	34–36 inches
Propellant charge:	Full charge—89 pounds SPD; reduced flashless charge—92 pounds SPCG
Muzzle velocity:	2,800 fps
Approximate barrel life:	715 rounds

Range

6,000 yards at 2.5 degrees to 31,860 yards at 41.0 degrees.

8-inch/50 Mk. VIII

This weapon was designed for Britain's Treaty cruisers of the 1920s. Similar to other cruisers of that era, the mountings for these weapons were given a high maximum elevation in order to provide an anti-aircraft capability. However, the training and elevation gear was inefficient, and both the elevation and training rates were too slow to allow these mountings to be useful in that role. The later Mk. II mountings appear to have been much more reliable, with the first gun trials for HMS *York* in February 1930 being so successful that they took only four hours to complete. As a weight-saving measure, the Mk. II version of this mounting, used only on HMS *Exeter*, had a significantly reduced maximum elevation. The original design was "A" tube, wire, "B" tube, overlapping jacket, breech ring, and breech-bush, and these guns were designated as Mk. VIII upon completion. Owing to troubles with the "A" tube forging, an inner "A" tube was added to half of the wire-wound guns. After relining with a tapered inner "A" tube, guns were then designated as Mk. VIII. Two prototypes and the last twenty-six guns built did not use wire and were designated as Mk. VIII. All guns used a Welin breech-block with hydraulic or hand-worked Asbury mechanism and were interchangeable with each other. A total of 168 guns were produced, including the two prototypes built without wire.

Gun Characteristics

Ship class used on:	*Kent*, *London*, *Norfolk*, and *York* classes; Australia *County* class
Date in service:	1927
Gun weight:	38,640 pounds
Gun length:	413.1 inches (overall)
Bore length:	400.0 inches
Rifling length:	346.3 inches
Grooves:	48
Rate of fire:	about 3–6 rpm

Ammunition

Projectile types and weights:	SAPC—256 pounds; HE—256 pounds
Projectile length:	26 inches
Propellant charge:	Full charge—89 pounds SPD; reduced flashless charge—92 pounds SPCG
Muzzle velocity:	2,805 fps
Approximate barrel life:	550 rounds

Range

5,000 yards at 2.1 degrees to 30,650 yards at 45.0 degrees.

6-inch /47 Mk. 16

These guns were used to arm the *Brooklyn* and *Cleveland*-class light cruisers, the latter being the most numerous class of cruisers ever built. Developed from experiments with old 6-inch/50 Mk. 8 guns with various modifications to test new ideas, this weapon was to a new design firing separate (semi-fixed) ammunition and was capable of using the super heavy armor-piercing projectile. These new projectiles had almost double the penetration performance when compared against the older 6-inch/53 armor-piercing projectiles used for the *Omaha*-class light cruisers. Constructed of monobloc autofretted barrel with liner secured to the housing by a bayonet joint. Mk. 16 Mod 1 differed from Mod 0 in having a tapered liner. All used a semi-automatic vertical sliding breech block accommodated in the housing. There was a 0.5-inch ring attachment at the muzzle.

Gun Characteristics

Ship class used on:	Brooklyn, St. Louis, Cleveland and Fargo classes
Date in service:	1937
Gun weight:	13,000 pounds (including breech)
Gun length:	300 inches (overall)
Bore length:	282.3 inches
Rifling length:	238.3 inches
Grooves:	N/A
Rate of fire:	about 8–10 rpm

Ammunition

Projectile types and weights:	AP Mk. 35 Mods 1 to 11 (super heavy)-130 pounds; HC Mk. 34 Mods 1 to 7-105 pounds; illumination Mk. 32 Mod 0—94.5 pounds; illumination Mk. 38 Mod 0—105 pounds
Projectile length:	27 inches
Propellant charge:	Full charge—89 pounds SPD; reduced flashless charge—92 pounds SPCG
Muzzle velocity:	AP Mk. 35—2,500 fps; HC Mk. 39—2,665 fps
Approximate barrel life:	750–1,050 rounds

Range

6,000 yards at 3.3 degrees to 26,118 yards at 47.5 degrees.

6-inch/45 BL Mk. XII and Mk. XX

First carried by the cruiser HMS *Birmingham* in 1914, this weapon was used as the secondary gun on the *Queen Elizabeth* and *Royal Sovereign* battleship classes and as the main gun on all cruisers built during World War I. These guns were 5 calibers shorter than the previous 50-caliber guns in order to make them easier to work on small cruisers. The lively nature of those ships had made the 50-caliber guns unwieldy and hard to manage. During World War II, some AMCs and gunboats were fitted with guns removed from scrapped ships. Constructed of inner “A” tube, “A” tube, full-length wire, full-length jacket, breech ring and breech bush, which screwed into the "A" tube. The guns used a hand-worked Welin breech-block. The Mk. XIIA had a modified chamber with parallel front end, while the Mk. XIIB had a modified chamber with a bore of 5.985 inches in an effort to improve accuracy. Where practical, it was preferred not to mix Mk. XIIB with Mk. XII or XIIA, but all guns were interchangeable. A total of 463 guns were manufactured for the Royal Navy, of which 431 remained in service as of 1939. Although none of these guns were specifically manufactured for the army, many were transferred from the navy during World War II for use in emergency coastal defense batteries.

Gun Characteristics

Ship class used on:	*Queen Elizabeth*, *Royal Sovereign*, *Arethusa*, "B," "C," "D," and "E" cruiser classes
Date in service:	1914
Gun weight:	15,428 pounds
Gun length:	279.7 inches (overall)
Bore length:	270.0 inches
Rifling length:	230.6 inches
Grooves:	36
Rate of fire:	about 5–7 rpm

Ammunition

Projectile types and weights:	CPBC 2 crh-100 pounds; CPC 4 crh-100 pounds; HE 4 crh—100 pounds; HE 6 crh—112 pounds
Projectile length:	CPC—23.5 inches; HE—22.9 inches
Propellant charge:	Full charge—89 pounds SPD; reduced flashless charge—92 pounds SPCG
Muzzle velocity:	AP Mk. 35—2,500 fps; HC Mk. 39—2,665 fps
Approximate barrel life:	670 rounds

Range

13,500 yards at 15.0 degrees to 21,500 yards at 40.0 degrees.

5-inch/38 Mk. 12

This was unquestionably the finest dual-purpose gun of World War II. Originally designed to arm new destroyers being built in the 1930s, the 5-inch/38 wound up being used on nearly every major U.S. warship built between 1934 and 1948 and was still being used on new construction as late as the 1960s. It was also used on many auxiliaries, merchant vessels, and smaller warships as well as on U.S. Coast Guard vessels. This standardization, unique in any navy, greatly helped the logistical supply situation of the Pacific War. These guns were hand-loaded, but power-rammed, which gave them a high rate of fire and a capability of being easily loaded at any angle of elevation, both of which are highly desirable qualities for an anti-aircraft weapon. The introduction of proximity-fused AA shells in 1943 made this weapon an even more potent AAA gun.

Gun Characteristics

Ship class used on:	Used on nearly all World War II-era warship destroyers
Date in service:	1934
Gun weight:	3,990 pounds (without breech)
Gun length:	223.8 inches (overall)
Bore length:	190 inches
Rifling length:	157.2 inches
Grooves:	45
Rate of fire:	Pedestal and other mounts lacking integral hoists-12–15 rpm; base ring mounts with integral hoists—15–22 rpm

Ammunition

Projectile types and weights:	AAC Mk. 34 Mod 10—55.18 pounds; AAC Mk. 35 Mods 1 to 12—55.18 pounds; AAC Mk. 47 Mods 0 and 1—55.18 pounds; AAC Mk. 49—55.18 pounds; AAC Mk. 52—55.18 pounds; AAC Mk. 56—55.18 pounds; common Mk. 32 Mods 1 to 4—54.0 pounds; AAVT Mk. 31 Mods 1 to 11—55.12 pounds; special common Mk. 38 Mods 1, 2, and 3—55.18 pounds; special common Mk. 46 Mods 1 and 2—55.18 pounds; RAP Mk. 57—54.3 pounds; illumination Mks. 27, 30, 44, and 45—54.39 pounds; WP Mk. 46—53.00 pounds; chaff Mk. 78—55.3 pounds (25.1 kg)
Projectile length:	27 inches
Propellant charge:	Full charge—89 pounds SPD; reduced flashless charge—92 pounds SPCG
Muzzle velocity:	AP Mk. 35—2,500 fps; HC Mk. 39—2,665 fps
Approximate barrel life:	750–1,050 rounds

Range

6,000 yards at 3.3 degrees to 26,118 yards at 47.5 degrees.

4.7-inch/45 QF Mk. XII

The 4.7-inch QF Mk. IX was used on most destroyers built in the 1930s and 1940s. The almost identical Mk. XII was designed for use in twin mountings and differed from the Mk. IX in being slightly heavier and longer. Both marks fired separate ammunition, otherwise they were similar to the preceding 4.7-inch BL Mk. I. A wet-mount version of the Mk. IX was developed for submarines, but only a few were in service and these were replaced by standard 4-inch/40 submarine guns prior to World War II.

Gun Characteristics

Ship class used on:	Prototype mounted on *Hereward Tribal*, "J," "K," and "N" destroyer classes
Date in service:	1930
Gun weight:	6,490 pounds
Gun length:	224.08 inches (overall)
Bore length:	212.6 inches
Rifling length:	179.3 inches
Grooves:	38
Rate of fire:	10–12 rpm

Ammunition

Projectile types and weights:	HE—50 pounds; SAP—50 pounds
Projectile length:	15 inches
Propellant charge:	11.58 pounds SC 109; 13.13 pounds NF/S 164–048; cartridge—30.5 pounds with propellant
Muzzle velocity:	2,650 fps
Approximate barrel life:	1,400 rounds

Range

15,800 yards at 30.0 degrees to 17,000 yards at 40 degrees.

4-inch/45 QF Mk. XVI

Intended for use as a DP weapon, the Mk. XVI was a reasonably good AAA gun, although many considered it as being too small for the anti-ship role. This weapon superseded the 4-inch/45 Mk. V HA gun on new cruiser construction during the 1930s. In addition, many older cruisers and capital ships had their Mk. V guns replaced with these more powerful weapons during refits. A popular weapon, production could not keep up with demand until late in the war, resulting in many ships being armed with older weapons. HMS *Carlisle*, a converted AA cruiser armed with these guns, shot down eleven aircraft during the war, the highest score among British cruisers. The auxiliary anti-aircraft ship HMS *Alynbank*, also armed with these guns, shot down six aircraft. The Mk. XVII was designed for some *County*-class cruisers with the intention of replacing two of their single 4-inch/45 Mk. V mountings with twin mountings without exceeding the Treaty weight limits.

Gun Characteristics

Ship class used on:	British capital ships, aircraft carriers, destroyers and frigates
Date in service:	1936
Gun weight:	4,502 pounds
Gun length:	190.5 inches (overall)
Bore length:	180.0 inches
Rifling length:	149.5 inches
Grooves:	32
Rate of fire:	15–20 rpm

Ammunition

Projectile types and weights:	HE—63.5 pounds; SAP—66.75 pounds
Projectile length:	45.13 inches
Propellant charge:	9.0 pounds SC 103; 10.5 pounds NF/S; reduced charge—5.1 pounds; cartridge—28.5 pounds
Muzzle velocity:	2,660 fps
Approximate barrel life:	600 rounds

Range

19,850 yards at 45.0 degrees. AA range at 80.0 degrees 39,000 feet.

40-mm/56 Mk. 1 and 40-mm/56 Mk. 2 Bofors

Bofors guns were both water-cooled and were used for all twin and quad mountings. The Mk. 1 was a left-hand weapon while the Mk. 2 was a right-hand weapon. Except for the barrel assemblies, the components were not interchangeable. These weapons could be fired in single-shot or automatic mode via a selector switch on the side of the slide. The 40-mm/56 M1 was an air-cooled version originally produced for the U.S. Army. The barrel assemblies for the M1 were interchangeable with those of British and Canadian produced air-cooled weapons. All U.S. Navy single mountings used a modified version of the army M1.

Gun Characteristics

Ship class used on: UK and USA—almost all major UK warships of World War II
Date in service: 1942
Gun weight: 1,036.5 pounds
Gun length: 148.8 inches (overall)
Bore length: 88.6 inches
Rifling length: 75.85 inches
Grooves: 16
Rate of fire: Cyclic—120 rpm per barrel nominal; 140–160 rpm when firing horizontal (gravity assist); practical—80–90 rpm

Ammunition

Projectile types and weights: PFHE—2.16 pounds; HE-T—2.05 pounds; AP-T—2.60 pounds; APHC-T—2.09 pounds
Projectile length: 7.2 inches
Propellant charge: 0.694 pounds NC 025; 0.661 pounds SPDN
Muzzle velocity: 2,890 fps
Approximate barrel life: 9,500 rounds

Range

6,844 yards at 10.0 degrees to 11,133 yards at 45.0 degrees, AA ceiling-22,299 feet.

20-mm/70 Mks. 2, 3, and 4

Widely used by many nations, this 20-mm automatic weapon originally designed by the Swiss firm of Oerlikon was probably produced in higher numbers than any other anti-aircraft weapon of World War II. By late 1944, the U.S. Navy had found that 20-mm shells were too light to kill/stop Japanese *kamikaze* planes and the higher approach speeds of these planes made manually controlled guns obsolete. As a result, Oerlikons were replaced by 40-mm Bofors where ever possible during 1944–45 and removed entirely from most U.S. ships by the mid-1950s.

Gun Characteristics

Ship class used on: Almost all Allied ships during World War II
Date in service: 1941
Gun weight: 87 pounds (with breech mechanism)
Gun length: 148.8 inches (overall)
Bore length: 55.1 inches
Rifling length: 49.1 inches
Grooves: 9
Rate of fire: Cyclic—450 rpm; practical—250–320 rpm

Ammunition

Projectile types and weights:	HE Mk. 3 Mods 1 to 64—0.271 pounds; HE-I Mk. 3 Mods 1 to 64—0.271 pounds; HE-T Mk. 4 Mods 1 to 28—0.262 pounds; HE-T Mk. 7—0.271 pounds; AP-T Mk. 9—0.269 pounds
Projectile length:	HE Mk. 3—3.275 inches; HE Mk. 4—3.025 inches; HE Mk. 7—3.025 inches; AP-T Mk. 9—3.051 inches
Propellant charge:	0.061 pound NC tube
Muzzle velocity:	2,725 fps
Approximate barrel life:	9,000 rounds

Range

3,450 yards at 10.0 degrees to 4,800 yards at 45.0 degrees, AA ceiling—10,000 feet.

0.50-inch/90 M2 Browning Machine Gun

Built since the 1930s, the 0.50-inch Browning machine gun M2 is still one of the world's most widely used heavy machine guns. Employed today on many USN ships for action against hostile small surface craft and commando-type attacks which might occur in restricted waters. This gun was initially designed near the end of World War I as an aircraft weapon. The design was modified for land use after the war and then designated as the Model 1921 machine gun. In 1932, the design was modified again, and this design became the M2. The M2HB version, introduced during World War II, is the most widely used model today and denotes guns using a thicker, air-cooled barrel, which was adopted in order to increase barrel life.

Gun Characteristics

Ship class used on:	Almost all Allied ships during World War II
Date in service:	1933
Gun weight:	Water-cooled: 100.5 pounds
Gun length:	65 inches (overall)
Barrel length:	45 inches
Rifling length:	41.9 inches
Grooves:	8
Rate of fire:	450–600 rpm

Ammunition

Projectile types and weights:	Varies depending upon ammunition type and weapon version
Projectile length:	5.45 inches

Propellant charge:	0.054 ounces NC tube
Muzzle velocity:	2,930 fps
Approximate barrel life:	about 3,000 rounds

Range

2,600 yards, AA effective ceiling—5,000 feet

Mk. 8 Fire Control Radar (FH)

Scanned via pulse-switching, the Mk. 8 Mod 0 could spot 16-inch splashes out to about 20,000 yards and the improved Mk. 8 Mod 3 could reliably spot 14-inch and 16-inch fire out to at least 35,000 yards.

War status:	Used by U.S. battleships, introduced in 1942–43
Installed:	Mounted on main battery directors
Purpose:	Fire control
Power:	15–20 kW, later 20–30 kW
Wavelength:	10 cm
Transmitter dimensions:	10.2 × 3.3 feet
Tracking range:	40,000 yards on battleship-sized target
Range accuracy:	15 yards
Bearing accuracy:	2 mils
Resolution:	400 yards and 10 degrees

Mk. 3 Fire Control Radar (FC)

It gave no height information, but used lobe switching to achieve high directional accuracy. By late 1944, it was already obsolete.

War status:	Used by U.S. battleships, introduced in 1941
Purpose:	Fire control
Power:	15–20 kW
Wavelength:	14 cm
Range accuracy:	40 yards
Resolution:	1,200 feet
Bearing accuracy:	2 mils

CXAM Detection Radar System

The CXAM radar system was the first production radar system deployed on U.S. Navy ships, operating in the mid-high VHF frequency band of 200 MHz. It followed several earlier prototype systems, such as the NRL radar installed in April 1937 on the destroyer USS *Leary*. Its successor was the XAF, installed in December 1938 on the battleship USS *New York* and the first RCA-designed system, the CXZ, installed in December 1938 or January 1939 on the battleship USS *Texas*. Based on testing in January 1939, where the XAF was more reliable, the U.S. Navy ordered RCA to build six XAF-based units for deployment and then shortly thereafter ordered fourteen more.

The first six units RCA produced, delivered in 1940, were denoted "CXAM" and were a fusion of XAF and CXZ technologies. These were installed on the battleship USS *California*, the aircraft carrier USS *Yorktown* (in September 1940), and the heavy cruisers USS *Pensacola*, USS *Northampton*, USS *Chester*, and USS *Chicago*. The next fourteen units RCA produced, also delivered in 1940, were denoted "CXAM-1" and were slight improvements over the CXAM design. These were installed in October 1941 on the battleships USS *Texas*, USS *Pennsylvania*, USS *West Virginia*, USS *North Carolina*, and USS *Washington*; on the aircraft carriers USS *Lexington*, USS *Saratoga*, USS *Ranger*, USS *Enterprise*, and USS *Wasp*; on the heavy cruiser USS *Augusta*; on two light cruisers; and on the seaplane tender USS *Curtiss*. It was able to detect single aircraft at 50 miles and to detect large ships at 14 miles.

21-inch Mk. 15 Torpedo

The Mk. 15 torpedo was the standard destroyer weapon of World War II. It replaced the earlier Mk. 11 and Mk. 12. It remained in service as long as U.S. destroyers carried 21-inch torpedo tubes. About 9,700 were produced between 1940 and 1944.

Ship class used on:	Destroyers and *Atlanta*-class cruisers
Date in service:	1935
Weight:	Mod 0-3,438 pounds; Mod 3-3,841 pounds
Overall length:	Mod 0-22 feet 7 inches; Mod 3-24 feet
Negative buoyancy:	1,260 pounds
Explosive charge:	Mod 0-494 pounds TNT; Mod 3-801 pounds TNT or 823 pounds HBX
Range/speed:	Mod 0-6,000 yards/45 knots; Mod 3-4,500 yards/45 knots
Power:	Wet-heater steam turbine
Guidance:	Mk. 12 Mod 3 gyro

APPENDIX III

Japanese Fleet at the Surigao Strait

Battleship Division 2

IJN Fusō (Captain M. Kinoshita)

IJN *Fusō*, a classical name for Japan, was the lead ship of the two *Fusō*-class dreadnought battleships built for the Imperial Japanese Navy. IJN *Fusō* did not take part in any combat during World War I, as there were no longer any forces of the Central Powers in Asia by the time she was completed. She patrolled off the coast of China during that time. The ship served as the flagship of the 1st Division during 1917 and 1918. During the ship's period in reserve in 1918, five 76.2-mm anti-aircraft guns were installed. She aided survivors of the Great Kantō earthquake between September 9 and 22, 1923. The first phase of the ship's first modernization began on April 12, 1930 at the Yokosuka Naval Arsenal. Machinery was replaced, armor was reinforced, and torpedo bulges were fitted.

IJN *Fusō* arrived on September 26, 1932 at Kure Naval Arsenal, where her armament was upgraded, and her torpedo tubes were removed. IJN *Fusō* began the first phase of her second modernization on February 26, 1937. The ship was again assigned to the 1st Division of the 1st Fleet on November 15. She briefly operated in Chinese waters in early 1939 before the second phase of her second modernization began on December 12, 1940. IJN *Fusō* left Brunei at 3:30 p.m. on October 22, 1944 as part of Nishimura's Southern Force, heading east into the Sulu Sea and then northeast into the Mindanao Sea. Intending to join Vice Admiral Takeo Kurita's force in Leyte Gulf, the force passed west of Mindanao Island into Surigao Strait, where it met a large force of battleships and cruisers lying in wait. The Battle of Surigao Strait became the southernmost action in the Battle of Leyte Gulf.

Shipyard:	Kure Naval Arsenal, Kure, Japan
Laid down:	March 11, 1912
Launched:	March 28, 1914
Commissioned:	November 8, 1915
Class and type:	*Fusō*-class battleship
Displacement:	35,300 tons
Length:	698 feet
Beam:	108 feet 7 inches
Draft:	31 feet 10 inches
Propulsion:	6 Miyahara water-tube boilers, 4 shafts; 2 steam turbine sets
Speed:	23 knots
Range:	11,800 nautical miles
Complement:	1,900
Armament:	6 × twin 14-inch guns 14 × single 6-inch guns 4 × twin 5-inch dual-purpose guns 8 × triple, 6 × twin 23 × single 25-mm anti-aircraft guns
Aircraft carried:	3 × floatplanes
Aviation facilities:	1 × catapult
Armor:	Waterline belt: 9–12 inches Deck: 1.3–2.0 inches Gun turrets: 9–11 inches Barbettes: 8–12 inches Conning tower: 13.8 inches
Sensors and processing systems:	1 × Type 21 air search radar 2 × Type 13 early warning radar 2 × Type 22 surface search radar

IJN *Yamashiro* (Captain C. Obata)

IJN *Yamashiro*, named for Yamashiro Province, the former province of Kyoto, was laid down at the Yokosuka Naval Arsenal on November 20, 1913 and launched on November 3, 1915. She was completed on March 31, 1917 with Captain Suketomo Nakajima in command and was assigned to the 1st Division of the 1st Fleet in 1917–1918. She did not take part in any combat during World War I, as there were no longer any forces of the Central Powers in East Asia by the time she was completed, but she did patrol off the coast of China briefly during the war. On March 29, 1922, a Gloster Sparrowhawk fighter successfully took off from the ship. She aided survivors of the 1923 Great Kantō earthquake in September 1923. As flagship of Nishimura's Southern Force, IJN *Yamashiro* left Brunei at 3:30 p.m. on October 22, 1944, heading east into the Sulu Sea and then to the northeast into the Mindanao Sea. Intending to join Vice Admiral Takeo Kurita's force in Leyte Gulf, they passed west of Mindanao Island into Surigao Strait, where they met a large force of battleships and cruisers lying in wait.

Shipyard:	Yokosuka Naval Arsenal, Tokyo, Japan
Laid down:	November 20, 1913
Launched:	November 3, 1915
Commissioned:	March 31, 1917
Class and type:	*Fusō*-class battleship
Displacement:	36,500 tons
Length:	665 feet
Beam:	94 feet 2 inches
Draft:	28 feet 7 inches
Propulsion:	6 Miyahara water-tube boilers, 4 shafts, 2 steam turbine sets
Speed:	24.5 knots
Range:	11,800 nautical miles
Complement:	1,900
Armament:	6 × twin 14-inch guns 14 × single 6-inch guns 4 × twin 5-inch dual-purpose guns 92 × 25-mm anti-aircraft guns
Aircraft carried:	3 × floatplanes
Aviation facilities:	1 × catapult
Armor:	Belt: 12 inches Deck: 2–6 inches Bulkheads: 4–12 inches Barbettes: 8–12 inches Turrets: 9–11 inches Conning Tower: 13.8 inches
Sensors and processing systems:	1 × Type 21 air search radar 1 × Type 13 early warning radar 1 × Type 22 surface search radar

IJN Mogami (Captain Ryo Toma)

IJN *Mogami* was the lead ship in the four-vessel *Mogami*-class of heavy cruisers in the Imperial Japanese Navy. She was named after the Mogami River in Tōhoku region of Japan. The *Mogami*-class ships were constructed as a light cruiser (per the Washington Naval Treaty) with five triple 6.1-inch dual-purpose guns.

Between 3:50–4:02 a.m. on October 25, after entering the Surigao Strait, IJN *Mogami* was struck by four 8-inch shells from the heavy cruiser USS Portland, which destroyed both the bridge and the air defense center. Both the captain and executive officer were killed on the bridge, and the chief gunnery officer assumed command. While attempting to retire southward, the flagship of Admiral Shima, IJN *Nachi*, collided with IJN *Mogami*. IJN *Nachi*'s bow was damaged and she began to flood. IJN *Mogami* was holed starboard above the waterline, but fires ignited five torpedoes that exploded and disabled her starboard engine. Between 5:30 a.m. and 5:35 a.m., the crippled IJN *Mogami* was hit again by ten to twenty 6-inch and 8-inch shells from the cruisers USS *Portland*, USS *Louisville*, and USS *Denver*. At 8:30 a.m., IJN *Mogami*'s port engine broke down. At 9:02 a.m., while adrift, she was attacked by seventeen TBF Avenger torpedo-bombers from Task Group 77.4.1 and was hit by two 500-pound bombs. At 10:47 a.m., IJN *Mogami*'s crew abandoned ship, and she stayed afloat for the next two hours. At 12:40 p.m., the destroyer IJN *Akebono* scuttled her with a single Type 93 Long Lance torpedo. She finally sank at 1:07 p.m.

Shipyard:	Kure Naval Arsenal, Kure, Japan
Laid down:	October 27, 1931
Launched:	March 14, 1934
Commissioned:	July 28, 1935
Class and type:	*Mogami*-class cruiser
Displacement:	13,670 tons
Length:	650 feet
Beam:	66 feet
Draft:	19.3 feet
Propulsion:	10 Kampon boilers, 4-shaft geared turbines
Speed:	35.5 knots
Range:	8,000 nautical miles
Complement:	850
Armament:	6 × 20-cm/50 naval guns
	8 × 12.7-cm/40 Type 89 naval gun
	30 × 25-mm Type 96 anti-aircraft guns
	12 × Type 93 torpedoes (4 × 3 tube rotating launchers + 12 reloads)
Armor:	Belt: 3.9–4.9 inches
	Deck: 1.4–2.4 inches
	Turret: 0.98 inches
Aircraft carried:	11 x Aichi E13A floatplanes

Destroyer Division 4

IJN Michishio (Commander Tomoo Tanaka)

IJN *Michishio* was the third of ten *Asashio*-class destroyers built for the Imperial Japanese Navy in the mid-1930s under the Circle Two Supplementary Naval Expansion Program. During the Battle of the Philippine Sea, Michishio was in Admiral Takatsugu Jōjima's Force B but did not see combat during that battle. Afterwards, she assisted the torpedoed tanker Itsukushima Maru at Negros Island, and escorted the battleship IJN *Fusō* from Davao to Kure. She accompanied the battleship IJN *Haruna* in August from Sasebo to Singapore and then escorted supply convoys to Brunei. During the Battle of Surigao Strait, IJN *Michishio* was in Admiral Shōji Nishimura's Southern Force. On October 25, she was struck by a torpedo fired by USS *McDermut*, and then finished off by USS *Hutchins*.

Shipyard:	Fujinagata Shipyards, Osaka, Japan
Laid down:	November 5, 1935
Launched:	March 15, 1937
Commissioned:	October 31, 1937
Class and type:	*Asashio*-class destroyer
Displacement:	2,408 tons
Length:	388 feet 1 inch
Beam:	33 feet 10 inch
Draft:	12 feet 2 inch
Propulsion:	2-shaft geared turbine, 3 boilers
Speed:	35 knots
Range:	5,700 nautical miles
Complement:	200
Armament:	6 × 12.7-cm Type 5 dual-purpose guns
	28 × 25-mm 96 anti-aircraft guns
	4 × 13-mm Type 93 anti-aircraft guns
	8 × 24-inch torpedo tubes
	36 depth charges

IJN Yamagumo (Commander Ono Shiro)

IJN *Yamagumo* was the sixth of ten *Asashio*-class destroyers built for the Imperial Japanese Navy in the mid-1930s under the Circle Two Supplementary Naval Expansion Program. During the Battle of Leyte Gulf of October 22–25, 1944, she was part of Admiral Shōji Nishimura's Southern Force. In the Battle of Surigao Strait, she was hit by torpedoes fired by the destroyer USS *McDermut* and exploded, sinking.

Shipyard:	Fujinagata Shipyards, Osaka, Japan
Laid down:	November 4, 1936
Launched:	July 24, 1937
Commissioned:	January 15, 1938
Class and type:	*Asashio*-class destroyer
Displacement:	2,408 tons

Length:	388 feet 1 inch
Beam:	33 feet 10 inch
Draft:	12 feet 2 inch
Propulsion:	2-shaft geared turbine, 3 boilers
Speed:	35 knots
Range:	5,700 nautical miles
Complement:	200
Armament:	6 × 12.7-cm/50 Type 3 dual-purpose guns
	28 × 25-mm Type 96 anti-aircraft guns
	4 × 13-mm Type 93 anti-aircraft guns
	8 × 24-inch torpedo tubes
	36 depth charges

IJN Asagumo (Commander Kazuo Shibayama)

IJN *Asagumo* was the fifth of ten *Asashio*-class destroyers built for the Imperial Japanese Navy in the mid-1930s under the Circle Two Supplementary Naval Expansion Program. In October 1944, she was assigned to Vice Admiral Shōji Nishimura's fleet at the Battle of Surigao Strait, IJN *Asagumo* was torpedoed by the destroyer USS *McDermut* and subsequently finished off by gunfire from U.S. Navy cruisers and destroyers. Of her crew, 191 were killed, but thirty-nine survivors (including her captain, Commander Shibayama) were taken prisoner by the Americans.

Shipyard:	Kawasaki Shipbuilding Corporation, Kobe, Japan
Laid down:	December 23, 1936
Launched:	November 5, 1937
Commissioned:	March 30, 1938
Class and type:	*Asashio*-class destroyer
Displacement:	2,408 tons
Length:	388 feet 1 inch
Beam:	34 feet 0.9 inch
Draft:	12 feet 2 inch
Propulsion:	2-shaft geared turbine, 3 boilers
Speed:	35 knots
Range:	5,700 nautical miles
Complement:	230
Armament:	6 × 12.7-cm/50 Type 3 dual-purpose guns
	28 × Type 96 anti-aircraft guns
	4 × Type 93 anti-aircraft guns
	8 × 24-inch torpedo tubes
	36 depth charges

IJN Shigure (Commander Shigeru Nishino)

IJN *Shigure* was the second of ten *Shiratsuyu*-class destroyers, and the first to be built for the Imperial Japanese Navy under the Circle One Program. In October 1944, IJN *Shigure* sortied from Lingga and Brunei and was at the Battle of Leyte Gulf on October 22–25. She took minor damage from a direct bomb hit to her forward gun turret on October 24, killing five crewmen and wounding six. She took further damage in the Battle of Surigao Strait in which a direct shell hit, and several near misses took out her radio, compass, and steering, but she was the only ship of the Southern Force to survive the battle and limped back to Brunei on October 27. Shigure returned to Sasebo for repairs in November, possibly sinking the submarine USS *Growler* off Mindoro on November 8 *en route.*

Shipyard:	Uraga Dock Company, Yokosuka, Japan
Laid down:	December 9, 1933
Launched:	May 18, 1935
Commissioned:	September 7, 1936
Class and type:	*Shiratsuyu*-class destroyer
Displacement:	1,712 tons
Length:	352 feet 8 inches
Beam:	32 feet 6 inches
Draft:	11 feet 6 inches
Propulsion:	2 shaft Kampon geared turbines, 3 boilers
Speed:	34 knots
Range:	4,000 nautical miles
Complement:	226
Armament:	5 × 12.7-cm/50 Type 5 naval guns
	2 × 13-mm anti-aircraft guns
	8 × 24-inch torpedo tubes
	16 × depth charges

Second Striking Force

IJN Nachi (Captain Enpei Kanooka)

IJN *Nachi* was the second vessel completed of the four-member *Myōkō*-class of heavy cruisers of the Imperial Japanese Navy. In October 1944, she was sent to the Philippines as part of a cruiser force under the command of Vice Admiral Kiyohide Shima. During the Battle of Leyte Gulf from October 24, Nachi and Ashigara were part of Vice Admiral Shōji Nishimura's force, which included the battleships IJN *Yamashiro*, IJN *Fuso*, and the cruiser IJN *Mogami.*

Shipyard:	Kure Naval Arsenal, Kure, Japan
Laid down:	November 26, 1924
Launched:	June 15, 1927
Commissioned:	November 28, 1928
Class and type:	*Myōkō*-class cruiser
Displacement:	13,500 tons
Length:	661 feet 9 inches
Beam:	68 feet
Draft:	20 feet 9 inches
Propulsion:	4 geared steam turbines, 12 boilers, 4 shafts
Speed:	36 knots
Range:	8,000 nautical miles
Complement:	773
Armament:	10 × 203-mm guns
	8 × 127-mm guns
	2 × 13.2-mm machine guns
	12 × 24-inch torpedo tubes
Armor:	Main belt: 3.9 inches
	Main deck: 1.5 inches
	Turrets: 0.98 inches
	Barbettes: 3.0 inches
	Aircraft carried: 2 × floatplanes

IJN Ashigara (Captain Hayao Miura)

IJN *Ashigara* was the final vessel of the four-member *Myōkō*-class of heavy cruisers of the Imperial Japanese Navy, which were active in World War II. In the Battle of Leyte Gulf on October 24, 1944, IJN *Ashigara*, with Captain Hayao Miura in command, was assigned to Vice Admiral Kiyohide Shima's force along with IJN *Nachi* and eight destroyers. This force entered Surigao Strait on October 25 after Admiral Shōji Nishimura's First Raiding Force had been destroyed. Following the loss of the battleships IJN *Fusō* and Nishimura's IJN *Yamashiro* and their escorts at the hands of Rear Admiral Jesse B. Oldendorf's fleet and aircraft, with Nishimura being killed aboard IJN *Yamashiro*, IJN *Ashigara*, and IJN *Nachi* fired their torpedoes and retreated. IJN *Ashigara* escaped to Palawan and from there to Brunei.

Shipyard:	Kawasaki Shipyards, Kobe, Japan
Laid down:	April 11, 1925
Launched:	April 22, 1928
Commissioned:	August 20, 1929
Class and type:	*Myōkō*-class cruiser
Displacement:	14,980 tons

Length:	668 feet 6 inches
Beam:	68 feet
Draft:	20 feet 11 inches
Propulsion:	4-shaft geared turbines, 12 Kampon boilers
Speed:	35.5 knots
Range:	7,000 nautical miles
Complement:	970
Armament:	10 × 8-inch guns
	8 × 12.7-cm/40 Type 89 naval guns
	8 × 25-mm Type 96 anti-aircraft guns
	2 × 0.52-inch quadruple machine guns
	16 × 24-inch torpedo tubes
Aircraft carried:	3
Aviation facilities:	1 × aircraft catapult

IJN Abukuma (Captain Takuo Hanada)

IJN *Abukuma* was the sixth and last of the vessels completed for the Imperial Japanese Navy in the *Nagara*-class of light cruisers, and like other vessels of her class, she was intended for use as the flagship of a destroyer flotilla. She was named after the Abukuma River in the Tōhoku region of Japan. In October 1944, she was redirected from Mako in the Pescadores to Manila to support Vice Admiral Shōji Nishimura against the U.S. Navy in the Philippines. IJN *Abukuma* was joined by the heavy cruisers IJN *Nachi*, IJN *Ashigara*, and seven destroyers in a flotilla commanded by Vice Admiral Kiyohide Shima. On October 25, IJN *Abukuma* met her fate in the Battle of Surigao Strait, part of the overall campaign of four naval battles collectively referred to as the Battle of Leyte Gulf. In the pre-dawn hours, as Shima's force entered the strait, the flotilla was attacked by a squadron of American PT boats. *PT-137* fired a torpedo at a destroyer, but it ran deep and passed beneath the target to strike IJN *Abukuma* at 3:25 a.m. in the No. 1 boiler room, killing thirty-seven crewmen.

Shipyard:	Uraga Dock Company, Uraga, Japan
Laid down:	December 8, 1921
Launched:	March 16, 1923
Commissioned:	May 26, 1925
Class and type:	*Nagara*-class cruiser
Displacement:	5,659 tons
Length:	531 feet 10 inches
Beam:	46 feet 7 inches
Draft:	15 feet 9 inches
Propulsion:	4 shaft Gihon geared turbines, 12 Kampon boilers

Speed:	36 knots
Range:	6,000 nautical miles
Complement:	450
Armament:	5 × 14-cm/50 naval guns
	2 × 12.7-cm/40 Type 89 naval guns
	4 × 25-mm triple Type 96 anti-aircraft guns
	2 × 25-mm twin Type 96 anti-aircraft guns
	24 × 25-mm single Type 96 anti-aircraft guns
	10 × Type 93 13.2-mm machine guns
	8 × 21-inch torpedo tubes
Armor:	Belt: 2.4 inches
	Deck: 1.2 inches
Aircraft carried:	1× floatplane
Aviation facilities:	1× aircraft catapult
Sensors and processing systems:	Type 21 air-search radar

IJN Akebono (Lieutenant Commander Shiro Yoda)

IJN *Akebono* was the eighteenth of twenty-four *Fubuki*-class destroyers built for the Imperial Japanese Navy following World War I. When introduced into service, these ships were the most powerful destroyers in the world. They served as first-line destroyers through the 1930s and remained formidable weapons systems well into the Pacific War. On January 1, 1944, IJN *Akebono* was reassigned to the Imperial Japanese Navy 5th Fleet. On January 14, she rescued eighty-nine survivors of torpedoed destroyer IJN *Sazanami en route* to Truk. Returning to Yokosuka for repairs and refit on January 25, she was reassigned to Ōminato Guard District for patrols of northern waters through October. However, as the situation continued to deteriorate for Japan in the Philippines, she was reassigned to Admiral Kiyohide Shima's Diversionary Force at the Battle of Surigao Strait on October 24. The following day, IJN *Akebono* rescued about 700 survivors of the heavy cruiser IJN *Mogami* and then scuttled her with a torpedo.

Shipyard:	Fujinagata Shipyards, Osaka, Japan
Laid down:	November 25, 1929
Launched:	November 7, 1930
Commissioned:	July 31, 1931
Class and type:	*Fubuki*-class destroyer
Displacement:	2,080 tons
Length:	388.5 feet
Beam:	34 feet 1 inch
Draft:	10 feet 6 inch
Propulsion:	4 Kampon type boilers, 2 Kampon Type Ro geared turbines, 2 shafts

Speed: 38 knots
Range: 5,000 nautical miles
Complement: 219
Armament: 6 × 127-mm Type 5 naval guns
22 × 25-mm Type 96 anti-aircraft guns
10 × 13-mm anti-aircraft guns
9 × 24-inch torpedo tubes
36 × depth charges

IJN Ushio (Lieutenant Commander Masami Araki)

IJN *Ushio* was the twentieth of twenty-four *Fubuki*-class destroyers, built for the Imperial Japanese Navy following World War I. When introduced into service, these ships were the most powerful destroyers in the world. They served as first-line destroyers through the 1930s and remained formidable weapons systems well into the Pacific War. IJN *Ushio* was one of only two of the twenty-four ships in its class to survive World War II, and it was also the only survivor out of the twenty-two combat ships involved in the Pearl Harbor assault force. During the Battle of Leyte Gulf, IJN *Ushio* was assigned to Admiral Kiyohide Shima's Diversionary Force at the Battle of Surigao Strait, remaining based in Manila after the battle to escort convoys in the Philippines. She was damaged on September 13, during an American air raid on Manila, during which her starboard engine was disabled, and twenty-three crewmen killed.

Shipyard: Uraga Dock Company, Uraga, Japan
Laid down: December 24, 1929
Launched: November 17, 1930
Commissioned: November 14, 1931
Class and type: *Fubuki*-class destroyer
Displacement: 2,080 tons
Length: 388.5 feet
Beam: 34 feet 1 inch
Draft: 10 feet 6 inches
Propulsion: 4 Kampon type boilers, 2 Kampon Type Ro geared turbines, 2 shafts
Speed: 38 knots
Range: 5,000 nautical miles
Complement: 219
Armament: 6 × 127-mm Type 5 naval guns
22 × 25-mm Type 96 anti-aircraft guns
10 × 13-mm AA guns
9 × 24-inch torpedo tubes
36 × depth charges

IJN Kasumi (Commander Hiroo Yamana)

IJN *Kasumi* was the ninth of ten *Asashio*-class destroyers built for the Imperial Japanese Navy in the mid-1930s under the Circle Two Supplementary Naval Expansion Program. During the Battle of Leyte Gulf from October 24–25, she was assigned to Admiral Shima's force in the Battle of Surigao Strait. On November 5, she rescued survivors of IJN *Nachi* in Manila Bay following an American air raid. She escorted a troop convoy to Ormoc on November 5 and was damaged by strafing in another American air raid later that month, which killed one crewman. At the end of November, she escorted the battleship IJN *Haruna* from Singapore to Mako, and a convoy from Mako to Cam Ranh Bay in French Indochina in December. In late December, she led a force in the bombardment of San Jose in the Philippines.

Shipyard:	Uraga Dock Company, Uraga, Japan
Laid down:	December 1, 1936
Launched:	November 18, 1937
Commissioned:	June 28, 1939
Class and type:	*Asashio*-class destroyer
Displacement:	2,408 tons
Length:	388 feet 1 inch
Beam:	33 feet 10 inches
Draft:	12 feet 2 inches
Propulsion:	2-shaft geared turbine, 3 boilers
Speed:	34.85 knots
Range:	5,700 nautical miles
Complement:	230
Armament:	6 × 12.7-cm/50 Type 5 dual-purpose guns
	28 × 25-mm Type 96 anti-aircraft guns
	4 × 13-mm Type 93 anti-aircraft guns
	8 × 24-inch torpedo tubes
	36 × depth charges

IJN Shiranui (Commander Teisaburo Ara)

IJN *Shiranui* was the second vessel to be commissioned in the nineteen-vessel *Kagerō*-class destroyers built for the Imperial Japanese Navy in the late 1930s under the Circle Three Supplementary Naval Expansion Program. On March 1, she was reassigned to the Imperial Japanese Navy 5th Fleet and was assigned to northern waters, making patrols from her base at Ominato Guard District in April, and returning with the cruisers IJN *Nachi* and IJN *Ashigara* to Kure at the start of August. During the Battle of Leyte Gulf on October 24–25, 1944, IJN *Shiranui* was assigned to Vice Admiral Shōji Nishimura's diversionary force at the Battle of Surigao Strait. After the battle, she departed Coron to search for the missing cruiser IJN *Kinu* and destroyer IJN *Uranami* and took on survivors from the destroyer IJN *Hayashimo*. On October 27, she was sunk with all hands by dive-bombers from USS *Enterprise*.

Shipyard: Uraga Dock Company, Uraga, Japan
Laid down: August 30, 1937
Launched: June 28, 1938
Completed: December 20, 1939
Class and type: *Kagerō*-class destroyer
Displacement: 2,066 tons
Length: 388 feet 9 inches
Beam: 35 feet 5 inches
Draft: 12 feet 6 inches
Propulsion: 3 Kampon water tube boilers, 2 Kampon impulse turbines, 2 shafts
Speed: 35.5 knots
Range: 5,000 nautical miles
Complement: 239
Armament: 6 × 12.7-cm/50 Type 5 dual-purpose guns
8 × 25-mm Type 96 anti-aircraft guns
8 × 24-inch torpedo tubes
18 × depth charges

IJN Wakaba (Lieutenant Commander K. Masakichi)

IJN *Wakaba* was the third of six *Hatsuharu*-class destroyers, built for the Imperial Japanese Navy under the Circle One Program. At the start of 1944, IJN *Wakaba* was reassigned directly to Combined Fleet headquarters, and continued in escort missions between Yokosuka and Truk. She returned to northern waters from the end of February to the end of June, with additional 25-mm anti-aircraft guns added during maintenance refits at Ōminato at the end of May and Yokosuka at the end of June. In July, she made two troop transport runs to Iwo Jima as part of the Japanese preparations against the American landings. A Type 13 Radar was added at the end of July. In August through October, she escorted troop convoys from Kure to Taiwan and Luzon. On October 24, 1944, in the Battle of Leyte Gulf, IJN *Wakaba* was sunk by aircraft from USS *Franklin*.

Shipyard: Sasebo Naval Arsenal, Sasebo, Japan
Laid down: December 12, 1931
Launched: March 18, 1934
Commissioned: October 31, 1934
Class and type: *Hatsuharu*-class destroyer
Displacement: 1,831 tons
Length: 359 feet
Beam: 32 feet 10 inches

Draft:	9 feet 10 inches
Propulsion:	2 shaft Kampon geared turbines, 3 boilers
Speed:	36 knots
Range:	4,000 nautical miles
Complement:	200
Armament:	3 × 12.7-cm/50 Type 5 naval gun
	2 × 25-mm anti-aircraft guns
	3 × 24-inch torpedo tubes
	18 × depth charges

IJN Hatsuharu (Lieutenant Commander M. Hiroshi)

IJN *Hatsuharu*, the second Imperial Japanese Navy destroyer of the name, was the lead ship of six *Hatsuharu*-class destroyers built under the Circle One Program. At the start of 1944, the *Hatsuharu* was reassigned directly to Combined Fleet headquarters, and continued in escort missions between Yokosuka and Truk. She returned to northern waters from the end of February to the end of June, with additional 25-mm anti-aircraft guns added during maintenance refits at Ōminato at the end of May and Yokosuka at the end of June. In July, she made two troop transport runs to Iwo Jima as part of the Japanese preparations against the American landings. A Type 13 radar was added at the end of July. In August through October, she escorted troop convoys from Kure to Taiwan and Luzon. On October 24, 1944, in the Battle of Leyte Gulf, IJN *Hatsuharu* rescued seventy-eight survivors from IJN *Wakaba*, which had been sunk by aircraft from USS *Franklin* off the west coast of Panay.

Shipyard:	Sasebo Naval Arsenal, Sasebo, Japan
Laid down:	May 14, 1931
Launched:	February 22, 1933
Commissioned:	September 30, 1933
Class and type:	*Hatsuharu*-class destroyer
Displacement:	1,831 tons
Length:	359 feet
Beam:	32 feet 10 inches
Draft:	9 feet 10 inches
Propulsion:	2 shaft Kampon geared turbines, 3 boilers
Speed:	36 knots
Range:	4,000 nautical miles
Complement:	200
Armament:	3 × 12.7-cm/50 Type 5 naval gun
	2 × 25-mm anti-aircraft guns
	3 × 24-inch torpedo tubes
	18 × depth charges

IJN Hatsushimo (Commander M. Sako)

IJN *Hatsushimo* was the fourth of six *Hatsuharu*-class destroyers, built for the Imperial Japanese Navy under the Circle One Program. At the start of 1944, IJN *Hatsushimo* was reassigned directly to Combined Fleet headquarters, and continued in escort patrol missions between Yokosuka and Truk. She returned to Sasebo on April 14, where additional 25-mm anti-aircraft guns were added along with an additional Type 22 radar. In June, she participated in the Battle of the Philippine Sea as part of the First Supply Force and continued in escort missions between Japan and the Philippines through September. In a maintenance refit at Kure Naval Arsenal, additional 25-mm anti-aircraft guns and a Type 13 radar were added. IJN *Hatsushimo* continued with transport and escort missions to the Philippines through November. On October 24, 1944, after the Battle of Leyte Gulf, IJN *Hatsushimo* rescued seventy-four survivors from the sunken Wakaba. On November 15, 1944, IJN *Hatsushimo* was reassigned to the Imperial Japanese Navy 2nd Fleet and assigned to escort missions between Singapore and Cam Ranh Bay in French Indochina through the end of the year.

Shipyard:	Uraga Dock Company, Uraga, Japan
Laid down:	January 31, 1933
Launched:	November 4, 1933
Commissioned:	September 27, 1934
Class and type:	*Hatsuharu*-class destroyer
Displacement:	1,831 tons
Length:	359 feet
Beam:	32 feet 10 inches
Draft:	9 feet 10 inches
Propulsion:	2 shaft Kampon geared turbines, 3 boilers
Speed:	36 knots
Range:	4,000 nautical miles
Complement:	200
Armament:	3 × 12.7-cm/50 Type 5 naval gun
	2 × 25-mm anti-aircraft guns
	3 × 24-inch torpedo tubes
	18 × depth charges

APPENDIX VI

Japanese Naval Weapons at the Surigao Strait

45-Caliber 41st Year Type 14-inch (36-cm) Gun

The Vickers 14-inch, 45-caliber gun was designed and built by Vickers and initially installed on the battlecruiser IJN *Kongō*, which it was building for the Imperial Japanese Navy. Guns similar to this Vickers design were also later built in Japan to arm IJN *Kongō*'s sister ships and subsequent Japanese-constructed super-dreadnoughts that were all built in Japan. Japanese-built versions of the guns were designated 14-inch 41st Year Type, and from 1917 when the navy went metric, they were redesignated 36-cm 41st Year Type.

Gun Characteristics

Ship class used on:	*Kongô*, *Ise*, and *Fuso* classes
Date in service:	1913
Gun weight:	189,586 pounds
Gun length:	648.4 inches
Rifling length:	540 inches
Grooves:	84
Rate of fire:	2 rpm

Ammunition

Projectile types and weights:	APC Type 91-1,485 pounds; common Type 0 HE-1,378 pounds; common Type 3 IS-1,371 pounds
Projectile length:	APC Type 91-60.03 inches; common Type 0 HE-47.25 inches; common Type 3 IS-55.1 inches
Muzzle velocity:	APC Type 91-2,526–2,543 fps; common Type 0 HE-2,641 fps; common Type 3 IS-2,641 fps
Approximate barrel life:	250–280 rounds

Range

5,470 yards at 2.6 degrees to 38,770 at 43.0 degrees.

20-cm/50 7.9-inch 3rd Year Type No. 2

These guns were developed in 1930–1931 in order to achieve the maximum caliber allowed for cruisers under the Naval Limitation Treaties of the time. All heavy cruisers built after 1932 were armed with these weapons while older cruisers that had been originally armed with the 7.9-inch No. 1 guns had them replaced with these more powerful weapons. In addition, the *Mogami*-class cruisers had their 6.1-inch triple mounts replaced by the 8-inch gun in twin mounts while the design of the *Tone*-class was altered during construction to use these guns. By the start of the Pacific War, the changeover was complete, and all Japanese heavy cruisers were armed with these weapons.

Gun Characteristics

Ship class used on:	*Furutaka*, *Aoba*, *Myôkô*, and *Mogami* classes
Date in service:	1932
Gun weight:	37,400 pounds
Gun length:	405.9 inches
Rifling length:	333.9 inches
Grooves:	48
Rate of fire:	3–4 rpm

Ammunition

Projectile types and weights:	AP Type 91—277.4 pounds; common Type 91 HE—277.4 pounds; common Type 0 HE—277.4 pounds; common Type 3 IS—277.4 pounds; illumination shell B—277.4 pounds
Projectile length:	AP Type 91—35.68 inches; common Type 91 HE—35.83 inches; common Type 0 HE—34. inches; common Type 3 IS—34.07 inches
Muzzle velocity:	All except illumination-2,756 fps; illumination—2,330 fps
Approximate barrel life:	320–400 rounds

Range

5,470 yards at 2.4 degrees to 32,150 at 45.0 degrees.

12.7-cm/50 (5-inch) 3rd Year Type 5

These weapons were used on most Japanese destroyers built between 1926 and 1945 in both single and twin mounts. The mountings for these guns were a revolutionary design, as the Japanese were the first to use weather and splinter-proof mounts on destroyers. The second batch of these destroyers were also the first to use medium-caliber guns with high elevations, giving them a DP function. However, the very slow training speeds and lack of power ramming made these mountings almost useless against the fast-moving aircraft of World War II. These weapons were of built-up construction, originally three layers (Model 1) and later two layers (Model 1–2) along with the usual breech ring and breech bush. About 700 guns were manufactured. Surprisingly for this size weapon, these guns fired bag ammunition and used a Welin breech-block.

Gun Characteristics

Ship class used on: *Fubuki*, *Shikinami*, *Akatsuki*, *Hatsuharu*, *Shiratsuyu*, *Asashio*, *Kagero*, *Yugumo* and *Shimakaze* classes
Date in service: 1928
Gun weight: 8,350 pounds
Gun length: 255.2 inches
Rifling length: 211 inches
Grooves: 36
Rate of fire: 5–10 rpm

Ammunition

Projectile types and weights: Common Type 0 HE—50.7 pounds; common Type 1 HE 1—50.7 pounds; common Type 3 IS—50.7 pounds; common Type 4 IS—50.7 pounds; ASW—46.2 pounds; illumination—50.7 pounds
Projectile length: 17.2 inches
Muzzle velocity: Common rounds—3,002 fps; ASW—820 fps; illumination—2,460 fps
Approximate barrel life: 550–700 rounds

Range

7,910 yards at 5.0 degrees to 20,100 at 45.0 degrees. AA ceiling at 75 degrees about 40,000 feet.

12.7-cm/40 (5-inch) Type 89

The Type 89 prototype was proved in 1931 and adopted for service use on February 6, 1932. The Japanese considered the Type 89 to be a good AAA weapon and it had a fast rate of fire and good elevation and training speeds, especially on the later Mods. Its primary shortcoming was a relatively low muzzle velocity and thus a short range and low AA ceiling. Used a spring rammer cocked by the recoil, similar to other Japanese AAA weapons.

These weapons were of simple construction with autofretted monobloc barrels and breech rings and used horizontal sliding breech-blocks. Total production of Type 89 guns amounted to 1,306 guns, with 836 being manufactured between 1941 and 1945. Of these, 362 were mounted ashore, including ninety-six in the Yokosuka area and fifty-four in the Kure area.

Gun Characteristics

Ship class used on:	Almost all Japanese capital ships, aircraft carriers, cruisers, *Matsu* and *Tachibana* class escorts
Date in service:	1932
Gun weight:	6,100 pounds
Gun length:	208 inches
Rifling length:	175 inches
Grooves:	36
Rate of fire:	14 rpm initially, 8 rpm sustained

Ammunition

Projectile types and weights:	Common Type 0 HE—51.7 pounds; common Type 3 IS—50.7 pounds; ASW—46.2 pounds; illumination—51.7 pounds
Projectile length:	Common Type 0 HE—17.2 inches; common Type 3 IS—17.2 inches; ASW—17.2 inches
Muzzle velocity:	Common Type 0 HE—2,360–2,379 fps; common Type 3 IS—2,360–2,379 fps; ASW—820 fps; illumination—2,362 fps
Approximate barrel life:	800–1,500 rounds

Range

16,185 yards at 45.0 degrees. AA ceiling at 75 degrees—30,840 feet.

25-mm/60 (1-inch) Type 96 Model 1

The 25-mm Type 96 was widely used throughout the Japanese Navy with about 33,000 guns being produced. The Japanese considered this gun to be an excellent weapon, but it did not compare well to either the Bofors 40-mm or the Oerlikon 20-mm weapons used by the Allies. The magazines for the Type 96 held only fifteen rounds, so frequent stoppages for change outs were required. By 1945, these weapons fired projectiles too light and too short ranged to effectively engage the heavier and faster U.S. aircraft then in service. The Japanese were the only major navy of World War II not to develop and deploy any AA machine guns larger than 1-inch. Used a forged monobloc barrel and the automatics were gas-operated.

Gun Characteristics

Ship class used on:	Almost all warships of World War II
Date in service:	1936
Gun weight:	253.5 pounds
Gun length:	90.4 inches
Rifling length:	53.2 inches
Grooves:	121
Rate of fire:	Cyclic—220–260 rpm; effective—110–120 rpm

Ammunition

Projectile types and weights:	AP—0.57 pounds; common—0.55 pounds; incendiary common—0.55 pounds; tracer—0.55 pounds
Projectile length:	AP—4.0 inches; common—4.4 inches; incendiary common—4.3 inches
Muzzle velocity:	2,953 fps
Approximate barrel life:	12,000 rounds

Range

7,439 yards at 45.0 degrees to 8,200 yards at 50.0 degrees. AA ceiling at 85 degrees; effective at 9,843 feet; maximum—18,040 feet.

13-mm/76 (0.52-inch) Type 93 Machine Gun

This weapon was originally designed by the French firm of Hotchkiss. Japan imported a number of twin and quadruple mountings for evaluation purposes in the early 1930s and officially adopted the weapon on February 4, 1933. Production of the Japanese version started in 1935. These guns were generally similar to the larger Japanese 25-mm/60 AA machine gun. The U.S. Naval Technical Mission to Japan reported that the Japanese considered the 13-mm to be almost as reliable as the 25-mm, since it is basically the same, but apparently not perfected to quite the same degree. Production reached 1,200 guns per month late in 1944. The magazine held thirty rounds and was similar in design to that for the 25-mm AA gun. Like most nations, Japan found that small-caliber MGs were inadequate against modern aircraft, but this gun was still produced in large numbers right up to the surrender. Used a forged monobloc barrel and the automatics were gas-operated. Actual bore diameter was 13.2 mm.

Gun Characteristics

Ship class used on:	Almost all warships of World War II
Date in service:	1933
Gun weight:	92.6 pounds
Gun length:	55.5 inches
Rifling length:	N/A
Grooves:	8
Rate of fire:	Cyclic—425–475 rpm; practical—250 rpm

Ammunition

Projectile types and weights:	AP—1.83 ounces; incendiary common—1.75 ounces; incendiary common—1.57 ounces; tracer—1.62 ounces
Projectile length:	2.4 inches; complete round—5.3 to 5.4 inches
Muzzle velocity:	2,641 fps
Approximate barrel life:	3,070 rounds

Range

6,560 yards at 45.0 degrees to 7,108 yards at 50.0 degrees. AA ceiling at 85 degrees—14,750 feet. Range against aircraft: maximum 6,550 feet; effective 3,300 feet.

61-cm (24-inch) Type 93 (1933) Model 1, Mod 1, Mod 2, and Mod 3 Torpedo

Model 1 was the prototype version of the famous Long Lance torpedoes. The first production version was Model 1, Mod 1. This differed by having stronger ribs in the fore body, the strength of the rear buoyancy chamber was increased, more cooling water was supplied to the piston rods to prevent overheating and cracking, and the slide valve gearing was improved. Mod 2 dated from 1936 and differed in many areas. The oxygen vessel was made of a deep pressing with one integral end instead of a hollow forging. This construction was followed in all subsequent versions. The bracing ribs of the rear buoyancy chamber were further strengthened and cooling water to the slide valves was increased together with modifications to the buffer chamber, lubrication of the cross-head and group valve gearing. Mod 3 was designed in 1944 and production started in 1945, but it did not enter service. This mod combined the oxygen vessel and warhead of Mod 1 with the propulsion system of Model 3.

Ship class used on:	Surface ships
Date in service:	1935
Weight:	5,952 pounds
Overall length:	354 inches
Negative buoyancy:	1,058 pounds
Explosive charge:	1,080 pounds Type 97
Power/range/speed:	200 hp/43,700 yards/36–38 knots; 300 hp/35,000 yards/40–42 knots; 520 hp/21,900 yards/48–50 knots
Propulsion:	Kerosene-oxygen wet-heater

APPENDIX V

Admiral Jesse Barrett Oldendorf Biography

Jesse Barrett Oldendorf was born in Riverside, California, on February 16, 1887, attended public schools there, and was appointed to the U.S. Naval Academy from the Eighth District of California in 1905. As a midshipman, he participated in swimming, tennis, and won the sharpshooter's marksmanship badge. Graduated in June 1909, he was commissioned ensign on June 5, 1911, after serving the two years at sea then required by law.

Upon graduation, he was assigned sea duty and served consecutively in USS *California* (armored cruiser), flagship of the Pacific Fleet, USS *Preble*, USS *Denver*, USS *Whipple*, USS *San Diego*, and USS *Hannibal*. When detached from the *Hannibal* on October 10, 1916, he was ordered to duty in charge of the Navy Recruiting Office at Pittsburgh, Pennsylvania. In June 1917, after the outbreak of World War I, he had command of the Armed Guard Unit attached to the U.S. Army transport *Saratoga*, which was sunk later in a collision off New York. On August 6, the same year, he reported aboard USS *President Lincoln*, of the Cruiser and Transport Force, and was gunnery officer of that vessel when she was sunk by a German submarine off the coast of Ireland on May 31, 1918.

Returning to the U.S., he had duty as engineer officer in USS *Seattle* from August 1918 until March 1919. Then reporting to the commander of U.S. Naval Forces operating in European waters, he was assigned duty as executive officer of the former German transport *Patricia*. From July to October 1919, he was officer in charge of the Pittsburgh Naval Recruiting Station and Special Disbursing Agent, and for the succeeding eight months served as naval inspector of machinery at the Baltimore Shipbuilding and Dry Dock Company and Bethlehem Steel Company, Baltimore, Maryland, with additional duty as naval inspector of engineering material for that district. From June to October 1920, he was officer in charge of the Branch Hydrographic Office in Baltimore.

In October 1921, he went aboard USS *Dolphin* as aide and flag secretary on the staff of the commander of the Special Service Squadron, then operating in Central and South American Waters. In July 1922, he reported for duty as aide to the commandant of the Navy Yard, Mare Island, California. When that duty was completed, he assumed command of the destroyer *Decatur* in competitive maneuvers. When detached from that command on May 30, 1927, he was ordered as aide to the commandant of the Navy Yard, Philadelphia, Pennsylvania, serving there until June 1928. Between June 1928 and July 1930, he completed courses at the Naval War College, Newport, Rhode Island, and Army War College, Washington, D.C. He then returned to sea, as navigator of USS *New York*, serving until June 1932.

For the next three years, he had duty as an instructor in the Naval Academy's Department of Seamanship and Navigation. In June 1935, he reported as executive officer of USS *West Virginia*, and after two years in that assignment, he was ordered to the Bureau of Navigation, Navy Department, Washington, D.C., as an officer in charge of the Naval Recruiting Section. In October 1939, he assumed command of USS *Houston* and when detached on August 30, 1941, was ordered to the staff of the Naval War College, Newport, Rhode Island. In February 1942, he was named commander of All Forces, Aruba–Curacao area, Netherlands West Indies, and from July 2, 1942 until April 21, 1943, he served as commander of Naval Operating Base, Trinidad, British West Indies. He was awarded the Distinguished Service Medal with the following citation:

> For exceptionally meritorious service ... as Commander All Forces Aruba–Curacao Area from March 2 to July 2, 1942, and as Commander Trinidad Sector, Caribbean Sea Frontier and Commandant of Naval Operating Base, Trinidad, from July 2, 1942 to April 19, 1943. Displaying excellent judgment and outstanding leadership, Rear Admiral Oldendorf assisted materially in the effective employment of the Naval Surface forces and combined Army–Navy aircraft assigned to his command in the anti-submarine warfare. By his forceful initiative and intelligent planning, he coordinated and directed the efforts of various services, which resulted in marked improvement and efficiency in the port if Trinidad.

He commanded a task force of the Atlantic Fleet from May 2 to November 25, 1943 and in January 1944 was ordered to the Pacific Area as commander of Cruiser Division 4. The following December, he was designated commander of Battleship Squadron 1, with additional duty in command of Battleship Division 2. For service in those commands he was awarded the Legion of Merit, Gold Star *in lieu* of a second Legion of Merit, two Gold Stars *in lieu* of the second, and third Distinguished Service Medal, and the Navy Cross. The citations follow:

Legion of Merit (with Combat "V"):
For exceptionally meritorious conduct ... as Commanding Officer of a Fire Support Group during the assault and occupation of Roi and Namur Islands, Kwajalein Atoll and Eniwetok Atoll of the Marshall Islands ... Rear Admiral Oldendorf directed the First Support Group in the fierce and effective bombardment of enemy–held islands during the assault phases of both these vital operations. Skillfully maneuvering the ships of his group close to known shoals, he directed the delivery of supporting gunfire to reduce to a minimum the enemy's opposition to the assault of our forces ... and contributed to the successful capture of these island...

Gold Star *in lieu* of Second Distinguished Service Medal:
For exceptionally meritorious service ... as Commander of all Fire Support Groups during action against the Japanese-held Saipan and Tinian Islands in the West Pacific, June 14 to August 1, 1944 ... Rear Admiral Oldendorf organized the firepower of all battleships, cruisers and destroyers comprising his support groups for furious onslaught. Disposing his ships for maximum striking power in a determined offensive executed in preparation for our amphibious attack on these important Japanese-held islands, he coordinated his component units and led the mighty armada into the dangerous waters of the assault area where his powerful guns assailed the enemy's strong coastal defenses in a smashing naval bombardment. Aggressive and unceasingly vigilant in his support tactics, (he) controlled the terrific fire of his vessels with extreme proficiency, effectively delivering all call fire, harassing and counter-battery fire as required by our troops ashore during and after the initial landings...

Gold Star *in lieu* of Second Legion of Merit:
For exceptionally meritorious conduct ... as Commander of the Fire Support Group in the assault of the strongly defended Japanese-held Peleliu and Anguar Islands, September 12 to 30, 1944. Entrusted with the direction of minesweeping, underwater demolition and shore bombardment preparatory to the assault, Vice Admiral Oldendorf ably carried out his duties without loss while under the continuous threat of, and often under actual enemy fire. He supervised the delivery of accurate and devastating fire against hostile defenses, thereby contributing to the success of our offensive...

Navy Cross:
For distinguishing himself by extraordinary heroism in action against the enemy on October 25, 1944, in support of landings on a heavily defended enemy-held island base. In the Battle of Surigao Strait, as Commander Support Force he engaged a powerful detachment of the Japanese Fleet, consisting

> of battleships, cruisers, and destroyers, and in a short but decisive action practically annihilated the enemy force. Fleeing remnants were closely pursued by units of his command, which, with the aid of cooperating aircraft, completed their destruction. His personal courage, determination, and perseverance, were reflected in the outstanding performance of the force under his command, which resulted in a brilliant naval victory and incalculable damage to the enemy…
>
> Gold Star *in lieu* of the Third Distinguished Service Medal:
> For exceptionally meritorious service ... as Commander Bombardment and Fire Support Group, prior to and during the invasion of Leyte, Philippine Islands. A master of amphibious warfare and all phases of capital ship operations, Rear Admiral Oldendorf rendered invaluable assistance to the Philippine attack Force Commander during the perfection of plans which culminated in the Leyte invasion on October 20, 1944. Under his forceful and brilliant leadership, battleships, heavy and light cruisers and destroyers blasted Japanese shore installations in sustained and devastating bombardment, silencing enemy batteries and thus making possible the landing of liberating forces with but light casualties.... [He] played a vital role in countering powerful resistance by hostile air and surface forces toward the liberation of the Philippines from Japanese domination…

In November 1945, he was ordered to duty as commandant of the Eleventh Naval District, San Diego, California, and from January 14, 1946 also served as the commander of the Naval Operating Base, San Diego. In February 1947, he became the commander of the Western Sea Frontier, with additional duty as the commander of the Pacific Reserve Fleet, HQ at San Francisco, California. On June 25, 1948, he was relieved of these commands, and reported to the Eleventh Naval District, San Diego, for duty pending his retirement on September 1, 1948. On June 28, 1948 at the Presdio, San Francisco, Admiral Oldendorf was presented the Army Distinguished Service Medal by General Mark Clark: "For service from January 1 to February 15, 1945 as Commander Battleships, U.S. Seventh Fleet in the Luzon Operations, General Order Number 46, dated June 2, 1948."

Admiral Oldendorf died in Portsmouth, Virginia, on April 27, 1974 and was interred at Arlington National Cemetery.

APPENDIX VI

Vice Admiral Shōji Nishimura Biography

Shōji Nishimura was from Akita prefecture in the northern Tōhoku region of Japan. He was a graduate of the 39th class of the Imperial Japanese Naval Academy in 1911, ranking twenty-first out of 148 cadets. As a midshipman, he served on the cruiser IJN *Aso* and battleship IJN *Mikasa*. After his commissioning as an ensign, he was assigned back to IJN *Aso*, and then to the battlecruiser IJN *Hiei*.

He attended naval artillery and torpedo school from 1914–1915, and was then assigned to the destroyer IJN *Yugiri*, cruiser IJN *Yakumo*, and battlecruiser IJN *Haruna*.

As a lieutenant from 1917, he specialized in navigation, and served as chief navigator on a large number of vessels, including the corvette IJN *Yamato*, destroyers IJN *Kawakaze*, IJN *Tanikaze*, IJN *Yura*, and IJN *Sunosaki*, cruisers IJN *Kitakami* and IJN *Ōi*, and battleship IJN *Hizen*. Nishimura was promoted to lieutenant commander in 1928. He was subsequently chief navigator on the cruiser *Nisshin*. He was given his first command on November 1, 1926 on the destroyer IJN *Kiku*. He subsequently was captain of the destroyers IJN *Wakatake*, IJN *Urakaze*, IJN *Mikazuki*, and, after his promotion to commander in 1929, IJN *Shirakumo*. In the 1930s, he was assigned commander of the 26th Destroyer Group. Promoted to captain in 1934, and briefly commander of the 19th Destroyer Group, Nishimura then served as captain of the cruiser IJN *Kumano*, from 1937 to 1938, and the reconstructed fast battleship IJN *Haruna*, from 1938 to 1940. He became a rear admiral on November 15, 1940, and a vice admiral on November 1, 1943.

Nishimura gained much fame as the commander of the 4th Destroyer Squadron during the Battle of the Java Sea. In June 1942, he was named the commander of the 7th Cruiser Division and participated in the Guadalcanal Campaign.

Near the end of the war, Nishimura was named the commander of the Southern Force in Operation Shō-Go, aimed at a final and decisive naval battle against the U.S. Navy in the Philippines. Nishimura's Force C consisted of battleships IJN *Fusō* and IJN *Yamashiro*, heavy cruiser IJN *Mogami*, and destroyers IJN *Shigure*, IJN *Michishio*, IJN *Asagumo*, and IJN *Yamagumo*. In the Surigao Strait between Leyte and Dinagat Islands on the evening of October 24, 1944, he contacted the U.S. Seventh Fleet under Rear Admiral Jesse Oldendorf, which consisted of six battleships, eight cruisers, twenty-nine destroyers, and thirty-nine motor torpedo boats. Nishimura's force was crushed when the Americans crossed the Japanese "T." Nishimura was killed during the battle when his flagship, the IJN *Yamashiro*, was sunk after being hit multiple times from the U.S. battleships. His awards included the Order of the Rising Sun (3rd class).

APPENDIX VII

Vice Admiral Kiyohide Shima Biography

A native of Miyazaki prefecture, Shima was a graduate of the 39th class of the Imperial Japanese Naval Academy in 1911, ranking sixty-ninth out of 148 cadets. As a midshipman, he served aboard the cruisers IJN *Aso* and IJN *Hashidate* and the battleship *Aki*. As an ensign, he was assigned to the battleship IJN *Iwami*, and as a sub-lieutenant, he served on the battlecruiser IJN *Ibuki* and cruiser IJN *Katori*. Shima was promoted to lieutenant in 1918, and after taking courses in torpedo warfare and navigation, he was assigned as chief communications officer on the battlecruiser IJN *Kirishima*. In 1921, he graduated from the Naval War College and was promoted to lieutenant commander. In 1925–1926, Shima was appointed *aide-de-camp* to HIH *Prince Takamatsu Nobuhito*, concurrently serving on the battleships IJN *Nagato* and IJN *Fusō*. In 1928–1929, he was sent to the U.S. and Europe. On his return, he served in a number of staff positions, primarily as an instructor at various naval ordnance schools.

In 1933, he was promoted to captain, and in 1936, he received his first command, the cruiser IJN Ōi. Shima became a rear admiral on November 15, 1939 and was chief of staff of the Maizuru Naval District. With the start of the Pacific War, Shima was given a combat command, and led the Tulagi invasion force that occupied Tulagi in the Solomon Islands on May 3, 1942 as part of Operation Mo Shima, or the Port Moresby Operation. He was promoted to vice admiral on May 1, 1943, and on February 15, 1944 became commander in chief of the IJN 5th Fleet.

During the Battle of Leyte Gulf, October 23–26, 1944, Shima led the Second Striking Force of three cruisers and seven destroyers in the Battle of Surigao Strait. Vice Admiral Shōji Nishimura's and Vice Admiral Shima's fleets were collectively called the Southern Force. Because of the strict radio silence imposed on the forces, Shima was unable to synchronize his movements with those of Nishimura's. Shima's force, two heavy cruisers, a light cruiser and four destroyers, reached the battle after Nishimura's forces had run into a deadly trap and suffered losses. During the nighttime battle, Shima fired sixteen torpedoes at two islands he mistook for American ships. Then, seeing what he thought were the wrecks of both Nishimura's battleships, actually the two halves of the wrecked IJN *Fusō*, he ordered a retreat: "At that time, things flashed in my head were thus:... If we continued dashing further north, it was quite clear that we should only fall into a ready trap." Retreating, his flagship, the heavy cruiser IJN *Nachi*, collided with Nishimura's heavy cruiser IJN *Mogami*, flooding the latter's steering room. IJN *Mogami* fell behind in the retreat and was sunk by aircraft the next morning. After this disaster, Shima was reassigned to command the Takao Guard District from May 10, 1945 to November 30, 1945. From May 10 to June 15, 1945, he was also final commander of the First Air Fleet. He died on November 7, 1973.

APPENDIX VIII

U.S. Ship Readiness and Material Conditions

Readiness

During the period of war, a ship was at all times in some condition of readiness, depending upon the requirements of the existing situation. The following conditions are prescribed:

Readiness for Action, Condition I

Entire crew, officers and men, at nettle stations. Complete readiness for action in all respects. All plane crews either in or standing by their planes, ready to take-off, with their planes equipped for their mission. Gun crews standing by their guns.

This condition of readiness shall be taken if reports of enemy movement indicated that action is possible; when proceeding to sea and before passing the last anti-submarine net or barrier and maintained until a different condition of readiness is signaled, or as previously directed by specific orders; immediately the enemy is sighted or reported in sight by any vessel in the vicinity. The organization of the ship must provide for passing promptly from condition II to condition I.

In clear weather, visibility substantially exceeding gun range and when a screen, other than the anti-submarine screen, is ahead and on the flanks of the battleship division, readiness for action, condition I may be modified to condition III.

When visibility is high and there is no screen other than the anti-submarine screen, or when adequately protected by a distant screen and the visibility does not exceed gun range but is not less than 6 miles, readiness for action, condition I, may be modified to condition II.

Readiness for Action, Condition II

Ship-control stations manned sufficiently to handle the ship, to insure watertight integrity, to maintain the standard lookouts and all communications with battle stations.

Fire-control stations manned sufficiently to be in all respects ready to open fire with, and to control, one-half of the turrets and two groups of the torpedo-defense battery and the anti-aircraft guns, and to maintain all communications with battle stations. Torpedo control manned with a full crew for one-half of the torpedo battery and all communications. Signal control shall keep one station maned and communication at all stations. All planes equipped for their mission; plane crews of one flight either in or standing by their planes.

During daylight when visibility is below 6 miles, or at night, in an area within which enemy surface vessels may be encountered but no reports of enemy have been received, readiness for action, condition II, will be taken.

Meeting the enemy when in condition II will be in the nature of a surprise. The essential requirement is to be able to open fire immediately with one-half of the main and secondary batteries.

In order that complete readiness for action may be attained without interference with the stations manned in condition II, the ship's organization must provide for passing from condition II to condition I, without changing the station of those officers and men at their stations for condition II. Attention is called to the fact that condition III may continue for a considerable length of time. The battle organization, therefore, should provide that officers and men standing watch should be entirely replaced by their reliefs in order that they may obtain complete rest unless called to action by general quarters.

Readiness for Action, Condition III

Ship-control station sufficiently manned to handle the ship, to insure watertight integrity, to maintain the standard lookouts and communication with all battle stations. Fire control manned sufficiently to maintain the standard anti-submarine and aircraft defense and communication with all battle stations. Torpedo control maintain communications. Signal control keep one station manned. All planes equipped for their mission; plane crews prepared to take off at short notice.

In taking condition II or condition III, readiness for action, condition I will first be taken and after all stations have reported ready, the stations which are not to be manned when in the prospective condition should be secured in such manner as to be ready in the least possible time and the men of such stations dismissed.

General Quarters

General quarters calls the ship's company to stations. General duties include manning batteries and taking battle stations, loading torpedoes, connecting fire hoses, standing by manifolds and valves, standing by cut-off switches and switchboards, and testing out all gear.

All the preparations and dispositions are in accordance with the activities of clearing the ship for action. Every officer and man must occupy his battle station at general quarters. Fleet working parties and ship's work and boating must give way to the general quarters routine.

Material Conditions

Material conditions establish the fighting integrity of the ship and maintain its survivability. The determination of the material condition set at any time is the responsibility of the commanding officer, who may authorize modifications of any material condition. XRAY provides the least tightness and the greatest ease of access throughout the ship. It is set when the threat to the ship is minimal, during working hours when in port, or when there is no danger of attack or bad weather. YOKE is set when at sea, or in port during wartime. ZEBRA provides the greatest degree of subdivision and tightness to the ship. It is set immediately and automatically when general quarters is sounded. It is also set when entering or leaving port during wartime, to localize damage and control fire and flooding, or at any time the commanding officer deems it necessary. Modified material condition ZEBRA—allows movement around the ship for special conditions such as underway replenishment, vertical replenishment, air operations, amphibious operations, and transit of known or suspected hazardous navigation areas.

One of the most important features of ship survivability is the ability to configure the ship to simultaneously allow the survivability system to function and the ship to be operated. Standard configurations representing varying degrees of closure and known as "material conditions" set the ship according to the degree of threat to the ship and the current operational directives. All fittings in the ship are marked to indicate how they are to be set during various material conditions. The determination of the material condition set at any time is the responsibility of the commanding officer, who may authorize modification of any material condition. Closures are defined as closable openings in overheads, decks, and bulkheads for access by personnel. Fittings are covers, valves, caps, and plugs for access other than for personnel and for control of fluid flow. They may be on or in piping and ventilation systems, or in overheads, decks, and bulkheads. For brevity, where context allows, the term fitting is used to include the meaning of both fitting and closure, and the term compartmentation is used to include both structural and fluid system segregation.

Condition XRAY provides the least watertight integrity and the greatest ease of access throughout the ship. It is set when the threat to the ship is minimal. Condition XRAY is set during working hours when the ship is in port and there is no danger of attack or from weather. The minimum degree of tightness permitted on an operational ship is condition XRAY. When condition XRAY is set, all fittings marked with a black "X" are closed.

Condition YOKE provides a greater degree of watertight integrity than condition XRAY, but to a lesser degree than the maximum condition. YOKE is normally set at sea and in port during wartime. When YOKE is set, all fittings marked with black Xs and Ys, circle "X" and circle "Y" are closed. A modified condition YOKE is sometimes used at sea when cruising independently in good weather and calm seas and in port in peacetime. In the modified condition, YOKE fittings above the waterline are left open to improve ventilation and habitability. All other XRAY and YOKE fittings are closed.

Condition ZEBRA provides the greatest degree of subdivision and watertight integrity to the ship. It is the maximum state of readiness for the ship's survivability system. Condition ZEBRA is set: Immediately and automatically when general quarters is sounded; when entering or leaving port in wartime; to localize damage and control fire and flooding when the crew is not at general quarters; and at any time the commanding officer deems the maximum condition of survivability should be set. When condition ZEBRA is set, all fittings marked with black Xs and Ys, circle "X," circle "Y," circle "Z," red Zs and DOG Zs are closed.

There may arise certain situations during which the commanding officer may wish to set a modified material condition ZEBRA. Setting of modified material condition ZEBRA will give a higher survivability stance than condition YOKE. At the same time, modified ZEBRA is less restrictive and will more readily allow the accomplishment of certain operational requirements. Modified ZEBRA may result as an upgrade from condition YOKE or as a downgrade from condition ZEBRA. Some of the situations that may make a modified material condition ZEBRA desirable are underway replenishment; vertical replenishment; air operations; amphibious operations; or transit of known or suspected hazardous navigation areas.

On larger ships, setting material condition ZEBRA in part or in total without all hands at general quarters will impede the ship's company from quickly manning battle stations. This situation could result in ZEBRA being set slower than had the ship been at material condition YOKE before the emergency. Large ships should therefore consider this when changing material condition.

References

Campbell, N. J. M., *Naval Weapons of World War Two* (Annapolis: Naval Institute Press, 1985)

"Field Manual 100-5," *Headquarters Department of the Army.* (Fort Monroe: U.S. Army Training and Doctrine Command, 1993)

Hornfischer, J. D., *The Last Stand of the Tin Can Sailor.* (New York: Bantam Books, 2004)

Hone, T. C., *Battleline: The United States Navy 1919–1939* (Annapolis: Naval Institute Press, 2006)

Hone, T., "U.S. Navy Surface Battle Doctrine and Victory," *The Pacific. Naval War College Review*, vol. 62, no. 1, 2009

Culora, T. J., *Japanese Operational Plans in World War II* (Newport: Naval War College, 1994)

Imperial Japanese Navy Archives, www.combinedfleet.com/kaigun.htm

MacArthur, D., *Reminiscences.* (New York: McGraw-Hill Book Company, 1964)

Morison, S. E., *History of the United States Naval Operations in World War II*, 15 vols. (Boston: Little Brown, 1984)

Musicant, I., *U.S. Armored Cruisers: A Design and Operational History.* (Annapolis: Naval Institute Press, 1985)

Naval History and Heritage Command, www.history.navy.mil

"Naval Weapons, Naval Technology and Naval Reunions," www.navweaps.com.

Saur, H., *The Last Big-Gun Naval Battle: The Battle of the Surigao Strait.* (El Cerrito: Glencannon Press, 1999)

Steinberg, R., *Return to the Philippines* (Chicago: Time-Life Books, 1980) (Annapolis: Naval Institute Press, 2006)

"Reports of General MacArthur," *The Campaigns of Macarthur in the Pacific*, Volume I (Washington: Library of Congress, 1966)

Thomas, E., *Sea of Thunder* (New York: Simon and Shuster, 2006)
Tully, A. P., *Battle of Surigao Strait*. (Bloomington: Indiana University Press, 2009)
Vego, M. N., *The Battle for Leyte, 1944: Allied and Japanese Plans, Preparations, and Execution* (Annapolis: Naval Institute Press, 2006)